Dylan Kissane

Beyond Anarchy

The Complex and Chaotic Dynamics of International Politics

Dylan Kissane

BEYOND ANARCHY

THE COMPLEX AND CHAOTIC DYNAMICS OF INTERNATIONAL POLITICS

ibidem-Verlag
Stuttgart

Bibliographic information published by the Deutsche Nationalbibliothek
Die Deutsche Nationalbibliothek lists this publication in the Deutsche Nationalbibliografie;
detailed bibliographic data are available in the Internet at http://dnb.d-nb.de.

Bibliografische Information der Deutschen Nationalbibliothek
Die Deutsche Nationalbibliothek verzeichnet diese Publikation in der Deutschen
Nationalbibliografie; detaillierte bibliografische Daten sind im Internet über http://dnb.d-nb.de
abrufbar.

Cover picture: © BeTa-Artworks – Fotolia.com.

ISBN-13: 978-3-8382-0231-0

© *ibidem*-Verlag / *ibidem* Press
Stuttgart, Germany 2011

TABLE OF CONTENTS

ACKNOWLEDGEMENTS

Many thanks to David Lundberg for his consistent support, constructive criticisms and openness to research on the edges of international relations theory.

Thanks, too, to Ruchi Anand and Arie Kacowicz whose comments and criticisms improved the text immeasurably.

Valerie Lange and the team at Ibidem Verlag have made the publishing process a pleasure.

Embryonic ideas and arguments in the book were presented at conferences hosted by the Central European University in Budapest, the American Graduate School in Paris, the Hebrew University in Jerusalem and the University of Ljubljana in Slovenia.

Early versions of some parts of the book were published as articles in the *Central European University Political Science Journal*, the *Revista de stiinte politice* and *Contemporary Issues* as well as a working paper for the Centro Argentino de Estudios Internacionales.

Much of the research that led to this book was supported by funding from an Australian Postgraduate Award and both the Division of Education, Arts and Social Sciences and the School of International Studies at the University of South Australia. The manuscript was completed and edited in the first months of my tenure as Research Coordinator at the Centre d'Etudes Franco-Américain de Management.

Any errors in the text are my own.

DK

Lyon, France

22 December 2010

For Jamie.

The chance is high that the truth lies in the fashionable direction.
But, on the off chance that it is in another direction who will find it?
Richard Feynman

FOREWORD

A history of international relations might be considered a history of the theoretical discourse of realism. Though the discipline of international relations has existed only from the early twentieth century, the field claims a literature that dates back to Thucydides, the first of the greats in the realist tradition. Tracing a chronology through international political scholars and the names most often realised are Thucydides' realist colleagues, with Machiavelli, Hobbes, Carr, Morgenthau, Waltz, Van Evera and Mearsheimer among them.[1] Realism has defined the theoretical fold and though it has been challenged consistently for centuries, it remains the primary or alternate theory of almost every working theorist today.[2]

Realism as a method of interpreting international affairs can be traced to Thucydides' *History of the Peloponnesian War*.[3] In what has been described as "probably the most famous text in the realist tradition" the Greek historian outlines what many hold is the ultimate reality of international politics: "…the strong do what they can and the weak suffer what they must".[4] Later realists such as Machiavelli and Hobbes further developed this notion, the former described by Jack Donnelly as the most prominent of pre-twentieth century realist and the latter held by Bertrand Badie to be the inspiration for the "hyper-realism" of Bismarkian strategists of the 19th and 20th century.[5]

---

[1] Niccolò Machiavelli. 2005. *The Prince*, translated by P Bondanella. Oxford: Oxford University Press; Thomas Hobbes. 2004. *Leviathan*. Whitefish, MT: Kessinger Publishing; Edward Hallett Carr. 2001. *The Twenty Years Crisis 1919-1939: An Introduction to the Study of International Relations*. New York: Palgrave; Hans Morgenthau. 1993. *Politics among Nations: The Struggle for Power and Peace*. 6th edition. New York: Alfred A. Knopf; Kenneth Waltz. 1979. *Theory of International Politics*. Reading: Addison-Wesley; Stephen Van Evera. 1999. *Causes of War: Power and the Roots of Conflict*. New York: Cornell University Press; John Mearsheimer. 2001. *The Tragedy of Great Power Politics*. New York: Norton.

[2] Jeffrey Legro and Andrew Moravcsik. 1999. 'Is Anybody Still a Realist?' *International Security* 24(2): 5-55, p.5.

[3] Thucydides. 1998. *The History of the Peloponnesian Wars*. New York: Prometheus Books.

[4] Jack Donnelly. 2000. *Realism and International Relations*. Cambridge: Cambridge University Press, p.23.

[5] Donnelly. 2000, p.25; Bertrand Badie. 2001. 'Realism under Praise, or a Requiem? The Paradigmatic Debate in International Relations.' *International Political Science Review* 22(3): 253-260, p.254.

Like Thucydides, both highlighted the essential anarchy of the international system: Machiavelli noted that in international matters, "there is no tribunal to which to appeal"; Hobbes, in what would become a realist catchphrase, noted the international realm is "solitary, poor, nasty, brutish and short".[6]

Following the founding of the first academic chair in international relations in 1919 in Aberystwyth, Wales, realist thought began to be challenged by a rising liberal institutionalist position.[7] US President Woodrow Wilson's 14-point plan and the rise of the League of Nations were the most practical outcomes of this theoretical turn but it would only be a short time before realism again returned to the centre of international theorising.[8] As the political situation on continental Europe began to once again resemble the pre-World War One competitive arena, realism re-emerged in the shape of EH Carr's *The Twenty Years Crisis*, published in 1939.[9] Carr took the chair at Aberystwyth in 1936 and "immediately redesigned the curriculum, replacing the previous focus on the League of Nations with an emphasis on power and history".[10] Carr warned against the utopianism of the theory and practice of international affairs which, in his opinion, led them to pay bare attention to the realities of the international system.[11]

Following the widespread destruction of World War Two, Carr's work and, more generally, realism was seen in a new light. Carr's realist ideas, which had been ridiculed by one reviewer in 1941 as furnishing "a facile gospel for all those who would venture nothing to implement the community of nations", gained currency after the conflict and provided a basis for Hans Morgenthau to present his influential realist

---

[6] Machiavelli. 2005, p.62; Hobbes. 2004, p.52.

[7] Brian Schmidt. 2006. 'On the History and Historiography of International Relations.' In *Handbook of International Relations*. Edited by W Carlsnaes, T Risse and B Simmons. London: SAGE, pp.3-22, p.4.

[8] Woodrow Wilson. 2006 [1918]. *President Woodrow Wilson's Fourteen Points*. Viewed 13 July 2006, http://www.yale.edu/lawweb/avalon/wilson14.htm; Lisa Martin. 2001. 'An institutionalist view: international institutions and state strategies.' In *International Order and the Future of World Politics*. Edited by T Paul and J Hall. Cambridge: Cambridge University Press, pp.78-98, p.80.

[9] Carr. 2001.

[10] Donnelly. 2000, p.27.

[11] John Mearsheimer. 2005. 'EH Carr vs. Idealism: The Battle Rages On.' *International Relations* 19(2): 139-152, p.140.

work, *Politics among Nations*.[12] Morgenthau, described as a "founding father of realism" by Mark Lacy, regarded Carr's work as a "lucid and brilliant exposure of the faults of contemporary political thought".[13] Moving in the same direction, Morgenthau outlined his own realist paradigm, epitomised in his six principles of political realism headed by the claim that the roots of political action lies in human nature.[14] As well as Carr, though, there were obvious links here to the classical positions of Machiavelli and Hobbes and therefore, in Morgenthau, realism had found a new theoretical protagonist whose work and ideas would go on to dominate the early post-World War Two period.[15]

By the mid-1970s, however, Morgenthau's recourse to human nature as the foundation for international interactions had, in the words of one realist, "lost its cachet in the academic world".[16] Mearsheimer presents two reasons for this decline in the popularity of Morgenthau's realism:

> First, the campus protests against the Vietnam War made it terribly unfashionable to promote realism, with its emphasis on the balance of power and the necessity of sometimes using military force in pursuit of the national interest. This is ironic since almost all of the realists of the day opposed the Vietnam War. Second, the social science revolution was just then taking hold on campuses and it was widely believed that Carr and Morgenthau were not 'real' social scientists. Thus, they got pushed aside, along with realism more generally, during the 1970s.[17]

However, realism was revived in 1979 with the publication of Kenneth Waltz's canon, *Theory of International Politics*, which would go on to define not only a new

---

[12] Percy Corbett. 1941. 'Review: *The Twenty Years Crisis* by EH Carr." *Pacific Affairs* 14(2): 237-238, p.238. A contrary review by Corbett's contemporary, Edgar Dean, argued that Carr's book "should be read by every professor... [and] if professors won't read it, then undergraduates should – it will enable them to discount their professor's lectures". See Edgar Dean. 1941. 'Review: *The Twenty Years Crisis; Britain; British Foreign Policy since Versailles* by EH Carr.' *The Journal of Modern History* 13(1): 119-121, p.119.

[13] Mark Lacy. 2005. *Security and Climate Change: The Limits of Realism*. New York: Routledge, p.4; Hans Morgenthau. 1948b. 'The Political Science of EH Carr.' *World Politics* 1(1): 127-134, p.128.

[14] Morgenthau. 1993, p.4. This would later lead Donnelly to label Morgenthau "the best-known and most influential biological realist", the 'biological' arising from this recourse to human nature to explain state action. See Donnelly. 2000, p.44.

[15] John Mearsheimer. 2006a. 'Conversations in International Relations – Interview with John J. Mearsheimer (Part I).' *International Relations* 20(1): 105-124, p.108.

[16] Mearsheimer. 2006a, p.108.

[17] Mearsheimer. 2006a, p.107.

realist approach but also the discipline of international relations to the present day.[18] In the words of Mearsheimer, Waltz became the "king of thought" in international relations theory and has since retained respect for three decades.[19] Mearsheimer's own work, particularly his book *The Tragedy of Great Power Politics* and a series of papers in *International Security,* have resulted in him taking a place at the head of international realist scholarship, too.[20]

Realism continues to define and divide the field of international relations to the present day. Though the variance between realists led Jeffrey Legro and Andrew Moravcsik to ask "is anybody still a realist?" in a 1999 paper, it is generally acknowledged that realism has had and continues to have a marked impact on the understanding, explanation and prediction of international affairs by those working within the field.[21] As Donnelly argues:

> Even in our post-Cold War era of globalisation, realist theories, although much less dominant, still provide a context and motivation for many of the most important theoretical debates in the field.[22]

In spite of this, realism has come under increasing attack by those within the discipline who consider that it has lost its ability to properly describe, explain and predict international politics, particularly in the wake of the Cold War. Realism, it is argued, is obsolete, so changed is the political environment in the wake of the collapse of the Soviet Union.[23] In particular, two significant post-Cold War phenomena stand as case studies of realism's alleged failure to properly explain modern international relations.

---

[18] Waltz. 1979.

[19] Mearsheimer. 2006a, p.109.

[20] Mearsheimer. 2001; John Mearsheimer. 1990a. 'Back to the Future: Instability in Europe after the Cold War.' *International Security* 15(1): 5-56; John Mearsheimer. 1994. 'The False Promise of International Institutions' *International Security* 19(3): 5-49; Mearsheimer. 2006, p.105.

[21] Legro and Moravcsik. 1999.

[22] Donnelly. 2000, p.1.

[23] For example, Richard Lebow. 'The Long Peace, the End of the Cold War, and the Failure of Realism.' *International Organization* 48(2): 249-277; Paul Schroeder. 1994. 'Historical Reality vs. Neo-Realist Theory.' *International Security* 19(1): 108-148; John Vasquez. 1997. 'The Realist Paradigm and Degenerative versus Progressive Research Programs: An Appraisal of Neotraditional Research on Waltz's Balancing Proposition.' *The American Political Science Review* 91(4): 899-912.

The first of these is the continued and quickening integration of the European continent. As John McCormick writes, "the creation of the European Union will go down in history as one of the most remarkable achievements of the twentieth century".[24] Though a project with roots in the intellectual traditions of Friedrich Naumann, TG Masaryk and Richard Coudenhove-Kalergi and with a true naissance in 1951 with the European Coal and Steel Community, the speed and extent of integration following the Cold War has been truly incredible.[25] The European Union grew from 12 member states at the time of the fall of the Berlin Wall, to 15 member states by 1995 and 25 member states in 2004. Europe today encompasses some half billion citizens, the world's single largest economic trading block and borders that stretch from the Atlantic Ocean to the Russian border and from the Arctic Ocean to the Mediterranean.[26] Yet achieving this remarkable union required the states to sacrifice elements of their own sovereignty voluntarily and, essentially, permanently – an action that challenges standard realist understandings of international behaviour for states.[27]

For realists this continued and excited programme of integration following the end of the global bipolarity of the Cold War was almost unthinkable. In a now infamous 1990 paper, John Mearsheimer argued that realist theory suggests that "the prospects for major crises and war in Europe are likely to increase markedly" at the conclusion of the Cold War.[28] He suggests four possible futures for the continent, all of which draw on his offensive realist theory and none of which can be said to have matched the political reality of post-Cold War Europe.[29] As Mark Pollack argued:

> In contrast to Mearsheimer's lucid and testable prediction, however, European integration has continued its uneven but impressive course throughout the 1990s, including the

---

[24] John McCormick. 2002. *Understanding the European Union: A Concise Introduction.* 2nd edition. New York: Palgrave, p.xi.

[25] Peter Bugge. 1996. 'The nation supreme: The idea of Europe 1914-1945.' In *The History of the Idea of Europe.* Edited by K Wilson and J van der Dussen, pp.83-149; McCormick. 2002, p.66.

[26] McCormick. 2002, pp.193-194; Kenneth Rogoff. 2004. 'Europe's Quiet Leap Forward.' *Foreign Policy* 143 (Jul/Aug): 74-75.

[27] Robert Keohane. 2002. 'Ironies of Sovereignty: The European Union and the United States.' *Journal of Common Market Studies* 40(4): 743-765, pp.746-749.

[28] Mearsheimer. 1990a, p.6. Later in the same paper Mearsheimer suggests a prescription of managed nuclear weapons proliferation as a stabilising strategy for the US to employ (p.54).

[29] Mearsheimer. 1990, pp.6-8.

creation of a European Union and a single currency in the 1992 Maastricht Treaty, and the subsequent deepening of integration in the 1997 Amsterdam Treaty...[30]

Pollack continues by stating that this integration poses puzzles not only for Mearsheimer's offensive realism but neorealists in general.[31] Indeed, the voluntary redaction of the notion of state sovereignty by the very actors that realists assume to have, in the words of Waltz, an "incentive to put [themselves] in a position to be able to take care of [themselves] since no one else can counted on to do so" is a challenge to the conception of the international political system for all realists.[32]

A second significant post-Cold War phenomenon that challenges realist theorists is international terrorism. Terrorism in itself is not new to the realm of politics; indeed, Walter Laqueur's study, *A History of Terrorism*, finds that terrorism, in different forms, has been part of the political life of humans for centuries.[33] However, in the post-Cold War world – and particularly in the post-September 11th 2001 world – terrorism has evolved to be something very different from the standard conceptions of "bomb-throwing, alien anarchists" made famous in the literature of Fyodor Dostoevsky and Joseph Conrad.[34] In 1999, former US Secretary of State, Madeleine Albright, differentiated this 'new' terrorism thus: "What is new is the emergence of terrorist coalitions that do not fully answer to any government, that operate across national borders and have access to advanced technology".[35] Albright further claims that this confrontation between terrorism and states is a "new kind of confrontation that looms as a new century is about to begin"; indeed, as the events that followed the terrorist attacks of September 11th 2001 illustrate, it would be a confrontation that would have a marked effect on all of international relations.[36]

The terrorists responsible for the attacks on New York and Washington that September morning were known to the government of the United States. Indeed, it was noted

---

[30] Mark Pollack. 2001. 'International Relations Theory and European Integration.' *Journal of Common Market Studies* 39(2): 221-244, p.223.
[31] Pollack. 2001, p.223.
[32] Waltz. 1979, p.107.
[33] Walter Laqueur. 2002. *A History of Terrorism*. New Brunswick: Transaction Publishers, p.3.
[34] Laqueur. 2002, p.3.
[35] In Gideon Rose. 1999. 'It Could Happen to Us.' *Foreign Affairs* 78(2): 131-137, p.131.
[36] In Rose. 1999, p.131.

by Thomas Friedman that the world's sole remaining superpower had previously engaged in a missile strike on the leader of al-Qaeda, Osama bin Laden, under the Clinton administration, an attack held by Freidman to be "the first recorded battle between a superpower and a super-empowered angry man".[37] In the aftermath of the 2001 attacks, however, the Bush Administration retaliated not with missiles but a land invasion of the terrorist-sympathiser state, Afghanistan. Later, in 2003, the Afghanistan intervention was followed by a land invasion of Iraq, a change in the ruling regime of that country and an occupation, the duration of which is now measured in years. However, though few if any realists claim terrorism is not an important element of security in the modern world, realist theory generally does not yet encompass the small, non-state actors in their theoretical modelling.[38]

The criticism of realism for not incorporating terrorism into its analysis of international relations has been consistent, particularly following September 2001. Charles Glaser admits that, given the threat of non-state actors in the shape of terrorist groups, realism is no longer "the key theory for analysing some of the dangers that currently top the international security agenda".[39] Others question the realist dismissal of liberalist calls to consider non-state actors, particularly when they "now present the dominant security threat on the political agenda".[40] Seán Molloy argues that the security dilemma posed by transnational terrorism is very different to that which preoccupied realists during the Cold War, leading him to conclude that the "outmoded, state-centric and excessively simplified paradigm" poses an "active danger to the study of IR theory and the practice of international relations".[41] All see the failure of realism to consider non-state actors such as terrorists as a flaw in the theory; after all, if the threat or behaviour of a non-state group is enough for a superpower to launch two

---

[37] Thomas Friedman. 2001. *The Impact of Globalization on World Peace*. Working Paper No. 27, Burkle Center for International Relations, University of California, Los Angeles, p.6.

[38] To be fair to the realists, however, realist theories have never sought to explain or predict terrorist attacks or the behaviour of terrorist groups. As Mearsheimer notes: "Realism is a theory about state behaviour. It assumes that the state is the principal actor in the international system and that there is no higher authority above it. So there is no place in the theory for non-state actors like Al-Qaeda." See John Mearsheimer. 2006b. 'Conversations in International Relations – Interview with John J. Mearsheimer (Part II).' *International Relations* 20(2): 231-243, p.234.

[39] Charles Glaser. 2003. 'Structural Realism in a more complex world.' *Review of International Studies* 29(3): 403-414, p.407.

[40] The Editors. 2003. 'American Realism and the real world.' *Review of International Studies* 29(3):401-402, p.401.

[41] Seán Molloy. 2003. 'Realism: A Problematic Paradigm.' *Security Dialogue* 34(1): 71-85, p.84.

wars, shouldn't the dominant theory of international relations adapt to explain such events?

While there are some who would argue against a move away from realism's standard assumptions about the international system, there are many that have offered some reorientation of the theory in order to address critiques arising from increased regionalism and the rise of significant non-state threats.[42] Jack Snyder, for example, draws on traditionally liberal claims of the importance of domestic factors in state actions in developing his own defensive realist theory.[43] Despite what can be considered a major change to traditional realism, Snyder claims that "arguments stressing domestic determinants of grand strategy are fully consistent with the defensive version of realism".[44] Fareed Zakaria is another realist who instigated changes to the traditional realist stance. In analysing the rise of the United States over the 19th and 20th centuries, Zakaria avoided realism's notion of a unitary state and distinguished between the apparatus of a state (state) and the society of that state (nation).[45] Legro and Moravcsik note other contemporary realists, among them Joseph Grieco, Randall Schweller, Stephen Van Evera and William Wohlforth, have so changed base assumptions in realism to better fit the world they regard.[46]

These changes to realist assumptions, however, have not made the theory immune from criticism. Indeed, realism has been described as less capable of interpreting the world than competing theories, even labelled a "degenerative" paradigm by some.[47] Liberalists still attack realism for its non-engagement with globally significant trends

---

[42] Mearsheimer is one, for example, who sees little utility in incorporating analysis of terrorist groups and non-state actors into wider realism: "I find that fans of offensive realism who are bothered by the fact that the theory does not have a place in it for Al-Qaeda sometimes will say to me, 'Why can't you adjust the theory to fit terrorist groups into it?' My answer is that you cannot do that, because the theory would end up getting watered down, and it would lose its analytical bite. We should all recognize that no theory – realism included – can explain every aspect of international politics". Mearsheimer. 2006b, pp.234-235.

[43] Jack Snyder. 1991. *Myths of Empire: Domestic Politics and International Ambition*. Ithaca: Cornell University Press.

[44] Snyder. 1991, p.12.

[45] Fareed Zakaria. 1998. *From Wealth to Power: The Unusual Origins of America's World Role*. Princeton: Princeton University Press.

[46] Legro and Moravcsik. 1999, pp.18-45.

[47] "Perhaps the most useful way to judge the power of a social scientific paradigm is by examining what it is able to exclude. By the standard, the realist paradigm is degenerating. Its conceptual foundation is being 'stretched' beyond all recognition or utility". Legro and Moravcsik. 1999, p.53.

such as regional integration and terrorism; non-realist constructivists remain critical of realisms failure to engage with notions of constructed security, constructed systems and constructed threats to the state.[48] No matter the evolution of the theory, realism remains incapable of explaining the world as it exists today. No matter the changes introduced to the key assumptions of realism – to conceptions of what a 'state' is, to notions of domestic impact on foreign policy aims, to the importance of absolute versus relative gains – none has allowed realism to regain its former position as the unquestioned and sole theory of international relations. Why, then, has realism been relegated to the larger group of international relations theories that, in the words of John Gaddis, have failed to come anywhere close to predicting any of the major events at the end of the Cold War?[49] This book will argue it is because the changes made to the theory were the wrong changes. Instead of changing the secondary assumptions of realism, the theorists should address the foundational claim of the theory: that the international system is anarchic.

For all the redefinition that realism has endured during centuries past, the assumption of an anarchic international realm has remained foundational to the paradigm. It remains, according to Legro and Moravcsik, "the first and least controversial" of realist assumptions.[50] Realists – whether classical, behavioural, structural, offensive of otherwise – maintain wide agreement that the sphere in which international politics takes place is anarchic.[51] Even those realists who would give greater emphasis to interna-

---

[48] See, for example, Alexander Wendt. 1992. 'Anarchy is what states make of it: the social construction of power politics.' *International Organization* 46(2): 391-425; Alexander Wendt. 1995. 'Constructing International Politics.' *International Security* 20(1): 71-81; Jeffrey Checkel. 1998. 'The Constructivist Turn in International Relations Theory.' *World Politics* 50(2): 324-348; Ted Hopf. 1998. 'The Promise of Constructivism in International Relations Theory.' *International Security* 23(1): 171-200; Dale Copeland. 2000. 'The Constructivist Challenge to Structural Realism: A Review Essay.' *International Security* 25(2): 187-212; Glaser. 2003; Molloy. 2003; The Editors. 2003; David Welch. 2003. 'Why International Relations theorists should stop reading Thucydides.' *Review of International Studies* 29(3): 301-319;

[49] John Gaddis. 1992. 'International Relations Theory and the End of the Cold War.' *International Security* 17(3): 5-58, p.18. Gaddis drew all theories of international relations into three groups (behavioural, structural and evolutionary) before passing this judgement. Realism – in its various iterations – was included in both the behavioural and structural groupings.

[50] Legro and Moravcsik. 1999, p.12.

[51] Kenneth Waltz. 1959. *Man, the State, and War: A Theoretical Analysis.* New York: Columbia University Press, pp.224-238; Waltz. 1979, pp.79-128; Joseph Grieco. 1988. 'Anarchy and the Limits of Cooperation: A Realist Critique of the latest Liberal Institutionalism.' *International Organization* 42(3): 485-507, p.488; Christopher Layne. 1993. 'The Unipolar Illusion: Why New Great Pow-

tional institutions or interstate cooperation still admit that such actions only offer states a 'modified anarchy', one where in ceding some sovereignty to a central authority states "take themselves out of anarchy" temporarily.[52] Anarchy, in the words of Joseph Grieco, is "the principal force shaping the motives and actions of states", a view echoed in works of Colin Elman, John Mearsheimer, Jeffrey Taliaferro.[53] Thus, the discipline of international relations finds itself with a popular approach to theorising and analysing international politics which, when critiqued for obvious flaws, evolves but remains imperfect – and, at the same time, refuses to compromise on its paradigm-wide foundational assumption. As realist assumptions flow from this base 'fact' of international relations, the possibility exists that the poor results which realists generate with their theories may be associated with a poor initial assumption about the nature of the system.[54] In short, if the international relations system is not anarchic then realism is describing a politics that may resemble reality but will not truly describe, explain or predict it.

What could replace anarchy in international relations theory? This book argues that, in the shape of complexity and a complex system, there exists an alternative conception of the international system that can and will allow for better explanations and short-term predictions about actors within the system. Complexity is a distinctly different ordering principle for a system than anarchy. Like anarchical systems, a complex international system does not demand a single overwhelming power exerting control on the system; similarly it does not require that the theorist accept that states are necessarily rational, irrational, competitive or cooperative. This is not to suggest that the assumption of a complex system does not have significant implications for the theory of international relations: it does. Furthermore, while realists have long

---

ers Will Rise.' *International Security* 17(4): 5-51, p.11; Mearsheimer. 1994, p.9; Robert Powell. 1994. 'Anarchy in International Relations Theory: The Neorealist-Neoliberal Debate.' *International Organization* 48(2): 313-344, p.330; Stacie Goddard and Daniel Nexon. 2005. 'Paradigm Lost? Reassessing *Theory of International Politics.*' *European Journal of International Relations* 11(1): 9-61, p.12.

[52] Robert Jervis. 1999. 'Realism, Neoliberalism, and Cooperation: Understanding the Debate.' *International Security* 24(1): 42-63, p.56.

[53] Colin Elman. 1996. 'Horses for Courses: Why *Not* Neorealist Theories of Foreign Policy.' *Security Studies* 6(1): 7-53, pp.18-21; Jeffrey Taliaferro. 2001. 'Security Seeking Under Anarchy: Defensive Realism Revisited.' *International Security* 25(3): 128-161; Mearsheimer. 2006a, p.112.

[54] On this 'flow' see the construction by Mearsheimer of Waltz's structural realism and his own offensive realism in Mearsheimer. 2006a, p.112. See also discussion of the realist reliance on anarchy in Wendt. 1992.

made grand predictions about the future of the international system under anarchy, a complex system is essentially impossible to predict with reliable accuracy long-term.[55] Thus, while complex and anarchic systems are in some ways similar, the implications of each system are markedly different and particularly significant for the explanation and prediction of international politics.

A large literature on complexity is emerging and standout works already exist. More widely cited in the field is Robert Jervis' 1997 book, *System Effects: Complexity in Political and Social Life*.[56] In this work Jervis suggests that the traditional methods of assessing international politics are inadequate to explain the complexity and dynamism of politics in the international realm. Jervis draws deeply on cross-disciplinary sources with many references to population dynamics, biology, ecology and physics in making his case.[57] Jervis concludes his volume with the following words:

> ...we need to take more seriously the notion that we are dealing with systems and to look at the dynamics that drive them. A distinguished student of genetics summarized his perspective in the phrase, "Nothing in biology makes sense except in the light of evolution". Very little in social and political life makes sense except in the light of systemic processes. Exploring them gives us new possibilities for understanding and effective action: in their absence we are likely to flounder.[58]

Realists – though long assessing the role of systems and theorising as to their impact on international interactions – have not yet developed a theoretical approach that considers the possibilities of complex processes in place of anarchical or hierarchical alternatives. The 'exploration' of the international system, to use Jervis' words, has remained narrow and realism has, thus, 'floundered'.

---

[55] Gleick. 1987, p.18; Robert Jervis. 1997. *System Effects: Complexity in Social and Political Life*, Princeton: Princeton University Press, p.4; p.29.

[56] Jervis. 1997. A Google Scholar search shows some 172 citations for Jervis' work in the disciplinary literature.

[57] Jervis. 1997: population dynamics – p.21; biology – p.47; ecology – pp.37-38; physics – p.286. Jervis also makes mention of other sciences which have begun to apply chaotic and complex systems analysis including chemistry, theories of evolution, economics, group dynamics and strategic studies.

[58] Jervis. 1997, p.295.

This book sets out to arrest this floundering trend. From the outset the argument will be made that realism – the dominant approach to theorising international relations – is flawed: not for any of the reasons that realists have attempted to address in their re-formulations of the paradigm but by reason of its base assumption of an anarchically ordered system. It will be argued that this assumption of anarchy, the implications that flow from it in conjunction with other realist assumptions leads to analysis that cannot describe or explain the reality of international politics. Instead of changing secondary assumptions in the theory (the nature of state preferences or the significance of non-state actors, for example) realism needs to reassess the assumption of anarchy, replacing it with an understanding of the system that can describe, explain and predict international interactions with greater accuracy than realism has experienced. As has been foreshadowed in this introduction, the systemic ordering to be suggested by this book as the replacement for anarchy is complexity.

The argument towards this end will be concluded in two general parts, each involving several sub-sections. The first section will involve a detailed review of the realist literature to be followed by a critique of the same. Particular focus will be placed on the major branches of the realist paradigm, with the opening chapter considering the so-called classical realism typified in the work of Hans Morgenthau.[59] This chapter will also consider the work of EH Carr, Machiavelli, Hobbes and Thucydides, focussing on the importance of the anarchical assumption in each of their theories. A second chapter will turn to structural realism, also known as neorealism, and critically consider the work of Kenneth Waltz. Again, the importance of the anarchical foundation of the structural realist theory will be evidenced and critiqued, particularly in relation to the poverty of accurate explanation and prediction offered by structural realist theories. Owing to the wide variation in realist theories, a third chapter will consider the other branches of the paradigm with the joint goals of proving the paradigm wide reliance on anarchy as the foundation of realism's international political analysis and proving that the predictions and explanations offered by these variants of the paradigm are just as poor as the more popular classical and structural branches of realism.

---

[59] 'Classical realism' is the preferred term for this branch of realism in this book. Other scholars, including Donnelly, refer to this branch of the paradigm as 'biological' realism, so named for its focus on human nature as a tool of explanation for state behaviour. See Donnelly. 2000, p.11.

The second part of the book draws on this suggestion by explicating a theory of international politics based upon a complex international system. The first chapter in this second section will draw together the previous three and summarise the reliance on anarchy of each of these realist theories of international relations. Pointing to the poor record, particularly the recent record, of realist theories in describing, explaining and predicting international affairs and – concurrently – pointing to the paradigm wide reliance of realism on a base anarchic system, this chapter will suggest that the real failure of realism is the failure to engage with alternate conceptions of the system under examination. Drawing on interdisciplinary examples from the natural and human sciences, this chapter will suggest that rethinking the base assumptions about systems and processes is a useful way of obtaining better descriptions, explanations and predictions about systems and events within them. It will conclude by suggesting that a complex interpretation of the international system opens up possibilities that the anarchical interpretation of realism remains blind to.

The final chapter in this part extrapolates from this new founding assumption a series of assumptions and implications for actors within the international system. In essence, this final chapter presents a complex theory of international relations that stands in opposition to the realist perspective and paradigm presented in the first part of the book. A short concluding commentary will then summarise the argument as presented in the book, suggest some further research possibilities arising from the conclusions of the book and draw attention to the most significant implications of the research program.

This book will provide the first explication of a theory of international relations based upon an assumption of complexity in the place of anarchy. Comparing the descriptions, explanations and predictions of this alternative complex theory with the traditional realist paradigm will demonstrate that there are considerable benefits to be gained through the application of this theory in the analysis of international affairs. In particular, the complex theory outlined in this book will allow theorists and practitioners to better analyse the world as it exists rather than the misleading anarchic model of the world with which all preceding analysis has dealt with. In particular, reliable long-term predictions about the international system and potential interactions/conflicts will be shown to be impossible to conceive under a complex system.

However, in balance, the explanation and description of the international system provided by this alternative method will be shown to be a credible alternative to those realist positions considered in this book. In essence, this book will provide the discipline of international relations with an alternative frame of reference through which to view the international realm, one that opens the door to exciting future research programs.

The fact that an opinion has been widely held
is no evidence whatever that it is not utterly absurd.
Bertrand Russell

ANARCHY AND CLASSICAL REALISM

Little can be said about realism as an approach to theorising international relations without differentiating between the various realist approaches which, together, compose the wider realist method. These approaches are so varied – Colin Elman describes realism as a "big tent" theory with plenty of room for varied approaches inside – that it is useful to begin any review of the literature with a typology of realist theories.[60] This allows for the various major streams of realist thought to be assessed in turn under headings less broad than 'realism' alone, though not so specific as to become bogged down in the details of every theoretical 'tweak' to each and every realist theory. As well, within the realist literature, such typologies are common with realists commonly also identifying themselves with a sub-stream of this theoretical approach to international relations.

Jack Donnelly offers a typology of realism in his 2000 book *Realism and International Relations*.[61] Donnelly argues that there are "two dimensions" by which realist approaches can be classified: "the relative emphasis they give to the propositions of egoism and anarchy and the stringency of their commitment to a rigorous and exclusively realist analysis."[62] Within the first of these dimensions, Donnelly argues that there are two primary sub-groups: structural realists and biological realists.[63] The first of these he defines as those realists who "give predominant emphasis to international anarchy".[64] Significant realists who would fall into this group would include John Herz, Barry Buzan and Kenneth Waltz whose work, it has been held, continues to define the structural realist research agenda.[65] Donnelly's demarcation of structural

---

[60] Elman. 1996, p.26.

[61] Donnelly. 2000.

[62] Donnelly. 2000, p.11.

[63] Donnelly. 2000, p.11.

[64] Donnelly. 2000, p.11.

[65] Donnelly. 2000, p.11; John Herz. 1957. 'Rise and Demise of the Territorial State.' *World Politics* 9(4): 473-493, pp.473-474; Barry Buzan. 1993. 'From International System to International Society: Structural Realism and Regime Theory Meet the English School.' *International Organization*

realism is very much in line with other definitions of this particular sub-realist approach, including those of Legro and Moravcsik, Steve Smith and Waltz himself.[66]

The second of the sub-groups in this first dimension of realism has been termed by Donnelly "biological realism".[67] Biological realists place theoretical emphasis on human nature in explaining the behaviour of states. The term, though, is peculiar to Donnelly's work, the author having ascribed it to what most would identify as classical realism, or even simply 'realism'. Donnelly explains his distinction thus:

> Although such theorists are often called "classical" realists, this label tells us nothing about the substance of their orientation. The category "classical" is a residual: those who are not structural (neo)realists. The label biological, by contrast, is substantive and positive, pointing to their emphasis on human nature. And, by refusing to define categories in terms of the currently dominant structuralist turn, it maintains neutrality between competing approaches to realism.[68]

Biological realism has a far richer history than structural realism and can claim among its most significant theorists Niccolò Machiavelli, Thomas Hobbes, EH Carr and, more recently, Hans Morgenthau.[69] All of these authors, to which one could add dozens of others in the post-World War Two era, held what Robert Gilpin described as a "pessimism regarding moral progress and human possibilities", constrained as humans are by their inherent nature.[70]

Within Donnelly's second dimension, he differentiates between three different groups. First, there are the radical realists, those who "adopt extreme versions of the three realist premises of anarchy, egoism, and power politics".[71] Donnelly cites the Athenian envoys to Melos in Thucydides' *History of the Peloponnesian War* as an example of such radical realism, though there are similar sentiments expressed by

---

47(3): 327-352; Waltz. 1979. On "…continues to define the structural realist…" see Mearsheimer. 2006a, p.109.

[66] Legro and Moravcsik. 1999; Steve Smith. 2001. 'Is the truth out there? Eight questions about international order.' In *International Order and the Future of World Politics*, edited by TV Paul and JA Hall. Cambridge: Cambridge University Press, pp.99-119, p.99; Kenneth Waltz. 1990. 'Realist Thought and Neorealist Theory.' *Journal of International Affairs* 44(1): 21-37, pp.29-37.

[67] Donnelly. 2000, p.11.

[68] Donnelly. 2000, p.11. This book will use the terms 'classical' and 'biological' interchangedly.

[69] See examples in Machiavelli. 2005; Hobbes. 2004; Carr. 2001; Morgenthau. 1993.

[70] Robert Gilpin. 1986. 'The Richness of the Tradition of Political Realism.' In *Neorealism and Its Critics*, edited by RO Keohane. New York: Columbia University Press, pp.301-321, p.304.

[71] Donnelly. 2000, p.12.

26

Pericles, the Athenian statesman, in the same volume.[72] Though others have argued that, at times, even Hans Morgenthau adopted a radical realist position, Donnelly submits that a consistently radically realist position is uncommon within the discipline today.[73] Donnelly prefers to interpret Morgenthau's work as typical of his second group: strong realists.[74]

Strong realists are those who "adopt realist premises in a way that allows only modest space for politically salient "non-realist" concerns".[75] Alongside Morgenthau, Donnelly ranks Waltz as an exemplary strong realist, indicating that being 'strong' has little to do with either a structural or a biological stance.[76] The 'modest space' for non-realist concerns might also allow for realists such as Stephen Walt and John Mearsheimer's recent work on domestic lobby groups and foreign policy to not exclude them from this strong realist category.[77] Finally there are the 'hedged realists', those who accept the 'realities' of realism (anarchy and egoism) but remain dissatisfied with the realist 'solution' of power politics.[78] Donnelly goes on to note, however, "hedged realism gradually merges into views that are fundamentally something else…making it impossible to label the resulting position or argument 'realist'".[79]

This book will begin its review of the realist literature with the biological realists and, among those, a focus on the work of Hans Morgenthau, considered the archetype biological or classical realist.

---

[72] Donnelly. 2000, p.12; Thucydides. 1998, p.100.

[73] Jan Willem Honig. 1996. 'Totalitarianism and Realism: Hans Morgenthau's German Years.' *Security Studies* 5(2): 283-313; Donnelly. 2000, p.12. See also Jack Donnelly. 1998a. 'Realism: Roots and Renewal.' *Review of International Studies* 24(3): 399-405, p.405.

[74] Donnelly. 2000, p.12.

[75] Donnelly. 2000, p.12.

[76] Donnelly. 2000, p.12.

[77] John Mearsheimer and Stephen Walt. 2006. *The Israel Lobby and US Foreign Policy*. Faculty Research Working Paper No. RWP06-011, John F. Kennedy School of Government, Harvard University, March 2006. See discussion on these realist authors and their allowance for domestic influence in Mackubin Owens. 2006. 'Letters: Debating the Israel Lobby.' *Foreign Policy* 156: 4.

[78] Donnelly. 2000, p.12.

[79] Donnelly. 2000, p.13.

Classical Realism: The Realism of Hans Morgenthau

Dermeval Aires said of Hans Morgenthau:

> Morgenthau was one of the few individuals who could understand [the Cold War era's] problems, rising up to the challenge of facing human nature in the eyes in such bleak days without subterfuges.[80]

Facing human nature with all of its faults was something at the core of Morgenthau's realism. Indeed, Morgenthau is clear in his 'Principles of Political Realism' to start by acknowledging that human nature is at the core of human politics. In the five other principles that follow, Morgenthau outlines a particular strain of realist thought that builds on this notion of human nature to describe and explain the politics of the international realm. These six principles – claimed by Hans-Karl Pichler to be "the theoretical manifesto of his body of thought" – have since gone on to be widely cited as *the* point of departure for modern classical realists.[81] In the section that follows these six principles will be outlined in turn and parallels will be drawn with other realists and with Morgenthau's wider work in order to provide a detailed outline of a prototypical classical realist.

Principle One

Morgenthau's first principle of political realism demonstrates exactly why Donnelly would place him amongst the biological realists.[82] Morgenthau writes:

> Political realism believes that politics, like society in general, is governed by objective laws that have their roots in human nature. In order to improve society it is first necessary to understand the laws by which society lives. The operation of these laws being impervious to our preferences, men will challenge them only at the risk of failure.[83]

---

[80] V Sundaram. 2006. 'Scientific Man vs. Power Politics I.' *News Today* (6 March 2006).

[81] Hans-Karl Pichler. 1998. 'The godfathers of 'truth': Max Weber and Carl Schmitt in Morgenthau's theory of power politics.' *Review of International Studies* 24(2): 185-200, p.187.

[82] Donnelly. 2000, p.11.

[83] Morgenthau. 1993, p.4.

This 'human nature' remains unchanged over time, with Morgenthau citing with respect the work of the Chinese, Indian and Greek civilisations which also endeavoured to discover laws of politics based on human nature.[84] The nature of humanity Morgenthau refers to is not one of altruism and kindness; indeed, it is almost the opposite. Morgenthau claims that "history bears out" that humans think and act in terms of self interest.[85] This brings Morgenthau into line with earlier realists such as Machiavelli who wrote that humans will always think about their own interests and that "men always turn out bad for you, unless some necessity makes them act well".[86] This pessimistic conception of human nature has come to be one of the most significant elements upon which classical realists base their analysis of international affairs.

By founding his realism on human nature, however, Morgenthau does open himself to criticism that his base assumption is entirely problematic. Consider, for example, that in claiming a single human nature common to all – from the early Chinese Xia Dynasty through to the post-Cold War world – essentially disregards philosophers, sociologists and political scientists who would counter that such a selfish human nature is not reflected wholesale among humanity. Philosopher David Hume, for example, is eloquent in his defence of a human nature not entirely selfish:

> It is sufficient for our present purpose, if it be allowed, what surely, without the greatest absurdity cannot be disputed, that there is some benevolence, however small, infused into our bosom; some spark of friendship for human kind; some particle of the dove kneaded into our frame, along with the elements of the wolf and serpent. Let these generous sentiments be supposed ever so weak; let them be insufficient to move even a hand or finger of our body, they must still direct the determinations of our mind, and where everything else is equal, produce a cool preference of what is useful and serviceable to mankind, above what is pernicious and dangerous.[87]

Hume's claims stand in direct opposition to Morgenthau's world where "moral principles can never be fully realised" owing to the imperfect "forces inherent in human nature".[88] There is no 'dove' in the human nature of the classical realists, only the

---

[84] Morgenthau. 1993, p.4: "Human nature...has not changed since the classical philosophies of China, India and Greece endeavoured to discover these laws."
[85] Morgenthau. 1993, p.5.
[86] Machiavelli. 2005, p.82.
[87] David Hume. 2003a. *An Enquiry Concerning the Principles of Morals.* e-text. http://tinyurl.com/zj6pj, p.49.
[88] Morgenthau. 1993, p.3.

'wolf' and 'serpent' as humanity aims solely at the realisation of the lesser of two evils.[89]

Hume extends this critique of a solely pessimistic and selfish human nature in his *Dialogues Concerning Natural Religion*.[90] First pointing to nature and the "perpetual terror and anxiety" that results from the strong praying upon the weak, Hume then makes a case for humans being an exception to nature's rules.[91] He argues that through engagement in a society, humans can and do overcome the terrors of nature and tame those with greater strength who would, in nature, have preyed upon others.[92] This of course echoes another realist, Hobbes, whose Leviathan can be considered one example of such a society enabling escape from the natural terror of the world.[93] But it also echoes the work of twentieth-century sociologists who claim that human nature is less directive for human behaviour than the society which has been constructed by humans and which impacts upon their behaviour to a remarkable extent. The post-modern 'social construction' thesis of Peter Berger and Thomas Luckmann sees a role for a biological human nature in determining the behaviour of humans, but argue that the socially constructed 'culture' and 'society' is much more important in analysing the behaviour that manifests itself.[94]

Political scientist Kristen Monroe is another who would take issue with Morgenthau's depiction of a selfish human nature.[95] As she asks:

> Most social and political theory since Hobbes is constructed on the norm of self-interest. As a guiding principle, self-interest informs many public policies and directs our daily lives. Yet even in the most vicious of Darwinian worlds, altruism and selfless behaviour continues to exist. Why?[96]

---

[89] Morgenthau. 1993, p.4.

[90] David Hume. 2003b. *Dialogues Concerning Natural Religion*. 10th edition. e-text. http://tinyurl.com/kr224.

[91] Hume. 2003b, pp.35-36.

[92] Hume. 2003b, p.36.

[93] Hobbes. 2004. See also discussion in Bertrand Russell. 1993. *History of Western Philosophy and its Connection with Political and Social Circumstances from the Earliest Times to the Present Day*. London: Routledge, pp.535-536.

[94] Peter Berger and Thomas Luckmann. 1971. *The Social Construction of Reality: A Treatise in the Sociology of Knowledge*. Hammondsworth: Penguin. See also commentary in Van Harvey. 1973. 'Some Problematical Aspects of Peter Berger's Theory of Religion.' *Journal of the American Academy of Religion* 41(1): 75-93;

[95] Kristen Monroe. 1998. *The Heart of Altruism*. Princeton: Princeton University Press.

[96] Monroe. 1998, p.3.

The answer from realist's intent on maintaining a place for human nature in their explanative theories of international relations is that such altruism is enacted for the benefit of the individual.[97] Though this argument for self-serving altruism has been made by realists as notable as Hobbes, it remains a somewhat limited defence of the classical realist position.

Principle Two

Morgenthau's second principle of political realism outlines how states and statesmen navigate through an international system defined by the pessimistic human nature. For Morgenthau – as for all classical and many other realists – the motivation or action by states in the international system is the self-interest as defined in terms of power.[98] He states outright:

> The main signpost the helps political realism to find its way through the landscape of international politics is the concept of interest defined in terms of power. This concept provides the link between reason trying to understand international politics and the facts to be understood.[99]

Morgenthau supports this contention by appealing to history, arguing that previous international political actions bear out an international system dominated by states acting in their own interest.[100] Morgenthau is sure to point out that the actual political

---

[97] Monroe. 1998, p.143. See also Elias Khalil. 2001. 'Adam Smith and the Three Theories of Altruism.' *Recherches économiques de Louvain* 67(4): 421-435, p.428. Khalil quotes John Aubrey on Hobbes: "One time, I remember, goeing in the Strand, a poor and infirme old man craved his (Hobbes') almes. He, beholding him with eies of pitty and compassion, pull his hand in his pocket, and gave him 6d. Sayd a divine (scil. Dr. Jaspar Mayne) that stood by–'Would you have donne this, if it had not been Christ's command?'–'Yea', sayd he.–'Why?' quoth the other.– 'Because', sayd he, 'I was in paine to consider the miserable condition of the old man; and now my almes, giving him some reliefe, doth also ease me'".

[98] Morgenthau. 1993, p.5.

[99] Morgenthau. 1993, p.5.

[100] Morgenthau. 1993, p.5. See also Hans Morgenthau. 1952. 'Another "Great Debate": The National Interest of the United States.' *The American Political Science Review* 46(4): 961-988, p.962; pp.963-964. In Hans Morgenthau. 1967. 'To Intervene or Not Intervene.' *Foreign Affairs* 45(3): 96-112, p.94 Morgenthau directly compares the Cold War period to earlier historical times, particularly the period of the Napoleonic Wars. Later (p.97) he alludes again to the historical veracity of his claims by stating that, "These rules [concerning intervention] must be deduced not from abstract principles...but from the interests of the nations concerned and from *their practice of foreign policy reflecting those interests*" (emphasis added).

policies of states and statesmen who address international affairs with regards to interests and power will not result in "moral goodness" or even morally defensible positions.[101] He cites the differing foreign policy positions of Neville Chamberlain and Winston Churchill in relation to their German rivals. The policy of appeasement of the former was "inspired by good motives" and not through considerations of personal or national power and interest; the policies of the latter are described by Morgenthau as "much more narrowly directed towards personal and national power".[102]

Despite political realisms contention that politics is guided by interests defined by power, Morgenthau does submit that, obviously, not all foreign policies pursued by international actors have been "rational, objective, and unemotional".[103] Besides his example in Chamberlain, in works other than *Politics among Nations* Morgenthau has pointed to particular policies of the United States and the League of Nations as exemplars of non-realist positions being taken in international affairs.[104] Morgenthau argues that nothing can be done to stop "personality, prejudice and subjective preference" from impacting on the decisions of states and statesmen – yet he still maintains that such departures from rational, objective and unemotional conduct of foreign affairs by states is simply a "persistence of mistaken attitudes that have survived...political experience".[105]

Countering such a charge is a wide literature with two general streams of critique: first, that ideas have a significant effect on the foreign policy of nation-states; second, that defining politics in terms of power is overly vague. An example of this first critique is found in Stephen Brooks and William Wohlforth's *Power, Globalization and*

---

[101] Morgenthau. 1993, p.6.
[102] Morgenthau. 1993, p.6. Sheila Lawlor also alludes to this distinction between the 'good motives' of Chamberlain and the narrow, national interest motives of Churchill: "Whereas Churchill gave the impression that 'he love[d] war', 'it broke...Chamberlain's better heart'." Sheila Lawlor. 1995. *Churchill and the Politics of War, 1940-41*. Cambridge: Cambridge University Press, p.55.
[103] Morgenthau. 1993, p.7.
[104] See Hans Morgenthau. 1977. 'The Pathology of American Power.' *International Security* 1(3): 3-20; Hans Morgenthau. 1939. 'International Affairs: The Resurrection of Neutrality in Europe.' *The American Political Science Review* 33(3): 473-486, p.478;
[105] Morgenthau. 1993, p.7.

32

the End of the Cold War.[106] Brooks and Wohlforth argue that it is not a matter of "whether but rather how and how much ideas matter" in foreign policy.[107] Specifically, they reject the thesis that Soviet policy during the Cold War was defined by calculations of power alone but rather influenced to a significant extent by ideas, competitive instincts and that "ideational factors" are very important in explaining finely grained foreign policy decisions.[108] More than Morgenthau's 'power as politics' thesis, Brooks and Wohlforth suggest that other factors, in particular ideas within the state, have a tangible effect on a state's international relations strategies.

The second critique of Morgenthau's second principle stems from the definition of power. For Morgenthau, power "may comprise anything that establishes and maintains the control of man over man. Thus power covers all social relationships which serve that end".[109] While later Morgenthau differentiates 'power' and 'influence' – defining the former as compelling and the latter as merely persuasive – and between legitimate and illegitimate power (defined legally and morally), his definition does include economic, military and political power.[110] In this way, then, almost everything within the sphere of 'high politics' falls within the realm of power.[111] As well, in light of the recent work of Joseph Nye in the realm of soft power, it would seem that almost everything – including matters not within the direct control of the state – has become 'state power' of a sort.[112]

Principle Three

Morgenthau's third principle of political realism flows from his second. Political realism is concerned with interest and 'interest' for Morgenthau is timeless. He writes,

---

[106] Stephen Brooks and William Wohlforth. 2000. 'Power, Globalization and the End of the Cold War.' *International Security* 25(3): 5-53.

[107] Brooks and Wohlforth. 2000, p.6.

[108] Brooks and Wohlforth. 2000; *ibid*, p.50.

[109] Morgenthau. 1993, p.11.

[110] Morgenthau. 1993, pp.31-32.

[111] 'High politics' is defined as, "issues that pertain directly to the political and economic integrity of the state". See Eric Holm. 2000. *High Politics and European Integration: From EMU to CFSP.* Discussion Paper No. 2, The Hellenic Observatory, London School of Economics and Political Science, November 2000, p.1.

[112] Joseph Nye. 2004. *Soft Power: The Means to Success in World Politics.* New York: Public Affairs Press.

"[t]he idea of interest is indeed of the essence of politics and is unaffected by the circumstances of time and place" and, in support of this contention, appeals to Thucydides of ancient Greece, George Washington in the 18th century and Max Weber in the 20th century.[113] Morgenthau does not deny that there is a certain influence on the interest of a state depending on the social, political and cultural context the state finds itself in during any point in time; indeed, he admits that interests are defined by contemporary issues for states.[114] Yet he also claims that, despite the possibility of interests changing in the international context a state finds itself operating in, change in international relations cannot occur by disregarding the notion of interests. As he argues, a realist "cannot be persuaded" that change in international politics can occur as a result of ignoring the role of interests.[115] The importance, then, of the national interest in defining the international politics of states cannot be underestimated by the political realist.

On this point Morgenthau find wide support within the literature. Machiavelli discusses the centrality of interests in international politics in Chapter XVIII of *The Prince*, arguing that good and evil must not define the politics of the ruler; rather the interests of the Prince must take precedence over such moral questions.[116] Similarly, EH Carr rejects any notion of an 'international interest' and labels the period between the two World Wars – where such an idea was popularly put – as "a period of disillusionment", the people who reject the notion of national interest-defined politics as "naïvely egotistical" and the thought which supported the non-realist stance as profoundly defective.[117] Even among non-realists the potency of interests in defining state action is admitted freely. James Caporaso, in extolling the benefits of multilateral liberal institutionalism, argued that multilateral activities can occur when states act in a rational, self-interested fashion.[118] Further, liberalists Robert Keohane and Lisa Martin argue that within their institutionalist theory national interest plays a sig-

---

[113] Morgenthau. 1993, pp.10-11.
[114] Morgenthau. 1993, p.11.
[115] Morgenthau. 1993, pp.11-12.
[116] Machiavelli. 2005, p.61.
[117] Carr. 2001, pp.72-73; p.81.
[118] James Caporaso. 1992. 'International Relations Theory and Multilateralism: The Search for Foundations.' *International Organization* 46(3): 599-632, p.604.

34

nificant role in defining the international landscape of war and peace.[119] Yet for all the cross-paradigm attraction of assessing international affairs with reference to the national interests of state actors, there remains an inherent weakness within the argument for the centrality of 'interests' in politics.

In essence, the weakness of talking to 'interests' in international politics is the intrinsic vagueness of the term. While Morgenthau, for one, acknowledges the context of the international political interests matters, this does not grant the term any further distinctiveness and, indeed, allows it to be defined so loosely as to be abused by many. Take, for example, the way in which the National Socialist German Workers Party (NSDAP) defined the German national interest as "anything that benefits the German people".[120] Similarly, in more recent times, nation-states such as Australia have defined the national interest to encompass "the security and prosperity of the Australian people", before continuing to broaden this already broad definition to include such elements as "global and regional security, trade liberalisation, transnational threats, the promotion of human rights and the environment".[121] With interests defined so broadly and – in the case of Australia's 'transnational threats' – vaguely, it is easy to argue that all international politics arises from interests: how could it not? The breadth of the term and its utility for politicians as the all-encompassing excuse for international action make it a liability to a theory of politics such as Morgenthau's. In explaining everything, it can also be held to explain nothing.

Principles Four and Five

Morgenthau writes that "[p]olitical realism is aware of the moral significance of political action" but maintains that "universal moral principles cannot be applied to the actions of states".[122] The international realm, thus, is an amoral sphere of action where states interact not according to the rules of justice and morality that apply to

---

[119] Robert Keohane and Lisa Martin. 1995. 'The Promise of Institutionalist Theory.' *International Security* 20(1): 39-51, p.50.

[120] Carr. 2001, p.74. Carr is citing AJ Toynbee and VM Boulter. 1936. *Survey of International Affairs 1935*. Oxford: Oxford University Press, p.319.

[121] Department of Foreign Affairs and Trade. 2003. *Advancing the National Interest: Australia's Foreign and Trade Policy White Paper*. Canberra: National Capital Printing, p.vii; p.x.

[122] Morgenthau. 1993, p.12.

individuals but according to the rules of "prudence", by which Morgenthau means a "weighing of the consequences of alternative political action".[123] In support, Morgenthau quotes Abraham Lincoln who, though honoured in contemporary times for the moral 'right' that he brought the slaves of the US South, demonstrated that politicians must remain unencumbered with moral principles to achieve the best political ends:

> If the end brings me out all right, what is said against me won't amount to anything. If the end bring me out wrong, ten angels swearing I was right would make no difference[124]

Morality, then, is within the realm of individuals and national politics; the international sphere is one of amoral calculation by states which value ends over moral means.

The related fifth principle expounds upon this stance. Morgenthau writes, "[p]olitical realism refuses to identify the moral aspirations of a particular nation with the moral laws that govern the universe."[125] Noting that politicians are universally tempted to define their actions as moral according to "moral purposes of the universe", the political realist must not presume to know the definition of good and evil in international affairs.[126] According to Morgenthau, the definition of interests in terms of power alone "saves" the state from both moral excess and the "folly" of international action based on morality as it is understood by the state.[127] He cautions the realist against showing any moderation on this point as, he explains, the state would be doomed to failure in the face of other, less moral states.[128]

Of course, such a position is reminiscent of earlier realist authors. Machiavelli goes so far as to claim that "in our times we have not seen great deeds accomplished except by those who were considered miserly".[129] For the Italian political philosopher,

---

[123] Morgenthau. 1993, p.12.
[124] Morgenthau. 1993, p.12. The original Lincoln quote (unsourced by Morgenthau) can be found in FB Carpenter. 1995. *The Inner Life of Abraham Lincoln: Six Months at the White House.* Lincoln: University of Nebraska Press, pp.258-259.
[125] Morgenthau. 1993, p.13.
[126] Morgenthau. 1993, p.13.
[127] Morgenthau. 1993, p.13.
[128] Morgenthau. 1993, p.13.
[129] Machiavelli. 2005, p.55.

"a prince must not worry about the infamy of being considered cruel when it is a matter of keeping his subjects united and loyal", a sentiment that is reflected in Lincoln's statement as well as Morgenthau's work. [130] Similarly, one could return to Thucydides and the Melian dialogues where it is noted by the Athenian negotiator that:

> But you and we should say what we really think, and aim only at what is possible, for we both alike know that into the discussion of human affairs the question of justice only enters where there is equal power to enforce it, and that the powerful exact what they can, and the weak grant what we must.[131]

Thucydides, like Machiavelli, argues that in a world without a greater power (that is, the international rather than the national polity) questions of justice and morality do not arise. This is not to suggest, however, that realists such as Machiavelli and Morgenthau do not have any interest in political morality – they do.[132] It is just that realists argue that abstract socio-cultural moral principles should have little to do with how state interests are defined or what action is taken in support of those interests.

Countering such contention, of course, are a range of theorists from the liberalist and humanist perspectives. They argue, for example, that practical international political actions, such as a global acceptance of the Universal Declaration of Human Rights, indicate that morality not only has a role to play in international action but also has some impact over the interests that are defined by states.[133] One cannot read Francis Fukuyama's essay *The End of History?* on the eventual international triumph of the liberal-democratic norm without understanding that Fukuyama's thesis rests on the

---

[130] Machiavelli. 2005, p.57.

[131] Thucydides. 1998, p.169.

[132] Morgenthau, in particular, was a prolific publisher on morality and ethics in political actions. See examples in Hans Morgenthau. 1945a. 'The Evil of Politics and the Ethics of Evil.' *Ethics* 56(1): 1-18; Hans Morgenthau. 1948a. 'The Twilight of International Morality.' *Ethics* 58(2): 79-99.

[133] Donnelly goes as far as to call the rights stemming from the Universal Declaration of Human Rights the "new international standard of civilisation". See Jack Donnelly. 1998b. 'Human Rights: A New Standard of Civilisation?' *International Affairs* 74(1): 1-23, p.1. Morgenthau's response to such claims is outlined later in *Politics among Nations* where he argued that universal political morality is untenable, pointing to two key weaknesses in that argument: first, the "impossibility of enforcing the universal application of human rights"; second, that no country can "consistently follow the path of the defence of human rights without manoeuvring itself into a Quixotic position". Instead, Morgenthau concludes that Abraham Lincoln's position – "I must study the plain physical facts of the case, ascertain what is possible and learn what appears to be wise and right" – is the only 'morality' one can expect of a state and its leaders. See Morgenthau. 1993, pp.247-249.

notion of an international morality (in this case, democratic values) can and does exist.[134] But more importantly, those who argue for universal human rights or universal governance by democratic means are in fact, by implication, endorsing the existence of an international, cross-cultural moral foundation for political action. As such, they make a direct counter-claim against Morgenthau's amoral world, deciding that it is impossible to separate the politics of the international from the morality of the individual. For the realist it is not a convincing argument but in recent times it has seen some significant practical policy implications which suggest increasing empirical support for the notion.

Principle Six

Morgenthau's final principle of political realism demands that the realist "maintains the autonomy of the political sphere" in their assessment of international politics.[135] By this he means that the realist must separate the political from the moral and the legal, assessing international action and foreign policy decisions by their relation to state interests and power alone.[136] First comparing it to the necessarily limited disciplines of economics and jurisprudence, Morgenthau offers three historical examples to support his claim: the British and French response to the 1939 Soviet invasion of Finland; the status of the Communist government of China in the international community; and the British defence of Belgium in the 1914 war.[137] In each case, Morgenthau suggests that a realist assessment of the political situation unencumbered by legalistic or moralistic notions proves a better policy for the state that the alternatives. Thus, for Morgenthau and realists of his ilk, legal and moral norms should never enter into international political calculations.

Carr makes a similar argument for ensuring a distinction between the moral and legal sphere of the domestic polity and the solely political sphere which is the international. He argues that there are four principal reasons why the state should be concerned with international politics and not international legality and morality: the in-

---

[134] Francis Fukuyama. 1989. 'The End of History?' *The National Interest* (Summer):3-18.
[135] Morgenthau. 1993, p.13.
[136] Morgenthau. 1993, pp.13-14.
[137] Morgenthau. 1993, pp.13-15.

herent difficulty of ascribing to the state the emotions that inform individual morality; the fact that actions which might be considered immoral or illegal when performed by individuals are not so when performed by groups, including states; there is no authority higher than a state to demand a legal or moral order; and, finally, legal and moral structures can only exist within a social context, necessarily implying an international society which, for Carr, does not exist.[138] Similarly, Machiavelli warns against leaders ascribing to an international law that cannot be enforced, writing, "where there is no tribunal to which to appeal" one must only consider the final result.[139] Thus, Morgenthau, Carr and Machiavelli consider that international relations take place in a political realm unbounded by law, morals or ethics where the success of a policy is judged never by the means of implementation by only ever by its ends.

Yet, in opposition to this perspective, there exists an extensive literature which seems to demonstrate that the international sphere cannot be separated from the moral sphere as easily or as practically as Morgenthau suggests. One striking and increasingly popular example can be found in the 'democratic peace' thesis.[140] As outlined by Bruce Bueno de Mesquita, James Morrow, Randolph Siverson and Alastair Smith, the democratic peace thesis argues that democracies do not go to war with other democracies.[141] It is implied, then, that the moral, social or cultural domestic norms of the state can influence greatly the most important foreign policy decisions in the international sphere. So significant is the correlation between internal democratic norms and external state policy that authors have claimed it is a perfect correlation and that the thesis is "the closest thing we have to an empirical law in the study of international relations".[142] On top of such theoretical and empirical studies, there is

---

[138] Carr. 201, pp.143-147. It should not be implied from this, however, that Carr is uninterested in international morality but only that he believes states should concern themselves with politics instead.

[139] Machiavelli. 2005, p.62.

[140] The use of the word 'thesis' in place of 'theory' is for reasons in line with Kenneth Waltz's as outlined in Kenneth Waltz. 2000. 'Structural Realism after the Cold War.' *International Security* 25(1): 5-41, pp.6-7.

[141] Bruce Bueno de Mesquita, James Morrow, Randolph Siverson and Alastair Smith. 1999. 'An Institutional Explanation for the Democratic Peace.' *American Political Science Review* 93(4): 791-807.

[142] Francis Fukuyama. 1991. 'Liberal Democracy as a Global Phenomenon.' *PS: Political Science and Politics* 24(4): 659-664, p.662; Jack Levy. 1989. 'Domestic Politics and War.' In *The Origin and Prevention of Major War*, eds. Robert Rotberg and Theodore Rabb. Cambridge: Cambridge University Press, pp.79-101, p.88. For background see Michael Doyle. 1983a. 'Kant, Liberal Lega-

even practical political support in the shape of the Association of South East Asian Nations (ASEAN) which claims it "has subscribed to the notion of democratic peace, which means all member countries believe democratic processes will promote regional peace and stability".[143]

The question is, then, are Morgenthau, Carr and Machiavelli actually theorising the real international system? If the evidence of empirical studies and even practical politicians in ASEAN seem to suggest that the moral, social and cultural norms of states are very much a part of the international political sphere, how can realists suggest that it is any other way? It would seem that the distinction that realists make is not supported by the evidence or, at the least, is as open to dispute as all of Morgenthau's principles have so far been shown to be. Yet despite all of Morgenthau's principles of political realism remaining open to criticism, there is one underlying element that remains central to his thesis but remains undeveloped in his six principles and the work of those who reflect his stance: anarchy.

Anarchy in Classical Realism

Anarchy in realist theory is not defined in the same manner as it is in wider political science or in the popular vernacular. The difference is more than subtle and requires an unpacking of the constructed implications most often associated with the term. Within the discipline's literature anarchy is defined in various ways. Consider the following three examples:

> *Robert Axelrod and Robert Keohane:* As used here, the term [anarchy] refers to **a lack of common government** in world politics, not to a denial that an international society – albeit a fragmented one – exists....To say that world politics is anarchic **does not imply that it entirely lacks organization**.[144]

> *Arthur Stein:* [Anarchy is] a metaphor to describe the state of affairs, providing an image of nation-states that consider every option available to them and make their choices

---

cies, and Foreign Affairs.' *Philosophy and Public Affairs* 12(3): 205-235; Michael Doyle. 1983b. 'Kant, Liberal Legacies, and Foreign Affairs, Part 2.' *Philosophy and Public Affairs* 12(4): 323-353.
[143] Tim Luard. 2003. 'ASEAN: Changing, but only slowly.' *BBC News.* (viewed 16 October 2006) http://news.bbc.co.uk/1/hi/world/asia-pacific/3173458.stm.
[144] Robert Axelrod and Robert Keohane. 1985. 'Achieving Cooperation Under Anarchy: Strategies and Institutions.' *World Politics* 38(1): 226-254, p.226. Emphasis added.

independently in order to maximise their own returns. In this view, states are **autonomous sovereign entities** that "develop their own strategies, chart their own courses, make their own decisions".[145]

Robert Powell: **No agency exists above individual states with authority and power to make laws and settle disputes.** States can make commitments and treaties, but no sovereign power ensures compliance and punishes deviation. This – **the absence of a supreme power** – is what is meant by the anarchic environment of international politics.[146]

The sections in bold above indicate the essential elements of a definition of anarchy in realist international relations theory. Firstly, there is a lack of a common government above the level of the state. Secondly, states within an anarchic system are autonomous and independent of each other. Thirdly, even without a central authority the international system is not disorganised; rather, *anarchy* is the organising principle of the international system.

Despite the importance and centrality of the notion of anarchy to the literature of Thucydides, Machiavelli, Hobbes, Carr and Morgenthau – the classical realists this chapter has so far considered – the word anarchy does not appear as often as one may imagine. The *idea* of anarchy, however, underlies almost all of the classical realist texts. Considering the work of these realists in turn, it will be shown that anarchy is a constant in the realist literature.

Thucydides – *The History of the Peloponnesian War*

Thucydides is not a political theorist but rather a historian, his most famous work being a recollection of the three-decade long conflict that came to be referred to as the Peloponnesian War.[147] Irish historian James Bury describes his work as "severe in its detachment, written from a purely intellectual point of view, unencumbered with platitudes and moral judgements", highlighting the reasons why modern realists claim

---

[145] Arthur Stein. 1982. 'Coordination and Collaboration: Regimes in an Anarchic World.' *International Organization* 36(2): 299-324, p.300. Emphasis added.

[146] Robert Powell. 1994. 'Anarchy in international relations theory: the neorealist-neoliberal debate.' *International Organization* 48(2): 313-344, 330. Emphasis added.

[147] Thucydides. 1998.

Thucydides as one of their own.[148] Most often cited within the discipline is his account of the negotiations between Athenian envoys and representatives of the population of the island of Melos known as the Melian Dialogue.[149] This short extract from his canonical *History of the Peloponnesian War* outlines an anarchical world and the difficulties faced by the theretofore neutral Melos when faced by an Athens involved in a wider regional conflict. Considering the dialogue between the two groups of envoys allows for an explication of Thucydides' conception of the anarchical realm within which the long Peloponnesian War was fought.

The Melian Dialogue is introduced by Thucydides by placing the Melians in the wider regional context. He begins by noting that the island of Melos was a colony of the hostile Lacedaemonians yet had, to that point, remained neutral in the wider war.[150] Athenian actions in the region, however, led to increased hostilities between the Melians and the Athenians but – before the Athenians launched an attack – the commanding officers, Cleomedes and Tisias, sent envoys to negotiate with the Melians.[151] Greeting the envoys, the Melians decided not to allow the people to be addressed by the representatives of Athens but rather pushed for the negotiations to take place between the envoys and local Melian magistrates from the "dominant class".[152] After some preliminary discussions as to the format of the discussions to take place, the dialogue begins with an Athenian request that the Melians "face the facts".[153]

The Melians recognise the magnitude of their situation, stating that the conference between the two sides is concerned with "the question of our preservation", mirroring the base assumptions of realists that the ultimate national interest is survival.[154] In response, the Athenians explain the underlying reality of the Melian Dialogue:

---

[148] JB Bury and Russell Meiggs. 1975. *History of Greece to the Death of Alexander the Great*. New York: St Martin's Press, p.252. Bury's assessment is tempered by Walter Connor who argues Thucydides is "an artist who responds to, selects and skilfully arranges his material, and develops its symbolic and emotional potential". See Walter Connor. 1984. *Thucydides*. Princeton: Princeton University Press, pp.231-232.

[149] Thucydides. 1998, pp.167-176.

[150] Thucydides. 1998, p.167.

[151] Thucydides. 1998, p.167.

[152] Thucydides. 1998, p.167.

[153] Thucydides. 1998, p.168.

[154] Thucydides. 1998, p.168.

...we will not go out of our way to prove at length that we have a right to rule...or that we attack you now because we are suffering any injury at your hands. We should not convince you if we did; nor must you expect to convince us...that you have never done us any wrong. But you and we should say what we really think, and aim only at what is possible, **for we both alike know that in discussions of human affairs the question of justice only enters where there is an equal power to enforce it, and that the powerful exact what they can, and the weak grant what they must.**[155]

Despite failing to employ the term itself, the Athenian envoys have clearly outlined an anarchical realm. The basic elements of this anarchy are clear here: a system without an arbiter, without a natural enduring morality and defined by the strength of the actors within the system.[156] The Melian response is argumentative, critical of the "set[ting] aside [of] justice" that the Athenian declaration necessarily encompasses.[157] The Melian negotiators argue that justice and regard for the claims of the Melians would serve the wider interests of the Athenians. Under the anarchy the Athenians present, they argue, the aggressor of the present "will incur the heaviest vengeance" should their empire fall.[158] In response, the Athenian envoys argue that this is a matter that should not concern the people of Melos; instead, the Melians should be concerned with the survival of their own island, an end achieved by acquiescence to the Athenian invaders.[159]

Despite the appeals of the Melians – "It may be in your interest to be our masters, but how can it be ours to be your slaves?" – the anarchical system in which both Athens and Melos find themselves makes the Athenian response clear: "To you the gain will be that by submission you will avert the worst".[160] In the anarchical political sphere of Thucydidean Peloponnesia, the most a weak actor can hope for is survival, perhaps

---

[155] Thucydides. 1998, p.169 (emphasis added).

[156] Thucydides. 1998, p.169.

[157] Thucydides. 1998, p.169.

[158] Thucydides. 1998, p.169. One might imagine that the Melians were expressing an early version of the rule of reciprocity ('The Golden Rule') later expressed by such religious and philosophical figures as Moses, Confucius, Hillel, Christ and Muhammad. Interestingly, a similar tactic founded on 'The Golden Rule' was found to be the most effective strategy for overcoming the anarchy of The Prisoner's Dilemma. See Robert Axelrod. 1980a. 'Effective Choice in the Prisoner's Dilemma.' *The Journal of Conflict Resolution* 24(1): 3-25, p.21; Robert Axelrod. 1980b. 'More Effective Choices in the Prisoner's Dilemma.' *The Journal of Conflict Resolution* 24(3): 379-403, pp.401-403; Michael Orkin. 1987. 'Balanced Strategies for Prisoner's Dilemma.' *The Journal of Conflict Resolution* 31(1): 186-191, pp.190-191.

[159] Thucydides. 1998, pp.169-170.

[160] Thucydides. 1998, p.170.

suggesting good reason why some small states will 'bandwagon' with a more power-ful state to ensure just this end.[161] The hopelessness of the relatively weaker Melian populace is reinforced moments later when the Athenian envoys are dismissive of their claims of impending injustice. "You are talking about justice again," they argue, "We say that we cannot allow freedom to insignificant islanders".[162] In reporting this, Thucydides reinforces the amorality of the political sphere, a sphere where notions of justice – Melian or otherwise – have little bearing on decisions of great powers like Athens. Thucydides, then, is defining the political as separate to the moral, a stance heretofore shown to be at the base of understandings of the anarchical even millennia later.[163]

Thucydides expands upon the reality of the anarchical Peloponnesian world as the debate between the two groups of negotiators continues. The Athenians explain that the subjection of the Melians by their forces will increase the security of Athens.[164] Here Thucydides is outlining the inherent threat that *any* state in an anarchic system presents to every other state by virtue of its existence. In time this recognition of the intrinsic threat offered by all states to all others would come to be a central feature of realist-described anarchy, particularly for the offensive realists.[165] The Melians de-nounce this argument as "a doctrine of expediency", again warning the Athenians of a possible future where the Periclean city state was not all powerful in the region.[166]

---

[161] Historian Paul Kennedy finds a similar theme underlying the expansionist agenda of Napoleon, quoting the French leader: "My power depends on my glory and my glory on the victories I have won. My power will fail if I do not feed it on new glories and new victories. Conquest has made me what I am, and only conquest can enable me to hold my position". See Paul Kennedy. 1987. *The Rise and Fall of the Great Powers: Economic Change and Military Conflict from 1500 to 2000.* New York: Random House, p.133. See also Randall Schweller. 1994. 'Bandwagoning for Profit: Bringing the Revisionist State Back In.' *International Security* 19(1): 72-107.

[162] Thucydides. 1998, p.170.

[163] Refer to previous discussion on Morgenthau's 'Six Principles of Political Realism' in this chap-ter.

[164] Thucydides. 1998, p.171.

[165] Taliaferro. 2001, p.128. See also Mearsheimer. 2006a, p.120: "The reason for this tragic situa-tion is that states cannot discern the intentions of other states with a high degree of confidence. Moreover, it is almost impossible to know the future intentions of other states. Therefore, leaders have little choice but to assume worst case about other great powers' intentions. The reason for be-lieving the worst is that there is no higher authority that states can turn to if they guess wrong about another state's intentions. States operate in an anarchic system, which means that they have nobody to turn to if they assume that another state has benign intentions, but that judgment proves wrong. As I said in my book, if you dial 911 in the international system, there is nobody at the other end."

[166] Thucydides. 1998, p.171.

But again, and with regard to the anarchical reality they see, the Athenian envoys dismiss such concerns by making clear that all are enemies to Athens and that islanders outside of Athenian control are "the most reckless and most likely to bring themselves as well as us into a danger which they cannot but foresee".[167] Clearly the anarchical political realm is not, for Thucydides and Athens, one in which no justice endures save the 'justice' of the strong to condemn the weak.

Having defined his anarchy as amoral, inherently competitive and dominated by the stronger powers, Thucydides adds one more element to his description of the anarchical Peloponnesian system: a separation between the national and the international. Having painted a picture of a relentlessly competitive and dangerous inter-state rivalry, the historian now makes it clear that this only relates to relations between states and not within them. The Athenians argue that no matter the morality of their enemies, the Lacedaemonians, at home – where they admit they are "exceedingly virtuous" – in relations with Athens and others they have little choice but to reject the notions of justice that, like the Melians, they would otherwise endorse.[168] Thucydides, therefore, is clear to differentiate the international, anarchical sphere from the national, controllable sphere – the same distinction which, at a disciplinary level, separates the study of international relations from political science and public policy.[169]

In Thucydides, then, classical realists find a description of anarchy which remains relevant today. As has been outlined above, Thucydides' anarchical system is defined by, firstly, the lack of an arbiter with the power to settle disputes between actors, secondly, a lack of an agreed systemic moral code and, thirdly, defined by the immediate power and interests of the actors and not by their wishes or not by thoughts of what could or should occur at some future date. This notion of anarchy was to emerge in later realist works and notably in the work of Italian political philosopher Niccolò Machiavelli.

---

[167] Thucydides. 1998, p.171. This again echoes the 'every state is an inherent threat' argument of the envoys previously.

[168] Thucydides. 1998, p.173. The Athenians refer to the Lacedaemonians "national standards of morality" which, it is imagined, would be similar to those of Melos as it was a Lacedaemonian colony.

[169] On the separation of political science into various sub-fields, including international relations, see Brian Schmidt. 1998. *The Political Discourse of Anarchy: A Disciplinary History of International Relations*. Albany: State University of New York Press, p.1; p.16.

Niccolò Machiavelli – *The Prince*

According to Bertrand Russell, while the Renaissance produced not a single theoretical philosopher, it did produce a political philosopher of "supreme eminence" in Niccolò Machiavelli.[170] Born in Florence in 1469, little is known of his life before he came to be an official in the Florentine chancery just before the turn of the century.[171] Between 1498 and his death in 1527, however, Machiavelli contributed some 14 years of his life in service of the Medici and delivered some of the most outstanding political philosophy in Western thought.[172] Though a prolific author across various genres including poetry, history and translations, Machiavelli's most enduring texts are *The Discourses* and *The Prince*.[173] Known variously as an "amoralist" and an "atheist", denounced for everything from an "unnatural sexual act" to being a "sycophant", a "nerd" and a "feeble lecher", Machiavelli's work has endured because of his "unique and original" contribution to political theory defines international politics in an anarchical system.[174]

Throughout *The Prince* Machiavelli makes consistent reference to the anarchical reality of and constant state of war in the international system encountered by Renaissance rulers though, like Thucydides, he avoids using the term 'anarchy' himself. Take, for example, Machiavelli's description of a "self-sufficient" system where princes "either through abundance of troops or of money, are capable of gathering together a suitable army and of fighting a battle against whoever might attack them".[175] Here Machiavelli describes the essence of the international system for the prince: self-sufficiency is necessary for survival under anarchy. Machiavelli continues, urging the wise prince to fortify and arm himself against all enemies, suggesting

---

[170] Russell. 1993, p.491.
[171] JN Stephens and HC Butters. 1982. 'New Light on Machiavelli.' *The English Historical Review* 97(382): 54-69, p.54.
[172] Norman Wilde. 1928. 'Machiavelli.' *International Journal of Ethics* 38(2): 212-225, p.212; Stephens and Butters. 1982, pp.54-55.
[173] Russell. 1993, pp.491-492; Machiavelli. 2005.
[174] See Russell. 1993, p.492; Donnelly. 2000, pp.24-25; Timothy Lukes. 2001. 'Lionizing Machiavelli.' *American Political Science Review* 95(3): 561-575, p.561; Machiavelli. 2005, pp.vii-viii; p.xxxix.
[175] Machiavelli. 2005, p.38.

further that if adequately armed the prince will never be successfully attacked.[176] It is obvious that such advice fits easily within the wider classical realist tradition.

Machiavelli's focus on security is also reminiscent of classical realism's understanding of anarchy. The likelihood of war under anarchy that Thucydides foresaw leads Machiavelli to urge the prince to "have no other object, nor any other thought, nor must he adopt anything as his art but war, its institutions, and its disciplines".[177] Under anarchy the security of the state is paramount and the first and only thoughts of the leader must be towards maintaining security. Machiavelli also suggests that, like other classical realists, the fundamentals of anarchy are unchanged over time. He extols the benefits for the prince of reading histories and studying the reasons for military defeats and victories.[178] This implies that Machiavelli sees that the system – but not the states or the leaders – as essentially unchanging in its political implications for rulers. Anarchy is sustained no matter the wishes of the Renaissance prince and the prince can only learn to survive and prosper by looking to his predecessors.

It is possible to interpret Machiavelli's famous pronouncement that, for a prince, "it is much safer to be feared than loved" as an endorsement of realisms amoral anarchical reality.[179] Machiavelli echoes the Athenian envoys in arguing that the prince who relies on the trust of others will eventually "come to ruin", betrayed by the friendships that "are not owned" and "cannot be spent" in the defence of the prince's land.[180] Indeed, Machiavelli notes that:

> ...one sees from experience in our times that the princes who have accomplished great days have thought little about keeping faith and who have known how cunningly to manipulate men's minds...[181]

Under anarchy it is not necessary for justice or trust to be considered when a leader makes a decision. There is no arbiter with overall authority and, as Machiavelli notes,

---

[176] Machiavelli. 2005, pp.38-39.
[177] Machiavelli. 2005, p.50.
[178] Machiavelli. 2005, p.52.
[179] Machiavelli. 2005, p.58.
[180] Machiavelli. 2005, p.58.
[181] Machiavelli. 2005, p.60.

even where there is a stronger power there is no reason to appeal to justice or morality to avoid conflict; fortification and the arming of the state is the only solution.[182] Finally, Machiavelli highlights the fickleness of alliances under anarchy. He warns the prince, "you should never wish to fall down in the belief that you will find someone to pick you up".[183] As he argues, allies cannot be elide upon to keep their word to defend any state that is not their own.[184] Machiavelli highlights the case of Alexander VI whom he describes as a ruler whose "deceptions were always successful" in as much as they maintained his position and the security of his land.[185] Indeed, Machiavelli extols the notion that "a wise ruler, therefore, cannot and should not keep his word when such an observance would be to his disadvantage".[186] Under anarchy alliances must be only temporary as agreements as there will never be an arbiter to enforce any pact or demand assistance for a 'friend' where such assistance would render the ally weakened.

Thus, Machiavelli reinforces the notion of anarchy outlined in Thucydides' classic history of Athens and Sparta. A world of self-sufficiency, a world without an underlying morality, a world without an arbiter to settle disputes and a world where alliances cannot possibly endure. Machiavelli describes the Renaissance world he sees as one of pure anarchy, a practical realm where good and evil are domestic constructs and not international realities. Some sixty years after Machiavelli's death another political philosopher would be born whose metaphor for the anarchy he theorised would be influential across political science and philosophy for centuries to come.

---

[182] Machiavelli. 2005, p.38. Machiavelli writes, "The cities of Germany are completely independent, they control little surrounding territory, they obey the emperor when they please, and they fear neither him nor any other nearby power. For they are fortified in such a manner that everyone considers their capture to be a tedious and difficult affair."

[183] Machiavelli. 2005, p.83.

[184] Machiavelli. 2005, p.61.

[185] Machiavelli. 2005, p.61.

[186] Machiavelli. 2005, p.60.

Thomas Hobbes - *Leviathan*

Thomas Hobbes is described by Russell in terms that suggest he was ahead of his time.[187] His commitment to empiricism, mathematics and the scientific method saw him become one of the most influential political philosophers of his day. Russell writes that his political theory of states "is more modern than any previous theory, even that of Machiavelli", a view endorsed by others that consider his work to top "all its successors in political theory".[188] His canonical *Leviathan*, the text "upon which his fame mainly rests", was written while Hobbes was in Parisian exile from Britain and it is variously described as "the greatest, perhaps the sole masterpiece of English political theory" and the fruit of "a lifetime of speculation on the science of politics".[189] Having previously published a translation of Thucydides' *History of the Peloponnesian War* in 1629, a text that for one commentator "crystallised" the ideas fundamental to his political philosophy, Hobbes was most surely a student of the realist tradition.[190] A close reading of *Leviathan* sees Hobbes describe an anarchy so basic and fundamental that it is presented as entirely natural and is, indeed, described as the 'state of nature' by the author himself.[191] This metaphor for anarchy is Hobbes' most important contribution to classical realist thought.

The thirteenth chapter of *Leviathan* is where Hobbes makes clearest his notion of an anarchical realm.[192] He begins by highlighting the reality of the political system and its lack of a central power:

---

[187] Russell. 1993, p.531: "English empiricism, on the other hand, was little influenced by mathematics, and tended to have a wrong conception of scientific method. Hobbes had neither of these defects. It is not until our own day that we find any other philosophers who were empiricists and yet laid due stress on mathematics. In this respect Hobbes's merit is great."

[188] Russell. 1993, p.531; Quentin Skinner. 1966a. 'The Ideological Context of Hobbes's Political Thought.' *The Historical Journal* 9(3): 286-317, p.286.

[189] Russell. 2005, p.533; Skinner. 1966a, p.286; Quentin Skinner. 1966b. 'Thomas Hobbes and His Disciples in England and France.' *Comparative Studies in Society and History* 8(2): 153-167, p.153. For a critical reading of Skinner's account of Hobbes' life and work see Jonathan Wiener. 1974. 'Quentin Skinner's Hobbes.' *Political Theory* 2(3): 251-260.

[190] Richard Schlatter. 1945. 'Thomas Hobbes and Thucydides.' *Journal of the History of Ideas* 6(3): 350-362, p.350.

[191] Thomas Hobbes. 2002. *Leviathan, or the Matter, Forme, & Power of a Commonwealth Ecclesiasticall and Civil.* e-text, http://tinyurl.com/yz47c6, p.56.

[192] Hobbes. 2002, pp.56-58.

Againe, men have no pleasure, (but on the contrary a great deale of griefe) in keeping
company, where there is no power able to over-awe them all.[193]

Where there is no arbiter and no all-powerful force there is no way for actors to be
sure of their own survival, daily life takes a shape that is famously described as "solitary, poore, nasty, brutish, and short".[194] Indeed, Hobbes makes clear that without
such an arbiter men are likely to fall into conflict. He writes, "them that have no
common power, to keep them in quiet, is far enough to make them destroy each
other", suggesting that violent conflict is not only common but expected.[195] Under
anarchy there is destruction, warns Hobbes, a result of both the nature of the actors
and the nature of the system they must exist in.[196]

Hobbes' anarchy is also one which alludes to actors interacting as necessary threats to
every other actor. Hobbes clearly outlines that – under anarchy – even the weakest is
a threat to the strongest as "the weakest has strength enough to kill the strongest, either by secret machination, or by confederacy with others".[197] This fundamental inse-
curity in political life remains key for Hobbes as he goes on to argue that force and
violence within such a political system is to be expected. Extrapolated to the international level – for Hobbes' primary concern was writing a theory of the state –
Hobbes' 'state of nature' provides explanation for the competitive, insecure reality
that states find themselves mired in.[198] Anarchy is reality for Hobbes, the basic nature
in which political affairs take place – it cannot be escaped from or denied.

Hobbes' realism and his anarchy tied together ideas of the historian Thucydides and
the politician Machiavelli. As Colin Wight argues, Hobbes rejects the "knowledge of
particulars" that historians such as Thucydides must report but without denying the

---

[193] Hobbes. 2002, p.56.

[194] Hobbes. 2002, p.57.

[195] Hobbes. 2002, p.56.

[196] Hobbes. 2002, pp.56-57.

[197] Hobbes. 2002, p.56.

[198] "It is almost universally admitted that Hobbes marks an epoch in the history of natural law and
of the theory of the State." See Leo Strauss. 1996. *The Political Philosophy of Hobbes: Its Basis
and Genesis*. Chicago: University of Chicago Press, p.xix.

"practical wisdom" of his work.[199] Similarly, Russell endorses the modernity of Hobbes *Leviathan*, noting that he, unlike his predecessors, is "completely free from superstition" and religiosity in building his arguments, and nowhere near as "limited" as Machiavelli.[200] Though it remains true that "there is not a word in *Leviathan* to suggest any relation between [states] except war and conquest, with the occasional interludes", Hobbes' anarchy is not a world completely without hope.[201] The state that arms itself, improves its "fighting quality" (for which we could supplement the term 'power') in relation to other states and which is constantly vigilant will survive.[202] The philosopher and mathematician Gottfried Leibniz described Hobbes as a man whose work was unsurpassed even by "Descartes with his super human intellect".[203] It is little surprise, then, that it would be just short of three centuries before another scholar would add to Hobbes classical realist anarchy in any significant way.

EH (Edward Hallett) Carr – *The Twenty Years Crisis*

EH Carr is described by Jack Donnelly as "the first major figure to attempt to reshape the field" of international relations.[204] Born in the last years of the 19th century, Carr joined the British Foreign and Commonwealth Office where he was assigned to various posts in Britain and Europe. He played a part in drafting the Treaty of Versailles – primarily in relation to minority populations in Central Europe – and, over the course of his 20 year diplomatic service career, became more and more persuaded that the Wilsonian League of Nations would become an abject failure, a position which in hindsight seems remarkably sensible.[205] Carr left the diplomatic service in 1936 to take up a new position as Woodrow Wilson Chair of International Politics at the University College of Wales Aberystwyth, a move that led the pro-Wilsonian College President David Davies to resign citing the "flagrant injustice" of appointing

---

[199] Colin Wight. 2006. 'Philosophy of Social Science and International Relations.' In *Handbook of International Relations*, edited by Walter Carlsnaes, Thomas Risse & Beth Simmons. London: SAGE, pp.23-51, p.27.

[200] Russell. 1993, p.540.

[201] Russell. 1993, p.540.

[202] Russell. 1993, p.536; p.541.

[203] AP Martinich. 1999. *Hobbes: A Biography*. Cambridge: Cambridge University Press, p.335.

[204] Donnelly. 2000, p.26.

[205] Michael Cox. 2001a. 'Introduction.' In *The Twenty Years Crisis, 1919-1939: An Introduction to the Study of International Relations*. EH Carr. Basingstoke: Palgrave, p.ix-lviii, p.xvii.

an anti-League of Nations scholar to the position.[206] Just three years into his tenure in Aberystwyth Carr published what would be his most significant contribution to classical realist theory and to international relations theory as a whole: *The Twenty Years Crisis*.[207]

The Twenty Years Crisis is described as a "most interesting and valuable discussion" and "admirably objective and unbiased" and, by some critics, a "facile gospel" and "little more than the familiar formula" of might makes right.[208] According to Michael Cox, many were provoked by his "mischievous but potentially influential volume with little moral compass" and reacted with outrage and criticism.[209] Whatever the early reaction, however, Carr's book has gone on to become mandatory reading for those within the discipline of international relations, its clear rejection of utopian liberalism and endorsement of a politics where ends are valued over means inspiring such influential scholars as Robert Cox, Andrew Linklater, Ken Booth and John Mearsheimer.[210] Carr's attempt to unravel the politics of the first half of the twentieth century, though, is more than just a history of the events between the peace of Versailles and the outbreak of the Second World War – instead it is a case study of politics in an anarchic world where realist ideas are the only sextant by which to guide the course of the state.

The anarchic nature of the international system features prominently in Carr's *Twenty Years Crisis*, if not in name then by implication. Carr exhausts considerable energy in outlining the realities of the anarchic international system in parts two and three of

---

[206] Department of International Politics. 2006. *Full History of the Department of International Politics: Edward Hallett Carr*. Available online, http://www.aber.ac.uk/interpol/history/history_5.html.

[207] Carr. 2001. Note that Carr was also considered a significant historian as well as an international relations theorist. For a review of his historical literature (primarily focussed on Russia and the Soviet Union) see Isaac Deutscher. 1955. 'Mr. E.H. Carr as Historian of Soviet Russia.' *Soviet Studies* 6(4): 337-350; Jonathan Haslam. 1983. 'E.H. Carr and the History of Soviet Russia.' *The Historical Journal* 26(4): 1021-1027.

[208] C. Delisle Burns. 1940. 'Review: The Twenty Years Crisis, 1919-1939: An Introduction to the Study of International Relations.' *Ethics* 50(3): 344-346, p.344; Bessie C. Randolph. 1940. 'Review: The Twenty Year's Crisis, 1919-1939.' *The American Journal of International Law* 34(4): 761-762, p.761; Corbett. 1941, pp.237-238.

[209] Michael Cox. 2001b. 'A Guide to the Secondary Literature on E.H. Carr.' In *The Twenty Years Crisis, 1919-1939: An Introduction to the Study of International Relations*. EH Carr. Basingstoke: Palgrave, pp.lxiv-lxxi, p.lxv.

[210] Cox. 2001a, pp.xlvii-liv; Mearsheimer. 2005.

his four part treatment of international relations.[211] Like Machiavelli, Carr rejects the notion of a pre-existing moral order in international affairs. Rejecting such ideas as "utopian", Carr argues that imagining an international order without self-asserting states is "wide of the mark".[212] In an anarchic system states pursue ends that serve the national interest; presuming an international "harmony of interests" is a misunderstanding of the essential nature of the system, and even paradoxical.[213] In anarchy, those who would reject reality and embrace the ideal of an international morality construct a "barrier to clear political thinking" and their assessments, in the words of Carr, simply "make no sense".[214]

Anarchy also requires states to arm themselves against all others, with the threat of attack in a realm without an arbiter a likelihood that must be prepared for. For Carr, all politics is power politics and the *"ultimo ratio* of power in international relations is war".[215] Carr suggests that there always exists a state of "potential war" in international relations, in essence the chance that without a central authority one state may challenge another in pursuit of its own interests.[216] Strategy under anarchy, then, means that states should arm themselves well in anticipation of war as the state can never be sure for what reason or at which time they might be attacked.[217] In this Carr echoes Hobbes and his 'state of nature', with anarchy providing security for none and forcing a military upon all.

Further in the style of Hobbes, Carr is clear that politics under anarchy forces states to continually search for more and more power. Citing support from Reinhold Niebuhr, Carr argues that "the exercise of power always appears to beget the appetite for more power".[218] With no power maintained in a central authority, in international law, in any international moral standards or in any place other than independent states, anarchy forces states to pursue power as a means to ensure security against

---

[211] Carr. 2001, pp.25-88; pp.91-155.

[212] Carr. 2001, p.92.

[213] Carr. 2001, p.44. More broadly see Carr. 2001, pp.42-61.

[214] Carr. 2001, p.88.

[215] Carr. 2001, p.97; p.102.

[216] Carr. 2001, p.102.

[217] Carr. 2001, pp.103-104.

[218] Carr. 2001, pp.104-105. Carr quotes Niebuhr's *Moral Man and Immoral Society* on the impossibility of drawing any line between the will to live and the will to power.

foreign threats.[219] While Carr acknowledges that there are different elements to power under anarchy – including military and economic components and what Carr refers to as 'power over opinion' – Carr is adamant that the power of states in an anarchic system are best measured by their military power.[220] Importantly, a hierarchical system or a system with a central power would not beget such an international quest for power in this way. It is the particular nature of an anarchic system that Carr recognises that both demands and accounts for the development of military power, the quest for building on that power and the propensity for states to engage in conflict with each other. Indeed, rejecting explanations for war that include gaining territory or trade benefits, Carr submits that wars are fought for reasons of increasing military power or reducing the military power of a rival.[221]

It becomes clear, then, that there is a strengthening of the notion of anarchy in the development of realism as a perspective or paradigm of international relations theory. The anarchy which left the Melians open to attack by Athens is the same anarchy that Machiavelli wrote of in the Renaissance. The 'state of nature' explored and theorised by Thomas Hobbes is the same anarchy that is central to Carr's 'realist' assessment of international affairs. This continuity, despite the slightly differing interpretations and depictions of the anarchic system these classical realists present in their works, allows for their texts to form a canon of classical realist thought from which scholars continue to draw inspiration.[222] It took another scholar, though, to so distil the notion

---

[219] Indeed, for Carr it is not *all* states that maintain power in world politics but the 'great powers' that dominate the international system:

> The alleged 'dictatorship of the Great Powers', which is sometimes denounced by utopian writers as if it were a wicked policy deliberately adopted by certain states, is a fact which constitutes something like a 'law of nature' in international politics.

See Carr. 2001, pp.98-99.

[220] Carr. 2001, pp.97-134. 'Power over opinion' is described by Carr as including persuasion, diplomacy and, particularly, propaganda. It would not be misleading to suggest that Carr's 'power over opinion' is an early description if what would come to be popularised as 'soft power' by Joseph Nye. See Joseph Nye. 1990. 'The Changing Nature of World Power.' *Political Science Quarterly* 105(2): 177-192; Joseph Nye. 2002. *The Paradox of American Power: Why the World's Only Superpower Can't Go It Alone.* Oxford: Oxford University Press; Nye. 2004.

[221] Carr. 2001, p.104.

[222] See, for example, critical treatments of Thucydides, Machiavelli, Hobbes and Carr in Ken Booth. 1991. 'Security in Anarchy: Utopian Realism in Theory and Practice.' *International Affairs* 67(3): 527-546; Michael Williams. 1996. 'Hobbes and International Relations: A Reconsideration.' *International Organization* 50(2): 213-236; Peter Feaver, Gunther Hellman, Randall Schweller, Jeffrey

of anarchy explored by his predecessors as to build a deliberate and cogent theory of classical realism. That author was German émigré Hans Morgenthau and the book – described by Michael Cox as *the* book on international relations – was *Politics among Nations*.[223] Already employed earlier in this chapter as a guide to the basic tenets of classical realism, an assessment of the notion of anarchy in this volume clearly demonstrates that the important components of anarchy thus far considered remain central to classical realism as it would be described in the mid and late twentieth century.

Hans Morgenthau – *Politics among Nations*

Leaving Munich in 1932 for the University of Geneva, Hans Morgenthau passed by way of Madrid, New York and Kansas City before being appointed to the faculty of the University of Chicago in 1943.[224] The man who would become a giant of the developing discipline of international relations would go on to publish a number of influential works including *In Defense of the National Interest*, *The Purpose of American Politics* and a three-volume series *Politics in the Twentieth Century*.[225] It would be his book *Politics among Nations: The Struggle for Power and Peace*, though, which would see his reputation among students and scholars of international politics assured.[226] Though heavily criticised by some on its publication and afterwards, Morgenthau's work was accessible to students and scholars alike and its "simple structure" allowed for realism to be defined in ways that the work Carr, Hobbes, Machiavelli and Thucydides could not.[227] But like the work of earlier classical realists,

---

Taliaferro, William Wohlforth, Jeffrey Legro, Andrew Moravcsik. 2000. 'Brother Can You Spare a Paradigm? (Or Was Anybody Ever a Realist?).' *International Security* 25(1): 165-193.

[223] Morgenthau. 1993; Cox. 2001a, p.xxxvii.

[224] Morgenthau. 1993, p.v.

[225] Hans Morgenthau. 1951. *In Defense of the National Interest: A Critical Examination of American Foreign Policy*. New York: Alfred A. Knopf; Hans Morgenthau. 1960. *The Purpose of American Politics*. New York: Knopf; Hans Morgenthau. 1962a. *Politics in the Twentieth Century: Volume One – The Decline of Democratic Politics*. Chicago: University of Chicago Press; Hans Morgenthau. 1962b. *Politics in the Twentieth Century: Volume Two – The Impasse of American Foreign Policy*. Chicago: University of Chicago Press; Hans Morgenthau. 1962c. *Politics in the Twentieth Century: Volume Three – The Restoration of American Politics*. Chicago: University of Chicago Press.

[226] Morgenthau. 1993.

[227] Cox. 2001a, p.xxxvii. On criticisms of *Politics among Nations* see, for example, Robert Tucker. 1952. 'Professor Morgenthau's Theory of Political Realism.' *American Political Science Review*

indeed perhaps even more so, anarchy remains a foundational assumption for Morgenthau and his enumerated theory of realism.

A review of the index of *Politics among Nations* presents a surprising but consistent anomaly in the classical realist literature: there is no mention of anarchy or the anarchic system in Morgenthau's text.[228] However, like all classical realists, Morgenthau implicitly assumes anarchy to be the pre-existing condition of international politics, an assumption evident in *Politics among Nations* as well as his other published works.[229] Consider, for example, Chapter 14 of *Politics among Nations* where Morgenthau describes the role of "morality, mores, and laws and restraints on power".[230] In this short chapter Morgenthau outlines the very reasons that Machiavelli's anarchic realm does not exist in a domestic political environment. Arguing that the social systems that define the modern national polity negate the influence of raw political power, Morgenthau states:

> From the Bible to the ethics and constitutional arrangements of modern democracy, the main function of these normative systems has been to keep aspirations for power within socially tolerable bounds. All ethics, mores, and legal systems…recognize the ubiquity of power drives and condemn them.[231]

He continues, citing examples ranging from Judeo-Christian commandments and societal conformity, judicial norms and punishment regimes to personal moral standards and legal prohibition as prototypical elements that "mitigate the struggle for power on the domestic scene".[232] Significantly, a mitigation of this drive for power is all Morgenthau claims, specifically noting that the struggle for domestic power has not been banished, just curtailed.[233]

46(1): 214-224, p.214 ("open contradictions, ambiguity, and vagueness"); Donnelly. 2000, p.28 ("claims for realism that can only be described as wildly extravagant"); p.29 ("an extreme, even excessive, theoretical claim").

[228] Morgenthau. 1993, pp.409-419.

[229] See, for example, Hans Morgenthau. 1945b. 'The Machiavellian Utopia.' *Ethics* 55(2): 145-147, p.146; Hans Morgenthau. 1950. 'The Mainsprings of American Foreign Policy: The National Interest vs. Moral Abstractions.' *The American Political Science Review* 44(4): 833-854, p.840; pp.850-854.

[230] Morgenthau. 1993, pp.219-223.

[231] Morgenthau. 1993, pp.219-220.

[232] Morgenthau. 1993, pp.220-223.

[233] Morgenthau. 1993, p.222.

Yet when it comes to matters international – a system without the societal constraints of the domestic political sphere and the hierarchies associated with it – Morgenthau implies that anarchy reigns. Chapter 16 of his study is titled "The Main Problems of International Law" and, within this discussion of the nature of international laws, Morgenthau summarises the essence of the anarchic system: "The decentralized nature of international law is the inevitable result of the decentralized structure of international society".[234] Like the other classical realists reviewed in this chapter, Morgenthau argues that there is no central authority in the international system. Thus, though international laws can exist, there can be no arbiter to neither enforce them nor meter punishment should they be broken. Anarchy defines international relations, he argues, stating that whereas:

> [d]omestic law can be imposed by the group that holds the monopoly of organised force…[yet in] international society, composed of sovereign states, which by definition are the supreme legal authorities within their respective territories… no such central law-giving and law-enforcing authority can exist[235]

For Morgenthau, this international anarchy is a problem to be solved, even a sickness to be "remedied".[236] He understands anarchy as a systemic quality but also as a problem to be overcome. Anarchy, for Morgenthau, breeds disorder and war and in *Politics among Nations* he asserts various means by which to overcome these problems.

Disarmament, arms control, collective security and even an international police force are the 'solutions' to anarchy that Morgenthau considers.[237] He rejects each in turn as too specific and attacking a "particular problem in which the lack of international order" is manifest instead of addressing the "general" problems that emerge for states and leaders under anarchy.[238] The only solution to the general problem of anarchy and the security dilemmas it engenders, then, is an international government of some

---

[234] Morgenthau. 1993, p.255.
[235] Morgenthau. 1993, p.255.
[236] Morgenthau. 1993, p.299: "The remedies for international anarchy and war which have been discussed thus far are all specific remedies."
[237] Morgenthau. 1993, pp.277-298.
[238] Morgenthau. 1993, p.299.

sort.[239] That this is not a novel solution of Morgenthau's: he cites the 1814 Holy Alliance in Europe, the Concert of Europe, the League of Nations and, later, the United Nations as conscious attempts to overcome the anarchic system of Westphalian states.[240] But even these attempts to "remedy" anarchy all fall short, evidenced clearly by the wars that swept the major powers of the international system in the wake of each collapse.[241]

Anarchy, then, is neither a modern invention nor an interpretation of the system unique to Morgenthau. He recognises that anarchy is a persistent international condition that, in combination with the natural urges of the men and women who are charged with governing sovereign states, creates an atmosphere ripe for war. Note, however, that it is not anarchy alone that creates conflict for Morgenthau; rather it is the setting for the conflict brought about by the desire for greater power that exists naturally within all. Morgenthau's anarchy is real, empowering (for conflict) and pervasive throughout history. It defines the system within which states exist and allows them freedom of action, slowed only by weak international laws and ineffective attempts at long-term international governance. Time and again Morgenthau railed against the ignorance of the effects of anarchy on international affairs. Consider his 1948 essay *The Political Science of EH Carr* where he writes:

> How, then, is one to explain their blindness to the realities of international affairs?... It [the blindness] manifests itself in Neville Chamberlain in the conviction that all men will act like businessmen from Birmingham and that international politics is in its essence a series of business transactions among peoples speaking different tongues.[242]

---

[239] Morgenthau. 1993, p.299.

[240] Morgenthau. 1993, p.299-318; pp.319-300. Morgenthau differentiates between the United Nations and the earlier manifestations of international government by describing the UN as 'Government by the Superpowers' and the others as 'Government of the Great Powers'. This also delineates the change in polarity between the pre-WWII multipolar world and the post-WWII bipolar international environment.

[241] Consider that with each collapse of these "international governments" a major war (or a war between major powers) shortly followed. The Holy Alliance collapsed following the death of Alexander I of Russia and the wars of Italian independence against the Austrians followed. The Concert of Europe collapsed in 1848 to be followed by the Crimean War and the Austro-Prussian War. The League of Nations was in demise at the outbreak of the Second World War, having previously failed to prevent the Italian invasion of Ethiopia. The United Nations, at the time of writing, continues to exist.

[242] Morgenthau. 1948b, pp.127-128.

Morgenthau, like Carr, is convinced that blindness to the different systemic structure of international politics, in comparison to the domestic politics of the state, leads to poor foreign policy choices, conflict between sovereign powers and destruction. Though he hints at the possibility of a 'World State' in *Politics among Nations*, the necessary elements for such a "remedy" to international anarchy are so extreme as to be almost unthinkable.[243] Thus, in the end, Morgenthau, like classical realists before him, accepts that anarchy, conflict and war are parts of the international system that – while regrettable – are without human-inspired solution.

Summary: Classical Realism and the Nature of Anarchy in Classical Realism

Thus far this chapter has considered both the tenets of classical realism and the nature of anarchy as understood by five central scholars of the classical realist tradition. Beginning with an account of what classical realists maintain – via the explication of Morgenthau's "six principles of political realism" – this chapter has demonstrated that classical realism is a coherent body of political theory which seeks to understand the nature of international politic and the actions of international actors in an anarchic system.[244] This anarchic system, in turn, has been shown to have certain characteristics which endure over time. These characteristics define both the system and the options available for actors or states which seek to survive and prosper within the system, a reality endorsed by authors from the pre-Christian era historian Thucydides through to Hans Morgenthau, a scholar who died in the last decade of the twentieth century's Cold War.[245]

Drawing on the review of Thucydides, Machiavelli, Hobbes, Carr and Morgenthau outlined above, the following common characteristics of anarchy within the classical realist tradition can be established and – through combination – a fundamental definition of anarchy can be reached. Principally, the characteristics of anarchy in classical realist literature are as follows:

---

[243] Morgenthau. 1993, pp.333-347.

[244] Morgenthau. 1993, pp.4-16.

[245] Thucydides is thought to have lived between 460 BC and 400 BC. Hans Morgenthau died on the 19th of July 1980. Since Morgenthau's death the Carnegie Council has sponsored an annual Morgenthau Lecture which has been delivered by such distinguished international relations scholars as Kenneth Thompson, Stanley Hoffman and Joseph Nye.

Anarchy as reality

All classical realists assert that anarchy is existential, that is, it is a reality for those who would conduct politics in the international sphere. It cannot be avoided – as Melian citizens learn in *The History of the Peloponnesian War* – but can, in certain circumstances, be mitigated through temporary international cooperation between great or superpowers, as Morgenthau asserts. It cannot, however, be ignored and attempts to do so can only end in failure for the state and the leadership of the state; indeed, both Hobbes and Machiavelli warn against misunderstanding the reality of international anarchy and the assumption of a moral international sphere. Carr is perhaps the most forthright of the classical realists in this respect, decrying the attempts of the Wilsonian League of Nations to regulate through law and international agreement the anarchic international environment. As he argues, the failure of the League and of "the attempt to build a world order" has failed though "muddled thinking" about the actual nature of the political setting in which the League was supposed to act.[246] For the classical realists, the student, scholar or statesperson who fails to acknowledge the existence of anarchy is bound to make poor foreign policy choices.

Anarchy defined by violence and conflict

Just as anarchy is real for classical realists it is also violent. Every author acknowledges that the 'normal' state of the international system is one of conflict, if not out-and-out war. From Thucydides ("the powerful exact what they can, the weak grant what they must"), Machiavelli (the Prince "must not adopt anything as his art but war") and Hobbes (men find themselves in a fight "to destroy each other") all argue that the anarchic environment is implicitly violent.[247] Carr maintains a similar conviction, arguing against those who saw the manifestation of war under international anarchy as a temporary, irrational state; indeed, Carr mocks Sir Norman Angell and his argument that war and international anarchy are fundamentally absurd and that given a rational assessment of the system, "enough people would be rationally convinced of

---

[246] Carr. 2001, p.38. Carr cites Quincy Wright's *Neutrality and Collective Security* in support of his contention. See Quincy Wright (ed.). 1936. *Neutrality and Collective Security*. Chicago: University of Chicago Press, p.8; p.18.
[247] Thucydides. 1998, p.169; Machiavelli. 2005, p.50; Hobbes. 2002, p.56.

its absurdity to put an end to it" – the 'it' being both anarchy and war.[248] Importantly, classical realists do not submit that anarchy *causes* violence, but rather that an anarchic system creates condition under which violence is likely and normal.

Anarchy defined by a lack of central government

Unlike anarchy in domestic politics, defined by Michael Taylor as "a condition of statelessness", consider that anarchy in international relations is defined not by a lack of states but by a lack of a central authority for the states that do exist.[249] Again and again the lack of a central arbiter in international affairs is referenced by the classical realists, both as a reality and in the context of the 'problem' of international order. For Thucydides it is what allows the Athenians to conquer the Melians; for Machiavelli it is what allows the Prince to increase his territory without fear of retribution from a higher international authority; for Hobbes it is the condition that allows the weak, alone "or by confederacy with others", to murder the strong in his state of nature; for Carr it is the reason that the utopian League of Nations could never prevent the Italian invasion of Ethiopia; and for Morgenthau, it is motivating reason for pursuing the idealistic world state.[250] The lack of an overarching authority – as opposed to the statelessness that defines domestic anarchy – differentiates the realm of the classical realist from that of the political scientist.

Anarchy as unchanging over time

Though any assessment of international affairs through the paradigm of classical realism would be expected to have something in common with other assessments from the same perspective, what is significant about the nature of anarchy for classical realists is the enduring character of systemic anarchy. Unlike changes in polarity between the multipolar pre-WWI era and the bipolar Cold War era, classical realists recognise continuity in anarchy across all of human history. Frequently within the work of the later realists assessed (Carr, Morgenthau) are references to the conditions of anarchy described by the earlier theorists (Thucydides, Machiavelli, Hobbes). Em-

---

[248] Carr. 2001, p.28.

[249] Michael Taylor. 1982. *Community, Anarchy and Liberty*. Cambridge: Cambridge University Press, p.4.

[250] Hobbes. 2002, p.56; Carr. 2001, p.105.

pires rise and fall, states emerge, grow, dominate, decline and collapse – anarchy is the constant condition, even the natural condition, of international politics. The Melian Dialogue is repeated with different emphasis and effect in the Renaissance world of Machiavelli, the emerging Westphalian Peace described by Hobbes and the invasions of West and East Europe by Nazi Germany witnessed by Carr and Morgenthau. For the classical realists, anarchy is a constant and the variance in political responses is explained by the different approaches of the states and actors of the time.

Anarchy as amoral

For classical realists the anarchic sphere is one in which a common morality does not exist. Questions of what is right and wrong or what is good and evil are subservient to practical questions of what can and cannot be achieved in terms of the national interest. As has been shown – particularly in relation to the work of the three earlier classical realists – morality is reserved for communities, societies and domestic political decisions. With no international society and only an imagined international community, morality should have no place in the decision making algorithms of the leaders of sovereign states or international actors. Thus, Machiavelli cautions the Prince against applying rules of justice and morality in international dealings, and warns against extending trust in international affairs.[251] In a similar fashion, Hobbes describes an international environment where the nature of the actors is fundamentally flawed, fundamentally amoral and destructive.[252] Further, though he would go on to publish widely on the nature of ethics in political life, even Morgenthau admits that there is a "sharp distinction between the desirable and the possible", the former being the moral option and the latter the realistic one.[253] International politics, then, is again differentiated from domestic affairs where moral and ethical mores exist and exert influence.

---

[251] Machiavelli. 2005, pp.58-60.
[252] Hobbes. 2002, pp.56-57.
[253] Morgenthau. 1993, p.7. See examples of Morgenthau's writings on ethics in Morgenthau. 1945a; Morgenthau. 1948a.

The Meaning of Anarchy in Classical Realism

Drawing together these threads and components from five of the most influential and representative classical realist scholars, a definition of anarchy can be assumed. Expressed in a sentence, anarchy for the classical realists can be considered to be:

> A real and tangible systemic state in which there exists no central government and no specific moral code, defined by conflict and unchanging over time.

This definition encompasses all of the major elements of the classical realist conception of anarchy and is one that would fit easily within the various slightly differing approaches to international affairs that defines the classical realist position. In the context of this definition the word 'conflict' should be considered to encompass both non-violent and violent conflict and the terms 'real' and 'tangible' should be understood to refer to the existential nature of anarchy claimed by the classical realists. The other terms are self-explanatory in the context of the discussion thus far presented in this chapter.

Conclusion

This chapter has outlined the basic tenets of the classical realist approach, reviewed the shape and nature of anarchy within the canon of the approach and devised a notion of what anarchy actually *is* for those who profess that a classical realist analysis is the superior reasoned approach to the study of global political affairs. As alluded to from the outset, however, classical realism is but one of a number of perspectives within a wider paradigm of realism. Before beginning to assess the centrality of anarchy to realism, it is of some utility to assess the other of the two major perspectives in realist theory: structural realism or neorealism. In the chapter to come, the tenets and shape of structural realism, as well as the fundamental place of anarchy within it, will be assessed.

It is best to do thing systematically, since we are
only human and disorder is our worst enemy
Hesiod

ANARCHY AND NEO-REALISM

Events in the international system, Kenneth Waltz recalled in a February 2003, were always thought to be motivated by one of two root causes: either human nature or the nature of the state.[254] Even for a scholar as distinguished as Waltz, such differing perspectives on the root causes of international events made for a disciplinary canon that could only be described as a "confusing literature" by the then Columbia University doctoral student. Noting the discrepancies between what he termed the different "images" of international politics, Waltz's PhD dissertation became the book *Man, The State, and War*, the first of two books through which Waltz would define a new realist paradigm and change the face of the discipline of international relations.[255]

Through *Man, the State, and War* and its sequel, *Theory of International Politics*, Waltz defined a theoretical framework which he termed structural realism but which became widely referred to as neorealism. Though drawing on a significant portion of the realist literature and citing all of the classical texts assessed in The first chapter of this book, these foundational texts of the neorealist theoretical agenda were different enough that, decades later, they remain the works of a man described in 2006 as the "king of thought in [international relations] theory for the past 25 years".[256] Doctoral students under Waltz's tutelage have gone on to become giants in the study of modern international relations, among them MIT's Barry Posen and Stephen Van Evera and Harvard's Stephen Walt.[257] So significantly different is Walt's neorealism to the classical approach outlined in The first chapter of this book that it is necessary to de-

---

[254] Kenneth Waltz. 2003. *Theory and International Politics: Conversation with Kenneth Waltz.* [12 February 2007] http://globetrotter.berkeley.edu/people3/Waltz/.

[255] Kenneth Waltz. 2001. *Man, the State, and War: A Theoretical Analysis.* New York: Columbia University Press.

[256] Mearsheimer. 2006a, p.109.

[257] The three scholars have contributed a number of major books and articles to the disciplinary literature in recent decades including Barry Posen. 1986. *The Sources of Military Doctrine: France, Britain and Germany Between the World Wars.* Ithaca: Cornell University Press; Van Evera. 2001. See also Mearsheimer. 2006a, p.109. Walt also famously teamed with realist John Mearsheimer to write *The Israel Lobby and US Foreign Policy*, a working paper which raised significant controversy upon its release in 2006. See Mearsheimer and Walt. 2006.

vote an entire chapter to reviewing the paradigm and its own reliance on anarchy as a central organising feature of international relations. This is precisely the goal of this chapter.

This chapter will begin by outlining Waltz's intellectual background and the context in which he came to develop the theory that would later evolve into his own structural interpretation of international affairs. Having outlined the context of Waltz's theoretical design, this chapter will use a similar methodology as the first in drawing out the most important elements of the neorealist approach through a review of the most significant works in the structural catalogue: Waltz's own *Man, the State, and War* and *Theory of International Politics*. This methodology will highlight the major revisions Waltz offers to the classical realist paradigm by contrasting the conclusions of Thucydides, Machiavelli, Hobbes, Carr and Morgenthau with those of Waltz and his neorealist contemporaries, including Robert Jervis and his book *System Effects: Complexity in Social and Political Life*.[258] As in the first chapter of this book, the reliance on anarchy as a basis for the assessment and explication of international politics will be highlighted as a precursor to later chapters in the book which will criticise this foundational belief. In concluding this chapter it will be clear that while the neorealist paradigm is very different to that reviewed in The first chapter's treatment of classical realism, it is not so different as to escape the criticisms which will follow as this dissertation progresses in its alternative to anarchy thesis.

The Intellectual Context of Kenneth Waltz

Kenneth Neal Waltz was born in 1924 in Ann Arbor, Michigan to a father who never attended high school and a mother who never graduated high school.[259] As a young student Waltz was attracted to mathematics and physics and upon graduating from Ann Arbor High School was admitted to Oberlin College in Ohio as a mathematics major.[260] Though Waltz was close to completing his mathematics degree his interests shifted to economics when he decided – ironically it would appear in hindsight – that

---

[258] Jervis. 1997
[259] Waltz. 2003.
[260] Waltz. 2003.

66

he did not wish to pursue studies that would force him to either teach or write.[261] Having completed his undergraduate studies at Oberlin, Waltz departed for New York and the graduate program in economics at Columbia University where it became clear to the young scholar that he would never be a "real" economist. In Waltz's own words:

> If you're not attracted to a field enough to read beyond the requirements, just to read more because you're curious and you want to know more than is required at any given course -- if that's not the case, then you're in the wrong field. So I finally began to ask myself, what did I really enjoy most in college? And the answer was English literature and political philosophy. So I took a lot of English literature courses and loved it, but realized that I would never write a novel or a poem, and I would, therefore, be a critic -- a very honourable profession, but it didn't inspire me. So political philosophy won, and I'm very pleased it did.[262]

Waltz claims to have been inspired by his undergraduate professor of government at Oberlin, John Lewis, but it would be the doctoral studies he completed under William Fox and Nathaniel Peffer which would begin to cement Waltz's place among the political theorists.[263]

Fox forced Waltz – at that point a major in political theory with only a minor in international politics – to study international law and international organisation. Both

---

[261] Waltz. 2003.

[262] Waltz. 2003.

[263] John Lewis is recalled by Waltz thus: "The teacher and the wife of the teacher who influenced me most was John Lewis and his wife, Ewart Lewis…I took just two half-courses from John Lewis, one in theory and the other in American government, but I lived with the Lewises for a semester. Ewart Lewis was a highly knowledgeable person in the field of medieval thought, and published a book, a one-volume version by Knopf and two volumes published in England, called *Medieval Political Ideas*. We had very interesting kitchen conversations about the interpretation of Saint Augustine, for example, and I enjoyed all of that immensely. So when trying to make the final decision, my wife and I went back to Oberlin and visited the Lewises and talked about it. That confirmed, by then, a strong inclination, and I shifted from economics to political science." See Waltz. 2003. William Fox was the first director of Columbia's Institute of War and Peace Studies and a prestigious scholar of international relations. Among his most famous works are William Fox. 1959. *Theoretical Aspects of International Relations*. Notre Dame: University of Notre Dame Press; William Fox (editor). 1970. *How Wars End*. Philadelphia: American Academy of Political and Social Science. Nathaniel Peffer was an East Asian journalist turned scholar who eventually became Professor of International Relations at Columbia University in 1943. Among Peffer's most significant works are Nathaniel Peffer. 1942. *Basis for Peace in the Far East*. New York: Harper & Bros; Nathaniel Peffer. 1958. *The Far East: A Modern History*. Ann Arbor: University of Michigan Press. Peffer was remembered by an obituary speaking to his accomplishments following his death in 1964 in the journal *Political Science Quarterly* (79:3) 484-486.

were areas Waltz had previously found uninteresting and which he had failed to study in any serious manner while a graduate at Columbia.[264] Approaching his final exams, Waltz found himself immersed in what he termed a "most confusing literature" of international relations, a literature that was confusing for the sole reason that the authors were thinking in different causal terms.[265] As Waltz would later put it during an interview at the University of California Berkeley:

> Some are thinking that the causes of what goes on in international relations are rooted in human beings, what human beings are like. And others are saying the causes are found in states. That good states don't fight wars, because they are democratic; bad states fight wars. And then the definition of good and bad varies; for a Marxist, it's a socialist state that is the good state. For a liberal, a good state is democratic. So everything is rooted in what states are like. And then there's the third way of looking at it, that it's at the international, political level that the causes are found, and although the causes do operate at those two other levels, they operate in this context, and the context is extremely important.[266]

This notion of the context of the international system and its centrality to the explanation of international events would become the central argument of Waltz's doctoral dissertation and the book *Man, the State, and War*.[267] Indeed, the designation of these three images of international politics – also known as the three 'levels of analysis', though Waltz rejected the term in preference to his wife's suggestion of 'image' which he found "more accurate and elegant" – would eventually define a generation of debate in international relations theory and inspire works by scholars ranging from J. David Singer of the Correlates of War Project to Alexander Wendt at the leading edge of the constructivist research agenda.[268] Waltz would never claim that the first two images – the individual and the domestic polity – were unimportant but from the outset he would focus on the third image, the system, as the underlying cause in and for international politics. A review of his argument in *Man, the State, and War* makes clear why he holds this to be the case.

---

[264] Waltz. 2003. Also Waltz. 2001, pp.vii-viii.

[265] Waltz. 2003.

[266] Waltz. 2003.

[267] Waltz. 2001.

[268] Waltz. 2001; J. David Singer. 1969. 'The Levels of Analysis Problem in International Relations.' *World Politics* 14(1): 77-92; Alexander Wendt. 1987. 'The Agent-Structure Problem in International Relations.' *International Organization* 41(3): 335-370.

Man, the State, and War: The Seeds of a Theory

Waltz's first book is a study of a political argument building logically, premise on premise, towards a stunning conclusion. That conclusion, however, cannot be considered fully contained on the pages of *Man, the State, and War* but only alluded to, with the greater explication to follow in the book's sequel.[269] Nonetheless, Waltz achieved enough with his premiere effort to analyse the international political system for it to be lauded at the time as a "highly intelligent and perceptive study" by Morton Kaplan and as a classic, timeless effort in *Military Review*.[270] As would become common in his later works, Waltz presents his argument in clearly designated pieces, the hallmark of a clear train of thought. *Man, the State, and War* takes the form of a three section review of the existing international relations literature bookended by a short introduction and an even shorter conclusion. Each of the three sections consists of two chapters: the first, titled in turn as 'The First Image', 'The Second Image' and 'The Third Image', outlines the existing literature from one of the three perspectives that Waltz suggests exists in the disciplinary literature; the second, titled in turn as 'Some Implications of the First Image', 'Some Implications of the Second Image' and 'Some Implications of the Third Image', allow Waltz the opportunity to dissect his review and point to theoretical missteps or the potential for superior explanation that lies within each image. Addressing each of these sections in turn allows this book to demonstrate the criticisms Waltz makes of the classical realist paradigm as well as provide a foundation for the discussion of the neorealist theory which would follow in *Theory of International Politics*.

---

[269] Waltz recalled: "I remember people, specifically a professor at Oberlin, George Lanyi, saying to me, "What's going to be the sequel to *Man, the State and War*?" And I said, "I don't have an idea about how I could write a sequel." From 1959 until the late sixties, I didn't have any sequel in mind. And then I began to think -- I don't know why these things develop in one's mind; who knows? -- I began to think of a way of asking myself, at least, the question of how might a theory of international politics be possible? And that's when I began to read more widely in anthropology and very widely in the philosophy of science. I finally developed the notion. It took a period of years to develop a notion and fill it out, figure out ways of presenting it effectively and so on, and that is what one finds in the book *Theory of International Politics*." See Waltz. 2003.

[270] Morton Kaplan. 1959. 'Review: *Man, The State, and War* by Kenneth N. Waltz.' *The American Political Science Review* 53(4): 1125-1127, p.1127; Gregory Ebner. 2003. 'Review: *Man, the State, and War: A Theoretical Analysis* by Kenneth N. Waltz.' *Military Review* 83(1): 68-69, p.69.

Section One: The First Image and Some Implications of the First Image

Waltz opens his discussion of the first image of international politics by stating simply:

> According to the first image of international relations, the locus of the important causes of war is found in the nature and behaviour of man. Wars result from selfishness, from misdirected aggressive impulses, from stupidity. Other causes are secondary and have to be interpreted in the light of these factors.[271]

From the outset, then, it seems clear that this first image is to deal with the work of the classical realists and, indeed, the names of the classical realists litter the pages of his opening section. Giants of political philosophy and international political theory are described as "serious students of human affairs" from the perspective of the first image, among them Confucius, Aristophanes, Reinhold Niebuhr, St Augustine, Spinoza and the leading light of the classical realist tradition, Hans Morgenthau.[272] Though these might be considered by some to be, superficially at least, opposed in some of their key traits – Spinoza, described as "a man of appalling wickedness", is mentioned alongside pacifist Beverly Nichols, a woman described as "brimming with charm and humour" – Waltz finds amidst the varied philosophical, political and historical literatures a unifying theme: all subscribe to the notion that the fundamental cause of war lies in the nature of humanity.[273]

There is a certain pessimism, Waltz argues, that pervades the world view of those of the first image.[274] Though accepting that humanity aims for moral perfection, they are consistent in "rejecting the possibility of achieving it".[275] Waltz suggests that such contentions result in an implicit assumption of an inherent potential for evil in the nature of humanity, a trait he suggests is recurrent "in the thought of Augustine, Spinoza, Niebuhr and Morgenthau".[276] Waltz has no argument with the notion of such theorists that humans cannot act contrary to their nature; indeed, this would

---

[271] Waltz. 2001, p.16.
[272] Waltz. 2001, pp.16-26.
[273] Russell. 1993, p.552; Bryon Connon. 2005. *Beverley Nichols: A Life*. Portland: Timber Press.
[274] Waltz. 2001, p.26.
[275] Waltz. 2001, p.26.
[276] Waltz. 2001, p.27.

seem to be a logical impossibility.[277] Yet he does not consider that pointing to the evil behaviour of humans and assuming this arises solely from human nature is a logical explanation, either, this being just the first of a number of criticisms of this classical position.[278]

Waltz asks, if human nature implies a potential for evil and is a cause of war and conflict in political systems:

> Do such evidences of man's behaviour as rapes, murders, and thefts prove he is bad? What about the counterevidence provided by acts of charity, love, and self-sacrifice? Is the amount of crime in a given society proof that the men in it are bad? Or is it amazing that under the circumstances there is not more crime?[279]

Such questions go to the heart of the classical realist position for, if it is in the nature of humanity to provoke war and act with evil intent, how is anyone to explain the common experience of humanity that would seem to suggest such behaviour is not at all natural? As Waltz notes, human nature may indeed be the cause for war but it may also be the reason for peace.[280] Such conclusions, however, are not very helpful no matter how correct they may in fact be for, if human nature is the cause of political conflict, then it is a "cause that human contrivance cannot affect".[281]

The first image scholars Waltz reviews have their positions summarised thus: "the evilness of men, of their improper behaviour, leads to war; individual goodness, if it could be universalised, would mean peace".[282] But, he argues, this is a position that amounts to little more than the first image scholars noticing that political conflict exists, asking themselves why the conflict exists and concluding that the reason lies in natural human behaviour.[283] Waltz is dismissive of this first-image position pointing to its essential political naïveté and its depiction of humanity as simple, nature-driven

---

[277] Waltz. 2001, p.27.

[278] Waltz. 2001, pp.27-28.

[279] Waltz. 2001, pp.27-28.

[280] Waltz uses the period before World War One to demonstrate this point. He writes, "Human nature may in some sense have been the cause of war in 1914, but by the same token it was the cause of peace in 1910". See Waltz. 2001, p.28.

[281] Waltz. 2001, p.29.

[282] Waltz. 2001, p.39.

[283] Waltz. 2001, p.39.

beings.[284] Waltz notes the problems of this position, not least that when the cause of political conflict is an unchangeable human nature then the cause of war and conflict can never truly be addressed; at best, the cause of war can only be mitigated through social sanction which would seem to involve, necessarily, force.[285] Thus, the assumption of a fixed human nature shifts the focus *away* from human nature as, by definition, a fixèd nature cannot be changed and focus must instead switch to the nature and extent of the nature-controlling social institutions.[286]

With this in mind, Waltz moves to consider the implications of a system in which a fixed human nature is the cause of political conflict and war.[287] Assuming that the first-image scholars are correct, how should they address this evil nature of man to mitigate conflict? In responding to this question, Waltz divides the first image adherents into two groups: the optimists who imagine that change in human nature is possible and the pessimists who imagine that change is not possible. Both agree with the fundamental potential for evil that exists in humans but – in addressing this – seek two different routes to secure peace among naturally conflicting parties.[288] However, whether the course chosen is institutional, educational or spiritual, Waltz argued they are all doomed to failure as strategies to prevent conflict.

In addressing this first-image cause of war, societies have used education, social and legal sanction, emotional appeals and appeals to religion in an attempt to control the war-hungry urges of humanity.[289] Waltz brackets such attempts under the broader umbrella of "behavioural science" for the reason that all are an attempt to change the natural behaviour of individuals' writ large across an entire society.[290] Waltz argues that Lawrence Frank is correct in suggesting that, for the behavioural scientists, society is the patient in need of a cure, to be provided by the enlightened behavioural sci-

---

[284] Waltz. 2001, p.39.
[285] Waltz. 2001, pp.40-41.
[286] Waltz. 2001, p.41.
[287] Waltz. 2001, pp.42-79.
[288] Waltz. 2001, pp.42-43.
[289] Waltz. 2001, pp.42.43.
[290] "The literature we shall consider in the present chapter is intentionally not representative of behavioural scientists as a group, although it is broadly representative of what has been written by them on the subject of war and peace". See Waltz. 2001, p.43.

entists, of course.[291] One particular 'cure' – closer understanding of other persons – is used by Waltz to demonstrate the key implication he draws in this chapter: addressing individual humans has not and will not address the problem of conflict in international politics.

Consider, writes Waltz, the claim of psychologist James Miller that "ignorance of the desires, aims, and characteristics of other peoples leads to fear and is consequently one of the primary causes for aggression".[292] Taking the Cold War, Waltz asks, "are we in a cold war with the Soviet Union because we do not understand Communist societies well enough"?[293] Considering the evidence, Waltz concludes it is not the case at all. In the Cold War period before 1959 – when *Man, the State, and War* was published – extensive studies of the Soviet Union were undertaken by scholars in the United States. Dozens of articles in *Foreign Affairs, World Politics* and other reputable journals saw the Soviet Union become one of the most studied regions on the planet for American political scientists.[294] Some have gone as far as to suggest that one such study – George Kennan's *The Sources of Soviet Conflict*, also known as the *X Article* – was so influential as to set the US on a containment policy for years to come.[295] But despite more than a decade of study and a growth in knowledge of the 'desires, aims and characteristics' of their Soviet rivals, Waltz's US remained in conflict with the Soviet Union as he wrote his book. Could it not be the case instead, argues Waltz, that the United States remains in a conflict with the Soviet Union not because there is ignorance of Soviet motives and goals but largely because there is great knowledge of both and a concurrent dislike of these ends? As he puts it himself in

---

[291] Waltz. 2001, p.45.

[292] Waltz. 2001, p.48. This example and James Miller are just one of the behavioural science examples Waltz outlines. It is used here as a prototypical argument of Waltz's from this section of *Man, the State, and War.*

[293] Waltz. 2001, p.48.

[294] Examples of such articles include Paul Zinner. 1952. 'The Ideological Basis of Soviet Foreign Policy.' *World Politics* 4(4): 488-511; Philip Mosely. 1953. 'The Kremlin's Foreign Policy Since Stalin.' *Foreign Affairs* 32(1): 20-33. An article search of *Foreign Affairs* over the period 1945-1959 finds 137 articles relating to the Cold War. See http://tinyurl.com/yw7nfq for search results.

[295] George Kennan is credited with the article which was originally published under the name 'X'. X. 1947. 'The Sources of Soviet Conduct.' *Foreign Affairs* 25(4): 566-582. The influence of this article on US policy was documented in the *Boston Globe* where, on the occasion of Kennan's 100th birthday, he was lauded as "the most influential American diplomat of the 20th century". See David Engerman. 2004. 'The Kennan century.' *Boston Globe* (29 February 2004): D4.

relation to the Soviets, "the more clearly we come to understand them the less we like them".[296]

With his example Waltz is demonstrating the problem he finds in first image assessments of political conflict: all routes to world order that attempt to address individual level predispositions to conflict have in common an attempt to erect a single philosophy, a single government, a single religion, a single culture or, in this case, a single solution: greater understanding.[297] This naturally stems from a presupposition that all humans are naturally flawed in similar ways and, thus, can be similarly 'medicated' (to continue Frank's patient analogy). Yet, as history has shown, wars have begun many times under one-system rule; further, Thucydides' account of the Melian-Athenian dialogue is a striking example how implementing this 'one-way' solution is just as likely to produce conflict as to remove it from the range of human choices. The history of the behavioural science approach to mitigating conflict has been singularly unsuccessful yet, and more problematic for Waltz, is that the first image approach seems to have had little success in consistently explaining and predicting political conflict.[298]

Section Two: The Second Image and Some Implications of the Second Image

If the position of scholars of the first image is problematic for Waltz, he would find no evidence that the second image perspective is any better for explaining the occurrence of war in the international system. The second image – which places the cause of war at the level of the state actor – is differentiated from the first with a neat analogy by Waltz involving water.[299] Waltz argues that the first image:

> ...concentrated on the contents rather than the container...Water running out of a faucet is chemically the same as water in a container, but once the water is in a container, it can be made to "behave" in different ways. It can be turned into steam and used to

---

[296] Waltz. 2001, p.48.
[297] Waltz. 2001, pp.48-49.
[298] Waltz would go on to discuss this in more detail in Chapter One of *Theory of International Politics*. See Waltz. 1979.
[299] Waltz. 2001, p.80.

power an engine, or, if the water is sealed in and heated to extreme temperatures, it can become the instrument of a destructive explosion.[300]

Considering the violence begotten by nation-states in the period since Westphalia and the causation attributed to the 'container' by second image scholars, Waltz's allusion to an "instrument of destructive explosion" seems entirely apt.[301] Yet as with the first image scholars, Waltz finds that key causation cannot be attributed to the level of the nation-state alone; to do so would be to fail to recognise the context of the choices made by states and their leaders.

Waltz opens his review of the second image literature with an outline of various second-image positions.[302] For example, a common second image position is to suggest that states provoke international wars to promote internal national cohesion.[303] Such charges were levelled at US President Bill Clinton during his term in office, with *Reason* magazine contributing editor Charles Freund suggesting that the Clinton administration repeatedly used the military to distract the American public from domestic scandals and their associated political instability.[304] Historically Waltz finds support in the literature from Bodin's study of conflict, in particular his consideration of the Roman empire. Waltz cites Bodin's claim that the Romans "could find no better antidote to civil war, or one more certain in its effects, than to oppose an enemy to the citizens".[305] This first argument for the cause of conflict lying in the hands of the state, then, is one that finds support both historically and in contemporary times, though it is not the only one second image position that Waltz considers in his review.

---

[300] Waltz. 2001, p.80.

[301] In support of this stance, author HG Wells once described the nation-state system and its proclivity to conflict thus: "The existence of independent sovereign states IS war, white or red, and only an elaborate mis-education blinded the world to this elementary fact." See HG Wells. 2006. *The Shape of Things to Come*. eBooks@Adelaide: Adelaide, Chapter 10.

[302] Waltz. 2001, pp.81-85.

[303] Waltz. 2001, p.81.

[304] Charles Freund. 2000. 'Secrets of the Clinton Spectacle.' *Reason* 31(11): 22-28, p.22. This position was parodied in the title of *The New York Times'* review *Wag the Dog*: 'If the Going Gets Tough, Get a Pet or Start a War'. See Janet Maslin. 1997. 'If the Going Gets Tough, Get a Pet or Start a War.' *The New York Times* (26 December): B10. See also Stanley Renshon. 1998. *High Hopes: The Clinton Presidency and the Politics of Ambition*. London: Routledge, Foreword.

[305] Waltz. 2001, pp.81-82. The original citation is from Jean Bodin.1955. *Six Books of the Commonwealth*. Oxford: Basil Blackwell, p.168.

He next turns to positions that seek to explain foreign "adventures" via reference to the internal defects of the state.[306] Such explanations, writes Waltz, "may be related to a type of government that is thought to be generically bad".[307] Such generically bad governance might be associated, in modern times, with authoritarian or dictatorial rule. Consider the debate surrounding nuclear proliferation in which some states are labelled trustworthy or not trustworthy based upon the model of governance that state employs domestically.[308] In contemporary debates of the supposed rationality of the leaders of the Islamic Republic of Iran and the Democratic People's Republic of Korea, for example, it is common for the governance model – theocratic and autocratic, respectively – to be cited as evidence of proclivity to conflict. Colin Rubenstein, writing in Australia's *The Age* newspaper, rejects that Iran is a typical sovereign state, opining:

> …it is not at all clear that deterrence will work with Iran. The regime is run by mullahs who are motivated primarily by an extremist religious worldview. And Iranian President Mahmoud Ahmadinejad has shown signs that he believes it is his destiny to bring about a final battle between his version of Islam and the West, which will usher in the messianic era.[309]

Rubenstein's view is echoed by others including *US News & World Report* editor Mort Zuckerman and the German newsmagazine *Der Spiegel*, both of whom consider the Iranian theocratic governance model important enough to mention in the context of arguments why the Middle Eastern power cannot be permitted to develop nuclear weapons.[310] In citing historical and intellectual precursors of Rubenstein, Zuckerman and *Der Spiegel*, Waltz demonstrates that this response to the modern dilemma of

---

[306] Waltz. 2001, p.82.

[307] Waltz. 2001, p.82.

[308] Waltz would later go on to become a celebrated scholar of nuclear politics. Both his article, 'The Spread of Nuclear Weapons: More May Be Better', and a co-authored book, *The Spread of Nuclear Weapons: A Debate*, are considered classical treatments of the topic of nuclear proliferation from a structural realist perspective. See Kenneth Waltz. 1981. 'The Spread of Nuclear Weapons: More May Be Better.' *The Adelphi Papers* 171: 1-32; Scott Sagan and Kenneth Waltz. 1995. *The Spread of Nuclear Weapons: A Debate*. New York: WW Norton and Company.

[309] Colin Rubenstein. 2006. 'Why we must stop Iran.' *The Age* (22 March): 13.

[310] Mort Zuckerman. 2006. 'The Mullah menace.' *Jewish World Review* (6 December 2006); Der Spiegel. 2006. *UN Veto Powers Give Tehran Ultimatum.* [21 February 2007] http://www.spiegel.de/international/0,1518,408771,00.html.

76

horizontal nuclear proliferation is but the most recent in a history of 'defective state, defective international policy' arguments employed by second image adherents.[311]

Finally there are those who argue that sovereign states act internationally to correct inequalities forced upon them by way of national economic, geographic or other such deprivations.[312] A state, writes Waltz, "may argue it has not attained its 'natural' frontiers, that such frontiers are necessary to its security" and that such a domestic reality leads to inevitable international conflict.[313] Bertrand Russell is quoted in evidence and his claim that there "can be no good international system until the boundaries of states coincide as nearly as possible with the boundaries of nations" presented as typical.[314] Indeed, disputed borders based on the nationality of a people remains an issue in international conflicts in Chechnya, Kashmir and Israel, all situations where state borders are, to some extent, disputed between national parties on ethnic terms.[315] With these three perspectives within the second image literature Waltz presents what, at the time, were the three most significant arguments stemming from the 'causation at state level' argument yet, though he would briefly consider Kant's perpetual peace argument within this section of *Man, The State, and War*, a more recent literature perhaps provides the best example of second image thinking.[316]

The international relations literature that considers the so-called democratic peace thesis is striking in its endorsement of the second image of international relations. The democratic peace thesis, simply stated, maintains that liberal democracies do not engage in conflict; essentially, proponents of this book argue that a domestic political situation (being a liberal democracy) begets an international policy (peacefulness) and eventually an entirely peaceful international system. According to John Owen,

---

[311] Waltz. 2001, p.82.

[312] Waltz. 2001, pp.82-83.

[313] Waltz. 2001, p.83.

[314] Bertrand Russell. 2003. *Political Ideals*. e-Book edition. Salt Lake City: Project Gutenberg, p.26. Waltz's citation (Waltz. 2001, p.83) of Russell is to the original edition. See Bertrand Russell. 1917. *Political Ideals*. New York: The Century Co., p.146.

[315] Gail Lapidus. 1998. 'Contested Sovereignty: The Tragedy of Chechnya.' *International Security* 23(1): 5-49, pp.8-10; Robert Wirsing. 1998. *India, Pakistan, and the Kashmir Dispute*. New York: St. Martin's Press, pp.9-10; Thomas Diez, Stephan Stetter and Mathias Albert. 2006. 'The European Union and Border Conflicts: The Transformative Power of Integration.' *International Organization* 60(3): 563-593, p.566.

[316] Waltz. 2001, p.83; p.101; p.105.

this thesis is "nearly a truism" in international relations, with other scholars suggesting that it is the "closest thing" to an "empirical law in the study of international relations".[317] The thesis has even contributed, in Owen's view, to the foreign policy platform of at least one US President who remarked during a State of the Union address:

> Ultimately, the best strategy to ensure our security and to build a durable peace is to support the advance of democracy elsewhere. Democracies don't attack each other, they make better trading partners and partners in diplomacy. That is why we have supported, you and I, the democratic reformers in Russia and in the other states of the former Soviet bloc.[318]

Added to this practical public policy example of the democratic peace thesis are literally hundreds of articles which have gone on to define a significant sub-field within the discipline of international relations. Strong arguments in favour have been made by James Ray, Fred Chernoff, Michael Doyle, Bruce Russett and Frank Wayman, among others, with counter arguments presented by Thomas Schwartz and Kiron Skinner, John Mearsheimer and Kenneth Waltz himself.[319] While Waltz's specific critique would wait until a decade after the Cold War, his review of the implications of second image positions on the causes of war in 1959 would be just as critical of this intellectual stance.

Provocatively subtitling the chapter on the implications of the second image 'International Socialism and the Coming of the First World War', Waltz quickly demonstrates his motivations for doing so: it is the Marxists who best embody the second image view of international relations.[320] The Marxist perspective, argues Waltz, cannot be reduced to 'capitalists cause war'; rather he argues that the Marxist employs an

---

[317] John Owen. 1994. 'How Liberalism Produces Democratic Peace.' *International Security* 19(2): 87-125, p.87; Levy. 1989, p.88.

[318] Bill Clinton. 1994. *State of the Union Address*. [21 February 2007] http://tinyurl.com/25psdv.

[319] James Ray. 1998. 'Does Democracy Cause Peace?' *Annual Review of Political Science* 1: 27-46; Fred Chernoff. 2004. 'The Study of Democratic Peace and Progress in International Relations.' *International Studies Review* 6(1): 49-78; Doyle. 1983a; Doyle. 1983b; Bruce Russett, Christopher Layne, David Spiro and Michael Doyle. 1995. 'The Democratic Peace.' *International Security* 19(4): 164-184, pp.164-175; Frank Wayman. 2002. *Incidence of Militarized Disputes Between Liberal States 1816-1992*. Paper presented at the Annual Meeting of the International Studies Association, New Orleans, USA, 23-27 March 2002; Thomas Schwartz and Kiron Skinner. 2002. 'The Myth of the Democratic Peace.' *Orbis* 46(1): 159-172; Mearsheimer. 1990; Waltz. 2000, pp.6-13.

[320] "Marx and the Marxists represent the fullest development of the second image." See Waltz. 2001, p.125.

"unchallengeable logic" whereby the *existence* of states implies the possibility of war:

> If the state is the domination of one class over another, socialism by abolishing all classes thereby abolishes the state. And if war is armed conflict among states, the abolition of states must be the end of war. The problem of war and peace can no longer exist.[321]

It obviously follows that if the cause of international conflict – and other international actions – is the nature of the state then a global system without states is certain to be free from conflict. Though Waltz admits there is some ambiguity as to whether Marx was actually implying the necessary destruction of capitalism or states, he also notes that it matters little to "those who follows Marx to the socialist millennium" who, in reality, advocate the destruction of both.[322] For the Marxists "capitalist states cause war, and socialism spells peace"; yet even socialism was not enough to prevent the major conflicts that took place in the post-Marx and Engels period.[323]

Waltz presents the First World War as his case study of socialist second image politics failing in practice. With socialist parties across Europe in the period immediately preceding the war unanimously opposed to war and all advocating anti-war strategies (including general strikes and other withdrawal of labour efforts) it seems strange that many socialist parties also supported the war efforts of their home states.[324] This apparent philosophical conflict is explained away by Waltz with reference to what became another commonly held position by European Marxists: "socialists could with a clear conscience support their own countries in a defensive war".[325] The question then becomes, for which states was the First World War a defensive war? Evidence presented from English, French and German socialists does – in every case – suggest that the war efforts of each of their home states were matters of defence; indeed, as Waltz would comment, "it turned out the war was defensive for everyone".[326] Con-

---

[321] Waltz. 2001, pp.126-127.
[322] Waltz. 2001, p.127.
[323] Waltz. 2001, p.128.
[324] Waltz. 2001, pp.128-130.
[325] Waltz. 2001, p.130.
[326] Waltz. 2001, pp.130-132; p.132.

venient for the capitalist classes, perhaps, but of little help in confirming that the second image perspective is the most valid.

Ironically, Waltz finds parallels to the socialist second image logic of the pre- and immediately post-First World War periods in the rhetoric of some of those most opposed to the socialist program. In the Cold War pronouncements of the United States' leadership, including Richard Nixon, Waltz finds a common theme: if it wasn't for the inherent evilness of those 'other' states then there would be no trouble in the world.[327] It would seem, then, that both in the theoretical and practical study and application of the second image there is some significant support. Further, this support exists across all ideological boundaries, from European Marxists to American Republicans.[328] That it is applied by many, though, does not make it less problematic or even suggest that it is a perspective of any utility in explaining international affairs. Like Antoine de St. Exupéry's Lamplighter in *The Little Prince,* who continues to work as he has always done despite the obvious futility of his position, that the second image has become so pervasive in theoretical and practical politics need be no proof of analytical superiority but rather evidence of a world of Lamplighters who refuse to acknowledge the absurdity of their beliefs.[329]

Waltz does not go so far as to suggest the second image position is absurd; he does, however, label it the equivalent of not entirely thought through to its logical conclusions:

> Socialist states, they [second image endorsers] assert, will be peaceful. This may be true, but even so it does not follow automatically that among socialist states there will always be peace. This is what the revisionists did not understand.[330]

Indeed, by placing the cause of war, conflict and other international behaviour of states at the level of the state there exist many of the same problems that arise within first image scholarship.[331] As much as there are good humans in a world of evil human nature there will exist good autocrats in a world of evil autocrats and bad democracies in a world of overwhelmingly good democracies. Internal dimensions or the

---

[327] Waltz. 2001, p.157.
[328] Waltz. 2001. P.157.
[329] Antoine de St Exupéry. 2000. *The Little Prince.* New York: Harvest Books.
[330] Waltz. 2001, p.157.
[331] Waltz. 2001. p.158.

80

internal organisation of a nation-state are not enough to define that state's behaviour within the international system. As with his review of the first image, Waltz does not deny that domestic and governance matters internal to a state *can* have an effect at the international level but, again, it is the context of the wider system that seems most important factor here and not the particular attributes of the state within that wider system. It is this point that leads Waltz to his final section and the real beginnings of his redefinition of the existing realist paradigm: the third image.

Section Three: The Third Image and Some Implications of the Third Image

Opening his review of the third image with a definition that is reminiscent of Athenian envoys to Melos in its blunt assessment of the nature of international politics:

> With many sovereign states, with no system of law enforceable among them, with each state judging its grievances and ambitions according to the dictates of its own reason or desire – conflict, sometimes leading to war, is bound to occur. To achieve a favourable outcome from such a conflict a state has to rely on its own devices, the relative efficiency of which must be its constant concern. This, the idea of the third image, is to be examined in the present chapter.[332]

Waltz does not claim to have been the first to describe this anarchic reality of international politics, citing examples from ancient historians to twentieth-century analysts and US Presidents in the introduction to his review of this third image. Yet unlike his previous treatments of the first and second images, this section of *Man, the State, and War* is largely a study of the thought and work of one man: Jean Jacques Rousseau. While acknowledging that there is certain discontinuity to this approach, Waltz suggests that Rousseau is to the third image just as Spinoza and Kant are to the first and second images, respectively: philosophers who "follow the pattern" of an image's implication throughout their philosophical scholarship.[333]

---

[332] Waltz. 2001. P.159. The parallel implied to exist in the Peloponnesian War is at Thucydides. 1998, p.169: "But you and we should say what we really think, and aim only at what is possible, for we both alike know that into the discussion of human affairs the question of justice only enters when there is equal power to enforce it, and the powerful exact what they can, and the weak grant what they must." Waltz would reference a different passage in support of his point (the fear of the Lacedaemonians of the growth in Athenian power) but the fact remains that the world Thucydides describes is inherently anarchical. See Thucydides. 1998, p.17; Waltz. 2001, p.159.
[333] Waltz. 2001, pp.161-165.

A scholar of the Enlightenment and the father figure of philosophy's romantic movement, Rousseau was someone better described as a "social force" than a typical philosopher.[334] Though he gave a detailed account of his life in his book *Confessions*, it is one that is "without any slavish regard for the truth".[335] Born in Geneva in 1712, Rousseau received minimal education and left school at the age of 12 to become an apprentice to a notary public and, later, to an engraver.[336] In the years that followed Rousseau would travel to France, convert to Catholicism (though later revert to Protestant Calvinism), live as a vagabond, work as a secretary and a servant and masquerade "as a Scotch Jacobite named Dudding".[337] His first notable contribution to the philosophical literature would not come until 1750 when, at the age of 38, he entered an essay in pursuit of a prize offered by the Academy of Dijon for the best answer to the question, 'have the arts and sciences conferred benefits on mankind?'[338] Rousseau won first place with his essay arguing the negative case and would go on to publish the manuscript as *Discours sur les sciences et les arts* (*Discourse on the Sciences and the Arts*).[339] This essay would be published later alongside *Discours sur l'origine de l'inégalité* (Discourse on the Origin of Inequality), the latter one of the key tracts by Rousseau upon which Waltz would base his third image review.[340]

Waltz compares Rousseau's conception of human nature and the nature of the state to both Spinoza and Kant, but focuses on Rousseau's different interpretation of the nature of the system in which humans and their states find themselves political actors. The anarchical international system that Rousseau describes, argues Waltz, implies that war and conflict among actors is not only likely but *necessary*; indeed, Rousseau argues "that in anarchy there is no automatic harmony".[341] Waltz suggests that for Rousseau, that there are only two 'solutions' to the 'problem' of conflict in an anarchical international system: first, "to impose an effective control on the separate and

---

[334] Russell. 1993, p.651; p.660.
[335] Russell. 1993, p.660.
[336] Russell. 1993, p.660.
[337] Russell. 1993, p.661.
[338] Russell. 1993, p.662.
[339] Jean Jacques Rousseau. 1992. *Discours sur les sciences et les arts: discours sur l'origine de l'inégalité*. Paris: Flammarion.
[340] Rousseau. 1992; Russell. 1993, pp.662-663.
[341] Waltz. 2001, p.182.

imperfect states", and second, "to remove states from the sphere of the accidental".[342] The former suggests systemic change which Waltz would later suggest has not occurred and the latter is suggested to be impossible.[343] But Rousseau's conception of an anarchical realm "does make possible a theory of international relations that in general terms explains the behaviour of states, both good and bad", and for Waltz this is the key to understanding the implications of the third image.[344]

Two significant conclusions are drawn from Rousseau by Waltz: first, that "in anarchy there is no natural harmony" and, second, that war is inevitable among sovereign states in an anarchical system.[345] At the conclusion of his sixth chapter Waltz admits that there is no *necessary* link between the two conclusions but undertakes, in Chapter Seven, to demonstrate that there is indeed a relation between anarchy and international conflict.[346] For Waltz anarchy is the essential context of international political action. Whilst prefacing his argument with discussion of various economic and financial matters of state – obviously drawing on his background in economics as an undergraduate and graduate student – Waltz eventually moves to that which had become familiar ground for the classical realists that had passed before him: the balance of power.[347] In line with John Bright, he argues that the balance of power is a "mischievous delusion", yet it remains a delusion of long standing.[348] Athenians, Romans, American Founding Fathers and European diplomats are among those who have endorsed this balance, yet Waltz urges that their generally superficial endorsement of the balance of power be supported with the "logic" that lies in the third image of international politics and the context that the anarchical system provides.[349] The logic of the balance of power – later alluded to as the 'logic of anarchy' in Barry Buzan's book of the same name – is driven by the anarchical system, the balance appearing

---

[342] Waltz. 2001, p.182.

[343] Waltz. 2000.

[344] Waltz. 2001, p.183.

[345] Waltz. 2001, p. 186.

[346] Waltz. 2001, p.186; Waltz. 2001, Chapter Seven.

[347] Waltz. 2001, pp.188-198.

[348] Waltz. 2001, p.198. Waltz cites John Bright. 1869.*Speeches*. London: Macmillan & Co, p.233; pp.460-461; 468-469.

[349] Waltz. 2001, pp.198-200.

not because of the wishes of the actors alone but because of the significant influence of the system in which they operate.[350]

Waltz reverts to game theory to make his point, drawing on the work of John von Neumann and Oskar Morgenstern and asking the reader to imagine a pie as the object of international politics:

> Under these conditions the game can tend toward either of two extremes. (1) It may become a simple problem in maximization: all the players may cooperate to make the largest possible pie. In international politics this corresponds to the hypothetical case in which all states band together with nature as their adversary. (2) All the players may be so intent on the question of how the pie already in existence should be divided that they forget about the possibility of increasing the amount each will have by working together to make more of it…the game then reverts to a zero-sum or constant-sum game… [3] It may be that nobody likes pie, or that everybody likes something else better. In this case the game is not played at all.[351]

The third of these possibilities – the only non-extreme for Waltz – is rejected out of hand: after all, states have "objects" and objectives which they seek and pursue political action towards such ends. States will, by their nature, always be a part of the 'game' of international politics. But which of the remaining two game strategies does Waltz suggest best fit the 'balance of power' reality of the international system?[352] Again drawing on von Neumann and Morgenstern's game theoretic arguments, Waltz concludes that there is not only good reason for states to cooperate under anarchy but also to form blocs and, ideally, two blocs in order to best divide the power 'pie' in the wider system.[353]

Thus, for Waltz, the key reality of the classical realist position – the balance of power – is explained not with reference to the desires of humans or the desires of states but rather with regard to the actions of both humans and states within a context that forces them to balance. In comparison to the third image, the first and second images

---

[350] Barry Buzan, Charles Jones and Richard Little. 1993. *The Logic of Anarchy: Neorealism to Structural Realism*. New York: Columbia University Press.

[351] Waltz. 2001, p.203.

[352] Waltz. 2001, p.203.

[353] Waltz. 2001, pp.204-205. Waltz notes that the «'two bloc' ideal is not always the reality within the system, citing Clausewitz in his defence. Nevertheless, Waltz maintains that game theoretic analysis of an anarchical system suggests the two bloc reality remains an ideal.

cannot explain war and international action; yet, with consideration of the third image and the actions of humans and states within it one can explain the occurrence of war, the arrival of conflict and the actions of states, if not every occurrence ahead of its arrival.[354] Waltz finds in the third image the superior explanation for the actions of states. It provides a theoretical basis for international relations that neither the classical realists positions that endorse the first and second images can provide. Yet embracing this third image requires diplomats and their governments to embrace a reality that is far different from what they have previously known or assumed of the international system.

The diplomat must, warns Waltz, heed the reality of the third image and accept the implications of systemic anarchy for foreign policy:

> Each state pursues its own interests, however defined, in ways it judges best. Force is a means of achieving the external ends of states because there exists no consistent, reliable process of reconciling the conflicts of interest that inevitably arise among similar units in a condition of anarchy. A foreign policy...is neither moral nor immoral, but embodies merely a reasoned response to the world around us.[355]

Urging policymakers to recognise the importance of the third image in considering their foreign policy, Waltz concludes his argument and leaves the reader asking the obvious question: what's next?

Between *Man, the State, and War* and *Theory of International Politics*

Man, the State, and War was published in 1959 and based largely on doctoral work Waltz completed in 1954 and *Theory of International Politics* followed in 1979. In the two decades between these books Waltz recalls being asked "what's going to be the sequel to *Man, the State, and War*?", and replying, "I don't have an idea about how I could write a sequel".[356] Indeed, he admits that throughout the 1960s he did not have a sequel in mind, though it would seem that the first book could only ever be a

---

[354] Waltz. 2001, p.237.

[355] Waltz. 2001, p.238. On the problems of cooperation under anarchy see Kenneth Oye (ed.). 1986. *Cooperation under Anarchy*. Princeton: Princeton University Press.

[356] Waltz. 2003.

first step in a wider theory.[357] Waltz published regularly in the intervening period and then, in 1975, Waltz published the essay, *Theory of International Relations*, that would form the launching pad for his second major book.[358] This essay would form most of the opening three chapters of *Theory of International Politics* but that book – by its end – would shape the debates within the discipline for decades to come.

Theory of International Politics: A Theory in Full

This chapter earlier described *Man, the State, and War* as 'The Seeds of a Theory'. The publication of *Theory of International Politics* saw Waltz nurture these seeds into a mature and paradigm defining theory in its own right. The book was greeted with much interest across the discipline at the time, William Fox decreeing its contribution "distinguished" and not to be ignored and Robert Randle highlighting the reason and logic underlying the text.[359] Later it would spawn an entire literature and engendered texts that have become standards on international relations syllabi worldwide including Robert Keohane's *Neorealism and Its Critics* and David Baldwin's *Neorealism and Neoliberalism*.[360] A contribution described as having the biggest impact on the entire field and the way people think about international relations theory and which was the base for either extension or critique for a new generation of scholars – among them Barry Posen, Steven Van Evera and Stephen Walt – who would define new theories of realism and structural realism, Waltz's book is deserving of a detailed review.[361] Further, as this is the text through which neorealism and the important role of systemic anarchy within that theory is best outlined, examination of *Theory of International Politics* is fundamental to the aims of this book.

---

[357] Waltz. 2003.

[358] Kenneth Waltz. 1975. 'Theory of International Relations.' In *The Handbook of Political Science: Vol 8*, edited by Fred Greenstein and Nelson Polsby. Reading: Addison-Wesley, pp.1-86.

[359] William Fox. 1980. 'Review: *Theory of International Politics*, by Kenneth Waltz.' *The American Political Science Review* 74(2): 492-493; Robert Randle. 1980. 'Review: *Theory of International Politics*, by Kenneth Waltz.' *Political Science Quarterly* 95(1): 136-137.

[360] Robert Keohane (ed.). 1986a. *Neorealism and Its Critics*. New York: Columbia University Press; David Baldwin (ed.). 1993. *Neorealism and Neoliberalism*. New York: Columbia University Press.

[361] Mearsheimer. 2006a, p.109.

Theory of International Politics is presented in nine chapters but, more generally, it is a work in two parts.[362] The first is an extended critique of existing international relations theories, an extension of some of the points raised within *Man, the State, and War* and his 1975 essay, *Theory of International Relations*. The second is Waltz's truly significant contribution to international relations theory and is entirely composed of an argument for an explanation of a theoretical approach with the international system being the core, rather than the background, to the behaviour of actors. This chapter of the book will assess the two parts in turn, with more attention being paid to the latter and the fundamental change to the classical realist position it provides.

Part One: Theories, Laws and The Critique

The opening chapter of Waltz's book is one of definition, the author moving to differentiate between laws, theories and models.[363] A rigorous theorist, Waltz would later return to this discussion decades later, arguing that the "law" or "theory" of democratic peace is actually neither.[364] What is significant for Waltz here is that the reader understands he is presenting a theory – "theories are statements that *explain* laws" – rather than a collection of laws.[365] Waltz is clear that while laws must describe the real world exactly, his theory and all theories are distinct from the actual world, claiming "reality will be congruent neither with a theory nor with a model that may represent it".[366] Models are based upon a theory but neither exactly reflects reality nor always reflects the theory upon which they claim foundation.[367] From the outset, then, Waltz sets the scene for what is to follow and effectively closes the door to attempts to critique his work as a poor model or an unsustainable law.

Theories – not models or laws – are Waltz's interest In preparation for the critique to follow, Waltz sets out a test for theories by which, even at this early point in the text, it is clear that previous theories will be rejected and Waltz's own eventually upheld:

---

[362] Fox. 1980, p.493.
[363] Waltz. 1979, pp.1-17.
[364] Waltz. 2000, pp.6-8.
[365] Waltz. 1979, p.5. Emphasis added.
[366] Waltz. 1979, pp.6-7.
[367] Waltz. 1979, p.7.

In order to test a theory, one must do the following:

- State the theory being tested.
- Infer hypotheses from it.
- Subject the hypotheses to experimental or observational tests.
- In taking steps two and three, use the definitions of terms in the theory being tested.
- Eliminate or control perturbing variables not included in the theory under test.
- Devise a number of distinct and demanding tests.
- If a test is not passed, ask whether the theory flunks completely, needs repair and restatement, or requires a narrowing of the scope of its explanatory claims.[368]

Waltz refuses to critique theories under the labels of 'realist' or 'liberalist'. Instead, he employs the terms reductionist and systemic, the first placing most focus on the elements and actors within a system, the latter on the system itself and the interactions which occur within it. This is different to how Waltz had previously assessed theoretical explanations in *Man, the State, and War* where three images of international politics were used to differentiate positions on world affairs.[369] Essentially, what Waltz does here is to label the first two images – individual and state – 'reductionist', and his favoured third image as 'systemic'. The first two images are reductionist because they seek to explain the whole of the system through reference to the parts of the system, thus reducing the level of analysis.[370] Systemic theories, conversely, attempt to consider the organisation of the units (individuals and states) within the system believing that their organisation impacts on the system and the events within it.[371] Waltz largely leaves the systemic theories and approaches for later in his argument, presenting first a sustained critique of the reductionist position.

In large part, though, this critique is a restatement of the arguments put forward in *Man, the State, and War*. Again, criticism of imperialist and socialist theories of international politics are offered and, again, Waltz rejects them for failing to place the

---

[368] Waltz. 1979, p.13. Note that this is simply a re-statement of a Popperian falsifiability model and will have little application to a complex model of international politics where prediction is expected to be difficult or even impossible in the long term.

[369] Waltz. 1979, p.18. Waltz admits as much writing, "elsewhere I have distinguished explanations of international politics, and especially efforts to locate the causes of war and to define the conditions of peace, according to the level at which the causes are located – whether in man, the state, or the state system". See Waltz. 1979, p.18 in reference to Waltz. 1959 [2001].

[370] Waltz. 1979, p.18.

[371] Waltz. 1979, p.39.

actions of man and the state within the wider context of a significant system. In particular, Waltz is savage in his criticism of neo-colonial theories, reducing them to positions that leave their proponents "in despair" or, alternatively, "in fantasy".[372] Waltz argues that reductionist theories *by definition* imply that there is no reason existing at the international level for conflict between states; indeed, reductionist realist theories imply that international conflict arises because of human or nature, state policy or economic policy.[373] Yet Waltz, citing support from Robert Jervis, suggests that it is impossible to imagine that if the state-level issues were resolved (for example, all states emerge as perfect socialist states) that conflict would disappear.[374] Concluding his argument against such reductionist theories, Waltz writes:

> Internationally, different states have produced similar as well as different outcomes, and similar states have produced different as well as similar outcomes. The same causes sometimes lead to different effects, and the same effects sometimes follow from different causes. We are led to suspect that reductionist explanations of international politics are insufficient and that analytic approaches must give way to systemic ones.[375]

Thus, by the end of his second chapter Waltz has again delivered his argument to the conclusions he made in *Man, the State, and War*, yet with a significant difference. No longer is Waltz simply critiquing the work that has gone before him in the realist literature: instead, he is opening the analysis he previously delivered from mere review and critique to the construction of a new, non-reductionist theory of international politics.

Waltz begins his third chapter by stating that simple doubt as to the adequacy of reductionist theories does not imply anything more than that a systemic theory is better suited to explaining international relations; it certainly does not imply *which* systemic theory would be best suited to international analysis.[376] For, just as there are a number of reductionist political theories, there are a number of theories or approaches that

---

[372] Waltz. 1979, p.35.
[373] Waltz. 1979, p.36.
[374] Waltz. 1979, pp.36-37.
[375] Waltz. 1979, p.37.
[376] Waltz. 1979, p.38.

strive to deliver systemic analysis.[377] In short order Waltz mentions Karl Marx and Immanuel Wallerstein, though others could easily be added to the list in more recent times including George Modelski and Charles Doran.[378] Differentiating these approaches from the reductionist examples, Waltz uses an intriguing example. He draws on the example of the natural sciences and argues that reductionist methods are akin to the approach of the classical physicists.[379] Yet while this has worked "wonderfully" where the units under study can be isolated as all "other things are held equal", it is of little use to within a system where this is not the case.[380] Indeed, where outcomes are "affected not only by the properties and interconnections of variables but also by the way in which they [the variables] are organised" it is only a systemic approach that can possibly account for the outcomes of the units within the wider system.[381]

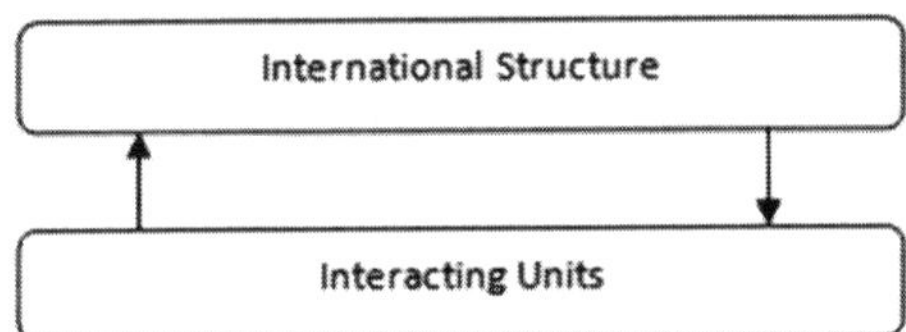

Figure 2.1: Conception of the International System in Systemic Theories of International Relations

Systems theories of international relations conceive of the international political system as in Figure 2.1 (above). A systems theory, though, must outline specifically the effects of the international structure on the units within the system, departing from the often vague descriptions attributed to the system in reductionist analysis.[382] Con-

---

[377] Waltz's use of the chapter title, *Systemic Approaches and Theories*, is significant in that it displays Waltz's implicit criticism of a number of systemic approaches that could not be considered theories in full. Contrast this with Waltz's previous chapter headed simply *Reductionist Theories*.

[378] See George Modelski and William Thompson. 1988. *Seapower in Global Politics, 1494-1993*. Seattle: University of Washington Press; Charles Doran and Wes Parsons. 1980. 'War and the Cycle of Relative Power.' *The American Political Science Review* 74(4): 947-965.

[379] Waltz. 1979, p.39.

[380] Waltz. 1979, p.39.

[381] Waltz. 1979, p.39.

[382] Waltz. 1979, pp.40-41.

sequently it is necessary that the systems theorist identifies "what units the system comprises, to indicate the comparative weights of systemic and sub-systemic causes, and to show how forces and effects change from one system to another".[383] And while Waltz considers three fellow theorists who adopt a systemic theoretical approach – namely, Richard Rosecrance, Stanley Hoffman and Morton Kaplan – he finds each lacking in at least one of these areas.[384] Rosecrance, for example, is failed by Waltz as not allowing for any systemic influence within his systemic theory; indeed, Waltz ultimately labels Rosecrance a reductionist.[385] Hoffman – at one time a teacher of Rosecrance – presents more of a systemic approach yet in his "failure to resist the temptation to tuck most everything into the structure" of his system, it becomes hard to determine a single, workable theory from his descriptions of the system.[386] Hoffman has included everything possible to the detriment of his wider theoretical work, implicitly rejecting the necessary limitations and parsimony demanded of a theory of international relations.[387] Kaplan, in turn, is failed by Waltz for failing to indicate the weights of the system and subsystem causes, a situation which he claims leads to a theory somewhat "weak and incomplete".[388]

Thus, at the close of this third chapter Waltz concludes that while a systems approach is superior to the reductionist realism that dominated the field, the approaches that are presented as systemic are lacking in the rigour required to properly explain international politics with a thorough, theoretical framework. Waltz argues:

> Students of international politics who claim to follow a systems approach fall into two categories. Some merely use such terms as "system" and "structure" as words of fashion in the ever-developing jargon of the field...Others pattern their work on the general-systems model.[389]

---

[383] Waltz. 1979, pp.40-41.

[384] Waltz. 1979, pp.41-59. The primary works of these theorists that Waltz considers are, in order, Richard Rosecrance. 1963. *Action and Reaction in World Politics: International Systems in Perspective.* Boston: Little Brown; Stanley Hoffman. 1961. 'International Systems and International Law.' *World Politics* 14(1): 205-237; Morton Kaplan. 1957. *System and Process in International Politics.* New York: Wiley.

[385] Waltz. 1979, p.43.

[386] Waltz. 1979, p.49.

[387] Waltz here also implicitly rejects a model or theory of international politics based upon the assumption of complexity, a reason why his Popperian test of theories is later held in this book not to apply to a complex approach to international affairs.

[388] Waltz. 1979, p.55.

[389] Waltz. 1979, pp.58-59.

The former category is clearly aimed at explaining the attempts of analysts in the vein of Rosecrance, the latter encompassing the attempts by Hoffman and Kaplan. The general systems model, however, with its reliance on clearly articulated and hierarchical orders, does not fit neatly with international politics.[390] As Thucydides, Machiavelli, Hobbes and Morgenthau had hinted at across millennia, the international system is not a hierarchical sphere and, therefore, models that assume such a system are necessarily flawed. What is needed is a systems approach leading to a theory of international politics that allows for an anarchical system's effect upon the systems constituent units. Such a theory is what Waltz now provides in the second part of his book.

Part Two: Structural Realism

As with the opening of his book, Waltz returns to definitions as he lays the foundations for his own theory of international politics. A system, he writes, "is composed of a structure and of interacting units".[391] Structure, meanwhile, is "the system-wide component that makes it possible to think of the system as a whole".[392] The first problem for a systems theorist, then, is to define the structure of a system without referring to the attributes or the interactions between the units within that system.[393] This structure must in turn be defined by the arrangement of its parts and, thus, only changes in the arrangements of the parts of the system are actually changes to the system's structure.[394] Here Waltz suggests that in political matters there are but two structures – hierarchical and anarchical – and that only the latter can properly be said to exist in the international system.[395] For neorealists, the discourse of hierarchy is that of the domestic political or societal political sphere; however, the domestic sphere does allow the theorist to apply useful tools of domestic systemic analysis to international anarchy.

---

[390] Waltz. 1979, p.59.

[391] Waltz. 1979, p.79. See also Figure 2.1 in this book.

[392] Waltz. 1979, p.79.

[393] Waltz. 1979, p.79. Waltz's challenge is analogous to an English teacher who demands that students define a word without using the word in need of definition.

[394] Waltz. 1979, p.80.

[395] Waltz. 1979, p.81; p.116. Waltz. 2000, pp.5-6. See also Kenneth Waltz. 1986. 'Reflections on *Theory of International Politics*: A Response to My Critics.' In *Neorealism and Its Critics*, edited by Robert Keohane. New York: Columbia University Press, pp.322-345, pp.325-330.

92

Waltz examines domestic systems according to three factors: the ordering principle of the system, the character of the units of the system and the distribution of capabilities between the units. His analysis concludes as depicted in Figure 2.2 (below).

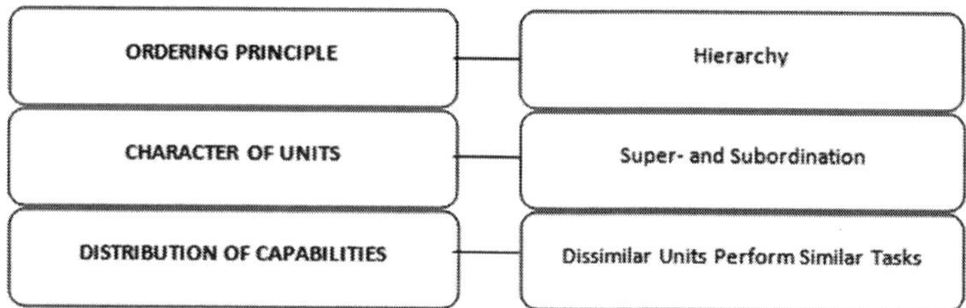

Figure 2.2 The Domestic Political System

Addressing next the international system, Waltz finds a significantly different system, one so different as to make international conjecture based on domestic examples worthless (see Figure 2.3, below).

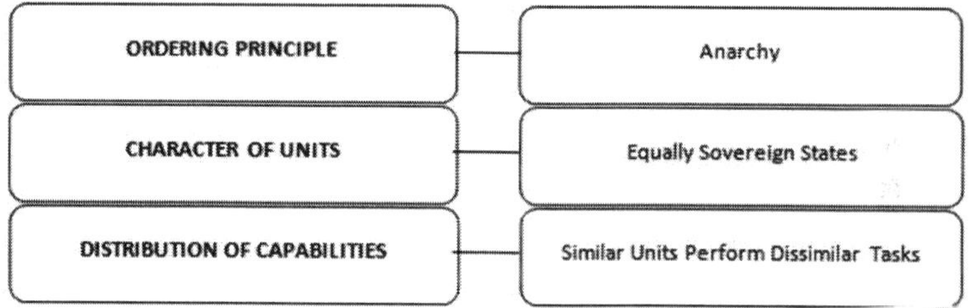

Figure 2.3 The International Political System

The ordering principle of the system, anarchy, will be considered on its own later in this chapter. However, at this point it is important to understand that anarchy is central to neorealist assessments and, in some ways, implies both the character of and distribution of capabilities between units of the system.

The neorealist focus on states as the key units of the international system is not surprising, the theory emerging as it does from a realist tradition where states have been the primary actors in international politics. Waltz does take pains to support his argument that states are like units despite their obvious differences in capabilities but he is much more concerned to support the choice of states as *the* most important international actor and the longevity of states.[396] He argues – as do others – that the influence of non-state actors is significant.[397] However, in comparison to states, non-state actors are significantly more transient. Consider that:

> [t]he death rate among states is remarkably low. Few states die; many firms do. Who is likely to be around 100 years from now – the United States, the Soviet Union, France, Egypt, Thailand and Uganda? Or Ford, IBM, Shell, Unilever, and Massey-Ferguson? I would bet on the states, perhaps even on Uganda.[398]

Neorealist's claim that states are 'like units', not only because of their longevity in a turbulent international system, but also because of their sovereignty.[399] Sovereignty, a concept disputed in its own right, is defined by the neorealists not as the *ability* to do as it pleases in the international system but that it can *freely decide* how to cope with internal and external issues.[400] No matter the differences in capabilities between states – including both physical and acquired characteristics – all states enjoy sovereign equality and remain, for neorealists, 'like units' in an anarchical system.

---

[396] Waltz. 1979, p.93.

[397] Waltz. 1979, pp.93-97. There is a significant and, in many ways, still emerging literature on the significant influence of non-state actors on the international system. Examples are considered in Kenneth Rodman. 1998. 'Think Globally, Punish Locally: Nonstate Actors, Multinational Corporations, and Human Rights Sanctions.' *Ethics and International Affairs* 12(1): 19-41; Tanja Börzel. 2000. *Private Actors on the Rise? The Role of Non-State Actors in Compliance with International Institutions*. MPI Collective Goods Working Paper 2000/14, Otto Suhr Institute for Political Science, Free University of Berlin; Peter Newell. 2000. *Climate for Change: Non-State Actors and the Global Politics of Greenhouse*. Cambridge: Cambridge University Press.

[398] Waltz. 1979, p.95. Today – more than a decade after the end of the Cold War – Waltz's examples may not prove his point quite as well as when originally conceived in 1979. All of the companies listed by Waltz continue to function while, of course, the Soviet Union has been consigned to history.

[399] Waltz. 1979, p.95. See also Gilpin. 1986, pp.316-317.

[400] Waltz's exact words are, "To say that a state is sovereign means that it decides for itself how it will cope with its internal and external problems, including whether or not to seek assistance from others and in doing so limit its freedom by making commitments to them...". See Waltz. 1979, p.96. On debates surrounding sovereignty see discussion in John Ruggie. 1986. 'Continuity and Transformation in the World Polity: Toward a Neorealist Synthesis.' In *Neorealism and Its Critics*, edited by Robert Keohane. New York: Columbia University Press, pp.131-157, pp.147; Kal Holsti. 1999. 'The Coming Chaos? Armed Conflict on the World's Periphery.' In *International Order and the Future of World Politics*, edited by TV Paul and John Hall. Cambridge: Cambridge University Press, pp.283-310, pp.284-289.

Yet while neorealists consider all states to maintain sovereign equality, it does not follow that all states are given equal weight in analysis of the international system. The distribution of capabilities among states is inherently uneven and results in some states assuming 'great power' status and relegating the remainder to the status of international 'others'. Neorealists consider the distribution of power amongst the great powers of the system the primary drivers of international action, arguing as Waltz does that "the story…of international politics is written in terms of the great powers of an era".[401] As the most capable – and by this the neorealists mean the states with the greatest relevant capabilities – these great powers "set the scene" for the actions and interactions of other states, as well as themselves.[402] Such a perspective is not solely a neorealist position, endorsed as it is by other systems theorists also, but it remains a neorealist staple, particularly as the theory turns to discussions of the balance of power.[403] First, though, neorealists take time to outline the particularly characteristics of anarchy in the international system that suggest that the balance of power is a likely outcome.[404]

Neorealists do not define anarchy as "chaos, destruction, and death" for the reason that – considering the history of domestic revolutions and dictatorships – there seems no reason why such factors alone would differentiate the international from the national sphere.[405] Instead, the first difference that neorealists find between domestic hierarchies and the international anarchies is the power responsible for exercising legitimate force in order to help themselves.[406] Self-help, claim neorealists, is the heart of the anarchic order in which states find themselves.[407] In this self-help anarchic system neorealists argue that the units are further differentiated from units in a hierarchical system by the time, effort and resources expended on protecting themselves from other units rather than achieving the close interdependence that hierarchies engender.[408] Indeed, Waltz argued that interdependence in international political systems is loose and despite talk of international integration, it is a rare occurrence within the

---

[401] Waltz. 1979, p.72.
[402] Waltz. 1979, p.72.
[403] See Doran and Parsons. 1980; Modelski and Thompson. 1988.
[404] Waltz. 1979, p.102.
[405] Waltz. 1979, p.103.
[406] Waltz. 1979, p.104.
[407] Waltz. 1979, p.104.
[408] Waltz. 1979, pp.104-105.

historical record.[409] Again, it is anarchy that Waltz blames for this lack of integration as under anarchy units worry more about their survival than seeking mutually beneficial interdependence with other states.[410]

The constraints of anarchy cannot be ignored or "wished away":

> In every age and place, the units of self-help systems – nations, corporations, or whatever – are told that the greater good, along with their own, requires them to act for the stake of the system and not for their own defined advantage…The very problem, however, is that rational behaviour, given structural constraints, does not lead to the wanted results. With each country constrained to take care of itself, no one takes care of the system.[411]

This necessitates a systems approach as the behaviour of the units is most definitely being affected by the nature and organisation of the system in which they find themselves. It also leads the states to clarify their ends pointedly: the sole underlying goal of a state in such a system is survival. Not the survival of the system, though, but the survival of the individual state actor so that, while the world's great powers are called upon "to do whatever they think is necessary for the world's survival", states will only ever act in their own interests.[412] Here neorealism splits from classical realism in that it is no longer the nature of humanity or the goals of governments that determine the national interest of a state; instead, it is the structure and organisation of the system that defines the survival instincts of the state.

Further distinguishing neorealism from classical realism is the introduction of the notion of the balance of power. Whereas alliances are common in political history – both in domestic political systems and the international environment – the classical realist explanation is not sufficient to explain its consistent recurrence as an organisational device. For neorealists, the balance of power between states is a fundamental theoretical construction based upon their assumptions about the states within the context of the system.[413] Neorealists assume, first, that states are unitary actors in the system; second, states seek their own preservation and survival in the system; third, at

---

[409] Waltz. 1979, p.105.
[410] Waltz. 1979, p.105.
[411] Waltz. 1979, p.109.
[412] Waltz. 1979, p.109.
[413] Waltz. 1979, p.118.

maximum effort to secure survival they seek domination over the other states of the system, this being the surest way to ensure ongoing survival; fourth, states attempt to act in a sensible and rational manner in pursuing these ends.[414] From these assumptions the neorealists then presume that states have two means by which to pursue their rational survival strategies: internal and external.[415] Internal strategies include increasing economic gains, gains in military strength and planning for potential crises in the system while external strategies include alliance building or the undermining of the alliances and power of other states.[416] The balance of power, then, becomes the optimal strategy for a state seeking survival and security for, in a system with only two poles, the chance of a state being undermined by a rival state is, for the neorealists, much reduced.

Closing Chapter Six of his book, Waltz provides a succinct summation of neorealism and its assumptions, starkly demonstrating the difference between the classical realists and the systems theorists who would go on to embrace his method:

> The theory leads to many expectations about behaviours and outcomes. From the theory, one predicts that states will engage in balancing behaviour, whether or not balanced power is the end of their acts. From the theory, one predicts a strong tendency towards balance in the system. The expectation is not that a balance, once achieved, will be maintained, but that a balance, once disrupted, will be restored in one way or another...Since the theory depicts international politics as a competitive system, one predicts more specifically that states will display characteristics common to competitors: namely, that they will imitate each other and become socialised to their system.[417]

The anarchic system with competitive, like-state units seeking survival and balancing against threatening states are, then, the essential elements of the international system as assessed by the neorcalists. While each element – system, state, balancing alliances – are significant for the understanding of the wider system, it is the assumption of anarchy and its place in the neorealist explanations that is most significant. As the following pages will demonstrate, what was a background to jealous-natured individuals or greedy states within classical realism is, in neorealism, not as much a background to action as an enabling and motivating factor for state action. The role of

---

[414] Waltz. 1979, p.118.
[415] Waltz. 1979, p.118.
[416] Waltz. 1979, p.118.
[417] Waltz. 1979, p.128.

anarchy in neorealism, then, is central to the theory, its method of analysis and to the work of the approach's adherents.

Anarchy in Neorealism

At this point in The first chapter it was argued that while the word 'anarchy' does not often appear in the works of Thucydides, Machiavelli, Hobbes, Carr and Morgenthau, the *idea* of anarchy does underlie all of their work within the classical realist canon. Neorealists, alternatively, not only mention anarchy explicitly, it forms the basis of their assessments of the systemic effects on states within the international system. Waltz's two texts will be analysed in the same manner as the texts of the classical realists were in the opening Chapter of this book. This will allow for the centrality and fundamentality of the notion of anarchy to neorealist theory to become strikingly clear.

Anarchy in *Man, the State, and War*

As could be expected, the opening sections of Waltz's text did not mention anarchy, save in passing reference to anarchism as a philosophical position.[418] This, though, is not the anarchy that concerns this book, as outlined in a similar discussion opening this section of The first chapter. Indeed, as related to the international political system, Waltz does not consider anarchy until, as expected, he reaches discussion of the third image of the international system.

Anarchy in neorealism implies competition, not harmony.[419] States under anarchy have goals and they value their own goals ahead of system-wide peace; as a result competition is often likely to lead to conflict.[420] In seeking to protect themselves states form alliances with other states and attempt to balance the distribution of power across the states within the system and keep safe from conflict. Anarchy for neorealists, then, is a dangerous systemic state of affairs and one that demands attention from units to the dangers of a system without an overarching authority. Waltz describes

---

[418] Waltz. 2001, p.23; p.26.
[419] Waltz. 2001, p.160.
[420] Waltz. 2001, p.160.

this balance of power under anarchy as "sometimes frightening" and, indeed, when one considers that a state is acting to ensure its own survival within the system, it is clear why international action and the system itself could seem frightening indeed.[421]

Anarchy is also significant for neorealists because it enforces the primacy of relative gains considerations for states.[422] An anarchic system does not reward states that seek trans-system benefits or 'win-win' situations where each side's 'win' is equal or not significantly greater than the other 'winner'. Absolute gains are the preserve of the hierarchical domestic polities where there exist a myriad of support mechanisms and safety nets to ensure that no individual actor falls too far behind. In an anarchic international realm where there is no arbiter of disputes, no social welfare system for nation-states and no laws of natural justice to consider when choosing how to act, survival is the only aim of states; thus, relative gains take precedence over potentially more immediately beneficial absolute gains. Anarchy's forcing of states to consider relative gains in their actions feed back into the competitive nature of neorealist anarchy, as Robert Powell comments:

> In the anarchy of international politics "relative gain is more important that absolute gain" (Waltz 1959, 198). A state's utility in structural realism is at least partly a function of some relative measures like powers…The more states care about relative gains, the more a gain for one state will tend to be seen as a loss by another and the more difficult, it seems, cooperation will be.[423]

Anarchy, then, reinforces itself: anarchy begets competition and competition begets more competition. Competition and relative gains concerns remain paramount for states under neorealist anarchy.

Anarchy in neorealism also provokes a paradox of sorts for state units within the system: while there is no central authority to limit the choices of the units as there would be in a hierarchical or domestic system, states are without choice as to their base concern under anarchy. While it is true that states can have significantly different goals and pursue considerably different ends than their rival states, the base concern for all

---

[421] Waltz. 2001, p.199.
[422] Waltz. 2001, p.198.
[423] Robert Powell. 1991, p.1303.

within the system is survival.[424] Under neorealist anarchy there are no chances to return from defeat, the notion of losing a democratic election to contest another in three or four years hence is foreign. Indeed, though history might convince one otherwise, there is no explicit endorsement of "living to fight another day" under neorealist anarchy. No matter what choices are made, no matter what goals are pursued, the foundational goal of survival within the system underlies every decision that a state actor will make. On this the neorealists are clear and Waltz, in his endorsement of such a zero-sum anarchical environment, allows little room for distortion from this 'survival first' path.[425]

Indeed, the third-image Waltz presents in *Man, the State, and War* is part of the shift in political science of the time towards using game theoretic notions to describe international affairs. On the heels of von Neumann and Morgenstern's *Theory of Games and Economic Behaviour* of 1944 and Downs' *An Economic Theory of Democracy* of 1957, Waltz's depictions of an anarchy that is a zero-sum game at its core means it presents a significantly different anarchy to those of the classical realists.[426] Game theory, described as "the secret of life" by one analyst, is useful in describing the anarchy of Waltz's third-image as the language introduced is directly from the game theoretic literature.[427] For example, under anarchy states don't make "policy" but *players* make *choices*.[428] Further, in denying the notion that states will work together and, instead, remain consistently competitive, Waltz writes of players avoiding a "simple maximum problem" and reverting to a "zero-sum or constant-sum" game.[429] In this way, anarchy under neorealism is not a background upon which international politics is pursued; rather it is the essential component which defines the structure and possible moves which a player may make.

---

[424] Waltz. 2001, p.203.

[425] Waltz. 2001, p.203.

[426] John von Neumann and Oscar Morgenstern. 1944. *Theory of Games and Economic Behaviour.* Princeton: Princeton University Press; Anthony Downs. 1997. *An Economic Theory of Democracy.* Boston: Addison-Wesley.

[427] Robert Wright. 2000. *Non-Zero: The Logic of Human Destiny.* London: Little, Brown and Company, p.4; Waltz. 2001, p.203.

[428] Waltz. 2001 , p.203.

[429] Waltz. 2001, p.203.

Anarchy in *Theory of International Politics*

Building on the third-image of international politics he outlined in the final section of *Man, the State, and War*, it is not surprising to find that Waltz's conception of anarchy is little different in his follow-up book. For example, Waltz continues to focus on the self-help and survival instincts of units in an anarchical system as well as making clear the 'balance of power' order that emerges in anarchical systems naturally.[430] As well, Waltz continues to highlight the primacy of state interests over systemic or international interests under anarchy as opposed to the altruism common under hierarchies.[431] What differs in *Theory of International Politics* is the systemising of anarchy in the wider theory of structural realism. Two decades after *Man, the State, and War* Waltz has moved from descriptions of anarchy to actual operationalisation of the system within the wider theory. Anarchy, then, remains constant and only its impact changes.

Summary: Neorealism and the Nature of Anarchy in Neorealism

The first chapter of this book argued that the nature of anarchy in classical realism was defined by five elements: its reality; its violence and conflict; its lack of central government; its unchanging nature over time; and its amorality. Further, The first chapter provided an overarching definition of anarchy in classical realism, being:

> A real and tangible systemic state in which there exists no central government and no specific moral code, defined by conflict and unchanging over time.

With regards to neorealism, the above definition does not demand much revision. However, there are at least three elements highlighted in neorealism that are not mentioned or are under appreciated within the classical realist texts.
Anarchy and competition

As noted above, neorealists consider that anarchy does not only engender conflict and violence but more broadly a system wide competition. Not reserved for war or con-

---

[430] Waltz. 1979, pp.103-106.
[431] Waltz. 1979, p.109.

flict, neorealists see such competition emerging in the realms of economics and diplomacy, too. Indeed, every action in the international system is essentially a competitive move by virtue of the zero-sum nature of the anarchy in which actions take
place.

Anarchy and relative gains

Related to competition under anarchy is the notion of relative gains. All but ignored
in classical realism, neorealists consider relative gains the most significant and certainly the top-of-mind considerations for states and their leaders in international affairs. It is not enough for the state to 'win'; the state must 'win' more than other
states and improve its relative position in anarchy. Notions of absolute gains and
'win-win situations' are foreign in neorealist assessments of anarchy.

Anarchy and survival

Foreign policy under neorealist anarchy has but one fundamental goal for the state
actor: survival. All actions be they violent or non-violent, overt or covert, diplomatic
or in warfare, economic or cultural, are all aimed squarely at the survival of the state.
Neorealists do not deny that states under anarchy may covet territory or resources –
they do. Nor do they deny that states may act in alliance with others or submit to the
will of another, stronger state in periods of relative weakness – again, they do. But at
the core of all such actions is a state's recognition of the reality of anarchy that ensures no state is guaranteed survival by a central arbiter and, thus, every state under
anarchy must act to ensure its own survival with every move it makes.

The Meaning of Anarchy in Neorealism

With these three elements in mind – and building on the definition of anarchy in classical realism offered in The first chapter - a definition of anarchy in neorealism can
be pronounced. Expressed in a sentence, anarchy for the neorealists can be considered to be:

> A real and tangible systemic state in which there exists no central government and no
> specific moral code, defined by competition for relative gains between states and a pro-
> pensity to conflict that is unchanging over time.

In this sentence, then, we find a definition that encompasses the anarchy of classical realism that Waltz built upon in developing his theory of neorealism as well as including the specific elements of an anarchic system that are highlighted within *Man, the State, and War* and *Theory of International Politics*. Anarchy in neorealism, then, while similar to the classical realist's conception of the same, is different in important ways and not only via its application as a systematising element of a new theory of international relations.

Conclusion

This chapter has outlined the essential development and elements of neorealism. Using Kenneth Waltz's seminal texts as a guide, the neorealist rejection of liberalism and classical realism is outlined and the seeds of what would become Waltz's structural realism were highlighted. Following this, the similarities and essential differences between anarchy in classical realism and anarchy in neorealism were outlined, three elements in particular being noted as distinguishing the two. However, at its core the definition of anarchy across classical and neorealism remains significantly consistent and few changes are required to the definition of anarchy established in The first chapter. Anarchy in realism – thought operationalised and systematised in Waltz's work – has been shown to be largely consistent with established understandings of the same. As this argument turns to its third and final chapter within this first part of the book and considers other realist theories and their conceptions of anarchy, it will be shown again that not only does the definition of anarchy remain largely similar throughout the paradigm but that its importance and centrality to the analysis of the international system only increases.

For reasons I can't put my finger on, I like
simple theories that address important issues.
John Mearsheimer

ANARCHY IN OFFENSIVE REALISM, GAME THEORY AND NEO-CLASSICAL REALISM

Kenneth Waltz's neorealism and the classical realism of Hans Morgenthau, EH Carr and their predecessors are but two of the 'realisms' within what Elman described as realism's "big tent".[432] While much of realist scholarship might be classified as either 'classical realism' or 'neorealism', the paradigm encompasses other perspectives that – while sharing some of the basic assumptions of realism – also take some theoretical positions that have not yet been assessed in this book. While still considered realists, such theoretical positions are different enough as to provoke new research agendas within the paradigm. Further, while it would be impossible to consider each and every realist position within realism's 'big tent', it is useful to consider the most influential of these other realist positions in order that this book can speak to realism generally and not be limited to only classical and neorealist approaches. Thus, this chapter will present five realist approaches whose positions cannot be easily placed in either the classical realist or neorealist camps and shows that – despite their differences – the founding assumption for all five remains an anarchical system.

This chapter considers five theorists under three approaches in turn, all of which have influenced the research agenda within realism and the discipline of international relations more generally. Considering first the offensive realism of John Mearsheimer and then, in turn, the game theory as applied in realist analysis of international relations, and the neoclassical realism of Victor Cha, Thomas Christenson and Gideon Rose, this chapter will complete the review and critical assessment of the realist paradigm in international relations.[433] As in Chapters One and Two, each of these scholars will be first introduced and their positions outlined with reference to their major works before the role of anarchy in their theories is explained. However, unlike

---

[432] Elman. 1996, p.26.

[433] Donnelly makes a convincing case that game theoretic analysis of international relations – specifically analysis using the 'Prisoners Dilemma' model – is a realist position. See Donnelly. 2000, pp.19-23.

105

the first two chapters, the diversity of the realist approaches evidenced here will not allow for a final, chapter-wide definition of anarchy. However, this chapter will be able to conclude that – just as with classical and neorealist positions – anarchy is fundamental to their approaches and remains the assumption on which the theory is built. Thus, at the conclusion of the chapter, this book will have considered a broad and representative sample of realist scholarship and will have argued that anarchy is the central component to all realist analysts considered herein.

John Mearsheimer and Offensive Realism

Born just two years after the end of the Second World War in New York, John Mearsheimer moved through West Point, Cornell University, the Brookings Institution and Harvard University before settling at the University of Chicago in 1982.[434] Though he never had ambitions of becoming an academic and, indeed, had a father who pushed him towards serving as an officer in the US Army, Mearsheimer quickly advanced in his chosen field towards his current position as R. Wendell Harrison Distinguished Service Professor of Political Science at the University of Chicago.[435] Like others of his generation, Mearsheimer was influenced greatly by the Vietnam War and the emerging scholarship which surrounded it. In particular, Mearsheimer found substantial wisdom in David Halberstam's book, *The Best and Brightest*, recalling that:

> I often used to say to myself in those days, "How in God's name did we get into this horrible war? How did it happen?" And reading David Halberstam's book, which provides a very powerful and cogent explanation, had a very significant impact on my thinking.[436]

Mearsheimer's desire to investigate the how and why of American security and foreign policy and his fascination "with international security issues – like deterrence theory – from the moment [he] was first exposed to them" has since evolved, leaving

---

[434] Mearsheimer. 2006a, p.105; John Mearsheimer. 2007. *Curriculum.* [30 April 2007] http://tinyurl.com/2hezst.
[435] Mearsheimer. 2006a, pp.105-107.
[436] John Mearsheimer. 2002. *Through the Realist Lens: Conversation with John Mearsheimer.* [1 May 2007] http://tinyurl.com/29fdy4.

in its wake a significant scholarly footprint and a new stream of realist theory: offensive realism.[437]

Mearsheimer's works span three books, one edited collection and dozens of articles, reports and influential contributions to the foreign policy debate, particularly in the United States. He is perhaps best known for his 2001 book *The Tragedy of Great Power Politics* where he first examined and then explained the shape of international relations and, in doing so, outlined his influential offensive realist approach.[438] Described as "provocative" and "seductive" by some as well as "disappointing" and "shallow" by others, the book would turn out to be just as controversial and influential as his previous body of articles and book chapters.[439] Indeed, controversial work seemed to define Mearsheimer's approach in the 1980s and 1990s. Articles such as 'Back to the Future: Instability in Europe after the Cold War' and his earlier book, *Conventional Deterrence* provoked others in the discipline to label him as "arresting and controversial" and inelegant to the point of lacking any "relevance to reality".[440] Debate continues to surround Mearsheimer to this day, most recently on the publication (with co-author Stephen Walt) of 'The Israel Lobby and US Foreign Policy', an examination of the domestic influence of pro-Israel advocates on the external policies of the world's sole remaining superpower.[441] As a critic of that particular working

---

[437] Mearsheimer. 2006a, p.105. So influential has Mearsheimer's work in offensive realism been that it has gone on to form the basis for classroom teaching tools such as 'The Power Politics Game'. See David Reilly. 2003. 'The Power Politics Game: Offensive realism in theory and practice'. *Simulation and Gaming* 34(2): 298-305.

[438] Mearsheimer. 2001.

[439] PF Coogan. 2002. 'Review: *The Tragedy of Great Power Politics.*' *The Journal of Military History* 66(3): 916-917, p.917; Pavel Baev. 2002. 'Review: The Tragedy of Great Power Politics.' *Journal of Peace Research* 39(5): 641.

[440] John Mearsheimer. 1983. *Conventional Deterrence*. New York: Cornell University Press; Mearsheimer. 1990; Stanley Hoffman, Robert Keohane and John Mearsheimer. 1990. 'Back to the Future, Part II: International Relations Theory and Post-Cold War Europe.' *International Security* 15(2): 191-199, p.191; p.192.

[441] Mearsheimer and Walt. 2006. One can conclude that Mearsheimer and Walt's paper was controversial for two reasons. First, the subject matter and the conclusions that the pair reached promoted great debate among scholars, press and political interest groups worldwide. Secondly, however, there were also questions raised from scholars as to why two confirmed realists – and, thus, externally focused theorists – would conclude that there is such a strong influence on state behavior residing within a state itself. Among the former see examples in Meghan Clyne. 2006. *Harvard's Paper on Israel Called 'Trash' by Solon.* [1 May 2007] http://tinyurl.com/26ord4; Noam Chomsky. 2006. *The Israel Lobby?* [1 May 2007] http://tinyurl.com/jvoam. On the latter see Marc Landy. 2006. 'Zealous Realism: Comments on Mearsheimer and Walt.' *The Forum* 4(1/6): 1-10; Ned Laza-

paper noted, it is an understatement to argue this piece does not represent Mearsheimer's best work.[442] His best work – and his most notable contribution to realist theory remains the offensive realist approach.

Offensive realism is, in some ways, a partial rejection of both classical realism and neorealism that still manages to include elements of both. Mearsheimer himself describes his approach in terms of its relation to Waltzian neorealism, highlighting the similar assumptions he and Waltz make but building upon the framework to deliver a more aggressive theoretical framework. Mearsheimer compares the two thus:

> The taproot of our disagreement lies in the assumptions that underpin our structural theories. Waltz says that his theory is built on two simple assumptions: (1) the system is anarchic, and (2) states seek to survive. He explicitly says that he does not assume that states are rational actors. My theory is based on five assumptions: (1) the system is anarchic, (2) all great powers have some offensive military capability, (3) states can never be certain about other states' intentions, (4) states seek to survive, and (5) great powers are rational actors or strategic calculators.[443]

These five points are the basis of the theory that Mearsheimer claims is superior to Waltz's position and are essential to understanding offensive realism as a theoretical position distinct from other realist positions. Offensive realists argue that the neorealist assumptions of anarchy and state survival are not enough to explain the aggressive behaviour of states or the consistent resort to violence to resolve international disputes. Specifically, as neorealists do not assume that states are rational actors they must rely on a separate theory of foreign policy; in contrast, offensive realism – through its additional assumptions about the system and its actors – assumes rationality and, in the eyes of Mearsheimer, is a superior theoretical approach.[444]

In assessing the interplay and application of offensive realism's five assumptions three papers by John Mearsheimer will be considered here. The first, 'Back to the Future: Instability in Europe after the Cold War', spawned responses from such signifi-

---

rus. 2006. 'Playing Pin the War on the Lobby.' *The Forum* 4(1/5): 1-10. The paper has since been developed into a book.

[442] Lazarus. 2006, p.1.

[443] Mearsheimer. 2006a, p.112. Importantly for this book, note that Mearsheimer never rejects Waltz's (or realism's) assumption of an anarchic system. This point will be further explicated in the pages to come.

[444] Mearsheimer. 2006a, p.112; pp.121-122.

108

cant theorists as Stanley Hoffman and Robert Keohane in major journals upon its publication in 1990, many due to its strictly offensive realist assessment of post-Cold War geopolitics.[445] The second, 'The False Promise of International Institutions', went on to be one of Mearsheimer's most cited works and provoked a response from Keohane and co-author Lisa Martin that, itself, would go on to be widely cited across the discipline.[446] Finally the third paper, 'Why We Will Soon Miss the Cold War', is a cautionary reflection by Mearsheimer on the likely post-Cold War landscape, clearly explicating the central assumptions of offensive realist theory.[447] Each will be addressed in turn, first, by introducing the context and primary argument of the article; secondly, the five elements Mearsheimer outlined as central to his offensive realist thesis will be identified in the article; and thirdly, the reliance of the article on the assumption of systemic anarchy will be highlighted. In this way, offensive realism will be clearly explained, applications of the theory in specific foreign policy situations will be considered and the consistent centrality of anarchy to the theory will become increasingly clear.

'Back to the Future: Instability in Europe after the Cold War.'[448]

While the end of the Cold War prompted many predictions of the future for Europe – and post-socialist Central and Eastern Europe in particular – few could match the influence or provocative prescriptions for policy embodied in Mearsheimer's 1990 effort.[449] Mearsheimer's paper not only neatly summarised the prevailing realist opinion on the presumed future of Europe but spawned a number of follow up articles both agreeing and disagreeing with his rather pessimistic conclusions for the peoples of the continent.[450] Written just months after the fall of the Berlin Wall and published

---

[445] Mearsheimer. 1990a.

[446] Mearsheimer. 1994; Keohane and Martin. 1995. See also Martin. 2001.

[447] Mearsheimer. 1990b.

[448] The arguments relating to 'Back to the Future: Instability in Europe after the Cold War' were first considered by the author in a 2007 conference paper presented in Budapest, Hungary. See Dylan Kissane. 2007a. *Realist Theory and Central & Eastern Europe after the Cold War*. Paper presented at the 3rd Central European University Graduate Conference in the Social Sciences, Budapest, Hungary, 25-27 May 2007.

[449] John Mearsheimer. 1990a.

[450] For example, Hoffman, Keohane and Mearsheimer. 1990; Bruce Russett, Thomas Risse-Kappen and John Mearsheimer. 1991. 'Back to the Future, Part III: Realism and the Realities of European

only months before the Belavezha Accords were signed by the leaders of Russia, Ukraine and Belarus, effectively dissolving the Soviet Union, Mearsheimer's article was a look towards a post-Cold War future after decades of confrontation.[451] For Mearsheimer, then the Political Science Department Chair at the University of Chicago, this was not his first foray into predicting the post-Cold War world: his essay 'Why We Will Soon Miss the Cold War' had appeared in *The Atlantic Monthly* just prior to the release of the *International Security* piece.[452] It was, though, a far more considered and Europe-centric assessment of the emerging international order and one that both drew together the existing literature on the topic and worked from his realist roots to forecast various possible futures for the former Cold War battleground of Central and Eastern Europe.

'Back to the Future' clearly corresponds to the five theoretical assumptions of offensive realism. Turning to the first assumption – that of anarchy – Mearsheimer is emphatic, writing, "the root cause of the problem [conflict] is the anarchic nature of the international system".[453] He argues that the anarchy of the system has two significant consequences for the system: first, states within the system cannot trust each other as the costs to the state of betrayal by a 'friend' directly impact on the likelihood of survival of that state; second, each state must be the guarantor of its own survival being unable to claim recourse to the systems non-existent arbitrating power. [454] Mearsheimer continues, noting that anarchy drives states to develop a capacity for self-defence which, for offensive realists, means a military capacity which is superior to rival states.[455] In this way, then, Mearsheimer has outlined in this article the first four of his five key theoretical assumptions in the opening passages of his article. The fifth would be expounded throughout.

Security.' *International Security* 15(3): 216-222; Stephen Van Evera. 1991. 'Primed for Peace: Europe after the Cold War.' *International Security* 15(3): 7-57.

[451] Richard Humphries. 2000. 'Running on Soviet time.' *The Japan Times* (27 December 2000): 1-7.

[452] John Mearsheimer. 1990b. 'Why We Will Soon Miss the Cold War.' *The Atlantic Monthly* 266(2): 35-50.

[453] Mearsheimer. 1990a, p.12.

[454] Mearsheimer. 1990a, p.12.

[455] Mearsheimer. 1990a, pp.11-12.

In 'Back to the Future' Mearsheimer makes a series of arguments based around the "virtues of nuclear deterrence" in post-Cold War Europe. [456] For example, Mearsheimer refers to the MAD (Mutually Assured Destruction) strategy as largely responsible for maintaining the peace in Europe during the Cold War. [457] This is succinctly described by Robert Jervis as:

> ...the idea that in a nuclear war, or even a large conventional conflict, each side should be prepared to destroy the other's cities and society. Of course, this objective was not sensible, but MAD proponents argued that was the point: the outcome would be so dreadful that both sides would be deterred from starting a nuclear war or even taking actions that might lead to it. [458]

Deterrence and the MAD strategy, though, implicitly assume rationality on behalf of the state which is the subject of the deterrent threat. After all, there can be no deterrence of an irrational actor who cares little for the life and livelihood of an actor's citizenry; indeed, this is a consistent criticism of attempts to deter non-state terrorist actors that endorse suicide bombings. [459] Further discussion in 'Back to the Future' also implies this assumed rationality among actors in an anarchic international system.

In the centrepiece of Mearsheimer's article – his four post-Cold War futures for Europe – his predictions involve a series of moves and countermoves by European states. [460] In his second future scenario for Europe, for example, Mearsheimer outlines

---

[456] Mearsheimer. 1990a, pp.19-20; pp.30-31; pp.37-40; pp.54-56. Mearsheimer's arguments reflect the 'nuclear logic' also found in Waltz. 1981; Waltz. 1986, pp.327-328.

[457] Mearsheimer. 1990a, p.20.

[458] Robert Jervis. 2002. 'Mutual Assured Destruction.' *Foreign Policy* (133): 40-42, p.40.

[459] The debate on rationality and deterrence is extensive. Robert Jervis offers a review of the literature in Robert Jervis. 1979. 'Deterrence Theory Revisited.' *World Politics* 31(2): 289-324, p.299-301. Jervis maintains that, when it comes to rationality, two things must be kept in mind: firstly, that 'perfect' rationality would not assist in deterring a rival; secondly, irrationality can reinforce deterrence in some circumstances. Frank Zagare responds to Jervis and others in Frank Zagare. 1990. 'Rationality and Deterrence.' *World Politics* 42(2): 238-260. Zagare makes an interesting distinction between 'procedural rationality' (on which he argues most critiques are focused) and 'instrumental rationality' (which he argues is safe from those same critiques). The argument that deterrence is impossible with regards to terrorists is a common one seen, for example, in Daniel Whiteneck. 2005. 'Deterring Terrorists: Thoughts on a Framework.' *The Washington Quarterly* 28(3): 187-199, p.187; Stephen Rademaker. 2006. *Countering WMD and Terrorism through Security Cooperation.* [3 May 2007] http://tinyurl.com/yqtcae.

[460] Mearsheimer. 1990a, pp.31-40.

a post-Cold War geopolitical landscape where the Cold War pattern of nuclear proliferation continues.[461] Noting that this scenario leaves nuclear weapons on the continent's flanks (in Britain, France and the USSR) Mearsheimer extrapolates the likely
strategic moves of the remaining European states.[462] He suggests that Germany would
conclude nuclear weapons are unnecessary to deter an attack from any of its Eastern
or Southern neighbours but would seek nuclear arms to deter the Soviet Union.[463] In
response to horizontal nuclear proliferation to Germany, Mearsheimer then suggests
the logical response of the smaller Eastern European states would be to develop nuclear arms of their own.[464] Neither Germany's presumed desire for nuclear weapons
nor the predicted response from smaller states caught between Germany and the
USSR are considered irrational strategic moves by Mearsheimer. Indeed, the language Mearsheimer employs can only be considered to endorse his fifth theoretical
assumption of rational and calculating actors.[465]

'Back to the Future', then, is an archetypical offensive realist tract, encompassing all
of the key theoretical assumptions of the approach and, while Mearsheimer is right
claim that it is his addition of three assumptions to Waltz's two that differentiate his
offensive theory from other realist approaches, this book is more concerned with the
common assumption that Mearsheimer maintains with his theoretical rivals: anarchy.[466] Anarchy is a constant background to the descriptions and predictions offered

---

[461] Mearsheimer. 1990a, pp.35-37.

[462] Mearsheimer. 1990a, p.36.

[463] Mearsheimer. 1990a, p.36.

[464] Mearsheimer. 1990a, p.36. Mearsheimer was not alone in suggesting that smaller states would
seek nuclear arms. Others at the time also predicted proliferation in a post-Cold War environment
where missiles and weapons of mass destruction "can be bought at market". See Charles Krauthammer. 1990. 'The Unipolar Moment.' *Foreign Affairs* 70(1): 23-33, p.30.

[465] Mearsheimer. 1990a, pp.36-37. See also the similar reasoning and language employed in
Mearsheimer's three other scenarios at Mearsheimer. 1990a, pp.32-33; p.38.

[466] "It's this anarchy that pushes states to compete for power. *So Waltz and I agree on that. But the
fundamental difference between the two of us is that I believe that states seek hegemony.* I believe
that they're ultimately more aggressive than Waltz portrays them as being. The goal for states is to
dominate the entire system. *To put it in colloquial terms, the aim of states is to be the biggest and
baddest dude on the block.* Because if you're the biggest and baddest dude on the block, then it is
highly unlikely that any other state will challenge you, simply because you're so powerful. Just take
the Western Hemisphere, for example, where the United States is by far the most powerful state in
the region. No state -- Canada, Guatemala, Cuba, Mexico -- would even think about going to war
against the United States, because we are so powerful. This is the ideal situation to have, to be so
powerful that nobody else can challenge you. But Waltz would argue that it's not a good idea to be
so powerful, because when you push in that direction, other states balance against you to try and cut

in the article. From the beginning, for example, Mearsheimer makes clear that the root cause of conflict and inter-state aggression in Europe is anarchy.[467] Later in the article Mearsheimer rejects the notion that economic liberalism has kept the peace by arguing that the Cold War peace is the result of a temporary and regional mitigation of the effects of anarchy by a temporary arbiter.[468] That is, while not turning away from the paradigm-wide claim that anarchy has no system wide arbiter, Mearsheimer argues that during the Cold War there was an effective regional arbiter in the shape of the United States in Europe.[469] Mearsheimer would, in the end, reject two other theories that would predict peace in post-Cold War Europe in large part because both reject the realities of an anarchic system and particularly anarchy where the superpowers have withdrawn from the continent.[470] 'Back to the Future', like the other articles in Mearsheimer's *vitae*, is one that assumes international actors can never escape the constraints of systemic anarchy.

'The False Promise of International Institutions.'[471]

Originally published as a working paper at Harvard University before being revised for publication in *International Security*, Mearsheimer's 1994 article 'The False Promise of International Institutions' would further establish the scholar and his offensive realist position in security studies and the wider discipline.[472] Described by Keohane and Martin as an article which "sharpened the theoretical issues dividing realist from institutionalist theory", the paper would go on to be cited in hundreds of scholarly works in the decade to follow and become a standard offensive realist in-

---

you down at the knees" [emphasis added]. See Mearsheimer. 2002; Mearsheimer. 2006a, p.112; pp.121-122.

[467] Mearsheimer. 1990a, p.11.

[468] Mearsheimer. 1990a, p.47.

[469] Mearsheimer. 1990a, p.47. This should not be considered an endorsement by Mearsheimer that states can escape the logic of anarchy completely as, in this case, the United States and its superpower rival, the Soviet Union, were still subject to an anarchic system at the global level.

[470] Mearsheimer. 1990a, pp.40-51. The specific arguments rejected, besides economic liberalism, are, firstly, that European powers had 'learnt' the costs of war from history and, secondly, the so-called 'democratic peace' thesis.

[471] Mearsheimer. 1994.

[472] The original article was published as Working Paper No. 10, Project on the Changing Security Environment and American National Interests, Institute for Strategic Studies, Cambridge, United States, November 1994.

clusion in edited collections.[473] Written in response to an emerging institutionalist order in Europe – an order that seemed to invalidate the predictions outlined in 'Back to the Future' – and the emergence of "neo-Wilsonian" internationalism under a Democratic President in the United States, with this article Mearsheimer again warned of the folly of states and policy makers trusting international institutions to mitigate the reality of anarchy.[474] A wide-ranging piece, 'The False Promise of International Institutions' first defines institutions and the key institutionalist arguments before engaging in a sustained critique of the theory and the logic that underlies it. His conclusion that "institutions have mattered rather little in the past" and that a "misplaced reliance on institutional solutions is likely to lead to more failures [like the war in Bosnia] in the future" were always going to be controversial in a domestic political environment where multilateralism and working through the United Nations were stated US objectives.[475] That Mearsheimer reached such conclusions, however, is not surprising as the article, like its fore mentioned counterpart, is a study in offensive realist thought.

The offensive realist assumption that all powers have some offensive military capability is clear from the outset as Mearsheimer describes the international system of competitive states as a "brutal arena" of "relentless security competition, with the possibility of war always in the background".[476] Mearsheimer is even more explicit later, laying out this same theoretical assumption clearly, stating "states inherently possess some offensive military capability, which gives them the wherewithal to hurt and possibly destroy each other".[477] He continues, describing the further theoretical assumptions offensive realists make about the international system:

---

[473] Keohane and Martin. 1995, p.39. On edited collections including the article see Michael Brown, Sean Lynn-Jones and Steven Miller (eds.). 1995. *The Perils of Anarchy: Contemporary Realism and International Security*. Cambridge: MIT Press, pp.332-376; Michael Brown, Owen Coté, Sean Lynn-Jones and Steven Miller. 1998. *Theories of War and Peace: An International Security Reader*. Cambridge: MIT Press, pp.329-383. For full details of the article's reprint status see Mearsheimer. 2007.

[474] Mearsheimer critiques widespread European institutionalism throughout the article and mentions President Clinton and his National Security Advisor Anthony Lake by name. The "neo-Wilsonian" quote is attributed to Lake. See Mearsheimer. 1994, p.5.

[475] Mearsheimer. 1994, p.49. On US objectives see Anthony Lake. 1993. *From Containment to Enlargement*. [5 May 2007] http://tinyurl.com/ysy27l; John Ruggie. 1994. 'Third try at world order? America and multilateralism after the Cold War.' *Political Science Quarterly* 109(4): 553-570.

[476] Mearsheimer. 1994, p.9.

[477] Mearsheimer. 1994, p.10.

The third assumption is that states can never be certain about the intentions of other states. Specifically, no state can be certain another state will not use its offensive military capability against the first...Uncertainty is unavoidable...The fourth assumption is that the most basic motive driving states is survival. States want to maintain their sovereignty.[478]

Mearsheimer's fifth assumption – that is, that states are rational and strategically thinking actors – and the assumption that separates offensive realism from its defensive and neorealist paradigmatic stable mates is also clearly explicated by the author. He writes that "none of these assumptions alone mandates that states will behave competitively" yet the assumption of rational strategy on the part of states "can create incentives for states to think and sometimes behave aggressively" towards other states.[479] All of this action takes place, of course, under anarchy, an environment clearly defined in and essential to the argument 'The False Promise of International Institutions' embodies.

Systemic anarchy is defined by Mearsheimer in terms that are largely uncontroversial. He draws on theorists such as Kenneth Waltz, Robert Art, Robert Jervis and Helen Milner in supporting his definition of anarchy, one he expresses thus:

> ...the international system is anarchic. This does not mean that it is chaotic or riven by disorder. It is easy to draw that conclusion, since realism depicts a world characterised by security competition and war. However, "anarchy", as employed by realists has nothing to do with conflict; rather it is an ordering principle, which says that the system comprises independent political units (states) that have no central authority above them. Sovereignty, in other words, inheres in states, because there is no higher ruling body in the international system. There is no "government over governments".[480]

From this elongated definition of anarchy it is possible to extract the key elements: states exist in a system; the ordering principle of the system is anarchy; and anarchy is defined by a lack of effective systemic governance. This definition of anarchy goes on to form the basis of Mearsheimer's argument against the assumed independent power of international institutions in that same system. For Mearsheimer, anarchy is

---

[478] Mearsheimer. 1994, p.10.

[479] Mearsheimer. 1994, pp.10-11. Here the author also contrasts his position with Morgenthau's. See Mearsheimer. 1994, p.9 (n.24).

[480] Mearsheimer. 1994, p.9. The "government over governments" quotation is from Inis Claude (see Mearsheimer. 1994, p.9 (n.23).

so pervasive as to render attempts to mitigate its effects – including the International Energy Agency, the League of Nations and the United Nations – something less than useless.[481] Indeed, he argues that the effect of the *belief* in international institutions as mitigators of anarchy has been more influential than the institutions themselves, though he casts even that impact as "pernicious" and "misplaced".[482]

Like 'Back to the Future', 'The False Promise of International Institutions' clearly outlines the offensive realist position of Mearsheimer and his ilk. Specifically endorsing the five theoretical assumptions of the offensive realist approach, the article builds on a foundation of anarchy a system that is competitive, dangerous, pessimistic in its depiction of a peaceful future and questioning of the motives of those theorists and policy makers that would seek to reject its 'realistic', even fatalistic conception of the international political environment. As in 'Back to the Future', Mearsheimer uses his article to attack the liberal institutionalists who believe that peace can be sustained via cooperative pacts, collective security agreements or trust between states. Indeed, like his classical realist and neorealist counterparts, Mearsheimer is explicit in the rejection of complete trust between parties under anarchy; it is unimaginable for the Chicagoan scholar that actors with offensive military capabilities in an anarchic realm will be anything other than suspicious, worried, fearful of others and always alert and anticipating potential threats to its survival.[483]

Yet offensive realism, under certain circumstances, also offers the theorist and politician alike some semblance of stability. In a situation of international bipolarity, for example, the balance of power between great power rivals is enough to bring peace to the system, or at least to the most significant elements of the system. Thus, during the Cold War offensive realists were keen to argue that the balance of power between the US-led West (including NATO) and the USSR-led coalition (including the Warsaw Pact states) was a good, realist peace-enforcing reality. The fall of the Berlin Wall, though, and the collapse of the Soviet Union and the global balance of power was, for offensive realists, then, something to be decried and the post-Cold War peace something to be warned against embracing too fully. In this sense, then, the title third of

---

⁴⁸¹ See Mearsheimer. 1994, p.25; p.27; pp.33-34.
⁴⁸² Mearsheimer. 1994, p.49.
⁴⁸³ Mearsheimer. 1994, p.10.

Mearsheimer's articles to be examined is particularly telling: 'Why We Will Soon Miss the Cold War'.[484]

'Why We Will Soon Miss the Cold War.'[485]

Where 'Back to the Future' predicted a pessimistic future for Europe and 'The False Promise of International Intuitions' did, in part, critique the institutions that arose and then evolved on that post-Cold War continent, this earlier paper was a broader warning to America's foreign policy elites that the world was about to descend into danger. Written in the months after the fall of the Berlin Wall and published less than a year after that event, 'Why We Will Soon Miss the Cold War' considered some of the themes that would arise in the other two papers but with a broader historical perspective and an American readership in mind. Indeed, eschewing the academic security journals and turning instead to *The Atlantic* as his publication outlet, Mearsheimer was putting his offensive realist ideas in front of a wider audience. One can only imagine what his vision of the post-Cold War world would have meant for the average reader of that monthly newsmagazine.

Mearsheimer leaves the reader in no doubt as to the likely impacts of a shift away from bipolarity in the international system. He writes that "the conditions that have made for decades of peace in the West are fast disappearing" and the world must prepare "to return to the multi-polar system that, between 1648 and 1945, bred one destructive conflict after another".[486] Arguing a similar line to that which he endorsed in 'Back to the Future', Mearsheimer suggests that the world is about to engage in a:

> ...vast test of the theories of war and peace put forward by social scientists, who never dreamed that their ideas would be tested by the world-historic events announced almost daily in newspaper headlines.[487]

---

[484] Mearsheimer. 1990b.

[485] Mearsheimer. 1990b. All page numbers in this section refer to the version of the article available from Mearsheimer's website.

[486] Mearsheimer. 1990b, p.1.

[487] Mearsheimer. 1990b, p.1.

Offensive realism, of course, is one of those theories and Mearsheimer uses the opportunity to predict an offensive realist future, not just for Europe but also for the wider West. He seems saddened by the practical inability of the West to prolong the Cold War preferring, as he does, the stability of the bipolar balance of power to the threatened multipolarity that would surely result from Soviet contraction.[488] More worrying for policy makers and readers might have been his policy prescriptions for the United States in the face of Soviet withdrawal from Central and Eastern Europe. These included encouraging the proliferation of nuclear weapons, countering a re-emergent German power by maintaining forces ready to engage that state and helping post-communist states to teach "honest national history" in schools.[489] Certainly, considered alone and with the benefits of hindsight, such proposals seem to present a series of strange and potentially dangerous recommendations for the surviving superpower to apply. In the context of Mearsheimer's offensive realism, however, they flow directly from the standard assumptions that such analysts make.

In 'Why We Soon Miss the Cold War' identifying the five theoretical assumptions is, again, not a difficult task. The assumption of states maintaining an offensive military capability is implicit in Mearsheimer's discussion of the benefits of bipolarity over multipolarity. The offensive realist argues that – in a system of any more than a single, bipolar dyad – the chance of conflict is greater as smaller states find it necessary to secure themselves against other rivals without the assistance of a superpower ally.[490] The uncertainty as to the intent of other actors in the system is likewise identified by Mearsheimer as he recounts a previous multipolar distribution of power in pre-World War One Europe where "Germany was not certain before 1914 that Britain would oppose it if it reached for Continental hegemony" – an uncertainty, he notes, that re-emerged for Germany in 1939.[491] Equally explicit is the author's explication of state survival as the goal of all international actors, Mearsheimer arguing simply that survival "is the highest goal a state can have".[492] Turning to his fifth assumption – rational and strategic thinking by states – Mearsheimer is again clear, and his discussion of nuclear strategy, proliferation strategies for the United States and

---

[488] Mearsheimer. 1990b, pp.15-16.
[489] Mearsheimer. 1990b, pp.16-17.
[490] Mearsheimer. 1990b, p.3.
[491] Mearsheimer. 1990b, p.3.
[492] Mearsheimer. 1990b, p.11.

118

the balancing of conventional forces with nuclear armed forces only further enmeshes this assumption further in the wider argument of the article.[493]

The founding assumption of realism – anarchy – is provided a central position in Mearsheimer's paper once again. In this case, though, Mearsheimer reaches back further than Waltz for inspiration, preferring to take Hobbes as his model.[494] Writing of the bipolarity of the Cold War and the temporary "taming" of anarchy in Europe that it beget, Mearsheimer reminds the reader that the Cold War reality was an anomaly in the history of the Westphalian system:

> For untamed anarchy is what Europe knew in the forty-five years of this century before the Cold War, and untamed anarchy – Hobbes's war of all against all – is a prime cause of armed conflict. Those who think that armed conflicts among the European states are now out of the question, that the two world wars burned all the war out of Europe, are projecting unwarranted optimism onto the future…They stand up to neither logical nor historical analysis. You would not want to bet the farm on their prophetic accuracy.[495]

Furthering his argument that anarchy is the "prime cause" of conflict – a standard neorealist proposition – Mearsheimer goes on to claim that it is anarchy that guarantees a scarcity of security in the international system and suggests that only the superpowers can mitigate its effects to any extent.[496] More than a simple 'first theoretical assumption' in his offensive realist arsenal, anarchy in 'Why We Soon Miss the

---

[493] See Mearsheimer. 1990b, pp.8-9. Arguments here are similar to those expressed in Mearsheimer. 1990a, pp.31-41.

[494] Mearsheimer. 1990b, p.1.

[495] Mearsheimer. 1990b, p.1.

[496] Mearsheimer. 1990b, p.11; p.12. Mearsheimer considers arguments that the European Community (today the European Union) was a non-superpower with the potential to maintain peace in Europe and, unsurprisingly, rejects it. Instead, he points to the omnipresent American superpower that 'guaranteed' the peace by making it unnecessary for Western European states and NATO members to invest in their own offensive military capability. Thus, it was the enforcement of the peace by the United States that kept states from conflict in Western Europe and allowed the EC to develop and not the EC that enabled for peace to become the standard position in Western European politics. More than a decade and a half after the Cold War came to an end Mearsheimer would face criticism of his offensive realism for its failure to consider the EU as a peace enforcer and an institution keeping rival states at bay in Europe. Mearsheimer continues to point to the role of the United States as the reason for the success, though he does concede that the continued deployment of troops in Europe by the US and the successes of the EU in its wake does make it difficult to evaluate his theory which – save a US withdrawal from the European theatre – may remain untestable. See Mearsheimer. 2006a.

Cold War' is presented as the key to understanding the emerging 'threat' of multipolarity to the West.

Conclusion: Anarchy in Offensive Realism

From the three articles considered above it is clear that anarchy is not quite as central to understanding events in the international system as it is for the neorealist Waltz. Nor is it quite as much the "assumed knowledge" that one might imagine it to be in classical realism, with that approach's focus on human nature and the manifestation of humanity's desires and jealousies in the political behaviour of international actors. For Mearsheimer and his offensive realism, though, the place of anarchy is somewhere in between. As alluded to in 'Why We Will Soon Miss the Cold War', there is a pervasive power to the anarchical assumption in offensive realism, so much so that it can be considered a 'key' or 'prime cause' of international events. Such a conclusion is much in the line of Waltz's neorealism where the system remains central to the analysis of international affairs. However, while Mearsheimer consistently ranks anarchy as the first theoretical assumption of the offensive realist, he is equally adamant that the other four are essential to explaining international conflict and international peace. Indeed, Mearsheimer is quite certain that without his fifth assumption – rationality and strategic thinking on the behalf of states – realism is not able to adequately explain the international system and the actions of the actors that reside within it.

Anarchy, then, for offensive realists such as Mearsheimer is an essential concept but not the *sole* essential assumption of the theory. Offensive realists are happy to borrow the definition of anarchy from the wider discipline – Mearsheimer himself, as has been discussed here, borrowing from classical realists and neorealists alike – but what separates the offensive realist approach is the positioning of anarchy as one of five equally important assumptions within a wider theory of international politics.[497] For the offensive realists anarchy is important but not overwhelmingly so, situated more as a background upon which the politics of interstate interactions are played out. This positioning, then, provides a useful contrast to the role of anarchy in the game 'Pris-

---

[497] It is argued here that the five assumptions are equally important because – as Mearsheimer notes – without any one of them the entire approach would fail to explain the occurrence of war, the resolution to peace or the actions of states.

oner's Dilemma', analysis of which follows, where anarchy is not only assumed – as in offensive realism – but operationalised as in neorealism to produce a representation of international politics that is at once simple in it operation and decidedly complex in its implications for actor strategy under anarchy.

Prisoner's Dilemma: Realism in a Game

Shortly after the classical realism of Thucydides, Machiavelli and Hobbes was re-popularised in the work of EH Carr and Hans Morgenthau, John van Nuemann and Oskar Morgenstern published *The Theory of Games and Economic Behaviour*.[498] In it, the pair explained game theory, a methodology by which the rational choices of economic actors could be analysed. Within a few decades this tool of economic analysis had been translated to the discipline of international relations where games like 'Chicken' and 'Stag Hunt' became common reference points within the literature, particularly in the specific literature concerned with nuclear strategy. While not all games are explicitly realist, one game, 'Prisoner's Dilemma', became a standard reference for modelling political decision making in the international system, largely on the back of much research by Robert Axelrod.[499] Further popularised through a series of competitions Axelrod organised to test decision making within the Prisoner's Dilemma framework, the game has become a staple of political analysis in international relations and, according to some, an easily understood yet devastatingly complex representation of actor decision making in realist theory.[500]

Jack Donnelly is convincing in advancing the Prisoner's Dilemma as a fundamentally realist pursuit in international relations theory.[501] Donnelly argues that – unlike the

---

[498] Oscar Morgenstern and John von Nuemann. 1947. *The Theory of Games and Economic Behavior*. Princeton: Princeton University Press. Robert Wright once described Morgenstern and von Nuemann's contribution to economic and political analysis as akin to finding "the secret of life". See Wright. 2000, p.4.

[499] Axelrod's *The Evolution of Cooperation* is considered the canonical work in this sector of international relations research. See Robert Axelrod. 1984. *The Evolution of Cooperation*. New York: Basic Books. See also Axelrod. 1980a; Axelrod. 1980b; Robert Axelrod. 1981. 'The Emergence of Cooperation Among Egoists.' *The American Political Science Review* 75(2): 306-318; Axelrod and Keohane. 1985.

[500] See Axelrod. 1980a; Axelrod. 1980b.

[501] Donnelly. 2000, p.13; pp.19-23. This section of the chapter is largely inspired by Donnelly's argument.

significant literatures that have developed around the classical realist and neorealist traditions – the Prisoner's Dilemma game offers a "different route to characteristic realist conclusions".[502] He argues that this game and its "striking realist paradigm" models the seemingly paradoxical international environment in which there is "conflict even where there are strong incentives to cooperate".[503] Within the Prisoner's Dilemma one can find the fundamentals of realist thought: uncertainty about the motivations and likely actions of other actors; a security dilemma whereby a defensive move is interpreted as offensive by other actors; a lack of an enforceable code of conduct from a central arbiter; and rational, selfish strategising on the part of the actors themselves. In the pages to follow, the game itself will be outlined and explained, the implications and strategies that emerge from game play will be considered and, finally, the nature and role of anarchy within this realist model will be explored to the point where it is clear, once again, the extent to which realist theory relies on anarchy to explain international affairs.

Prisoner's Dilemma: The Game

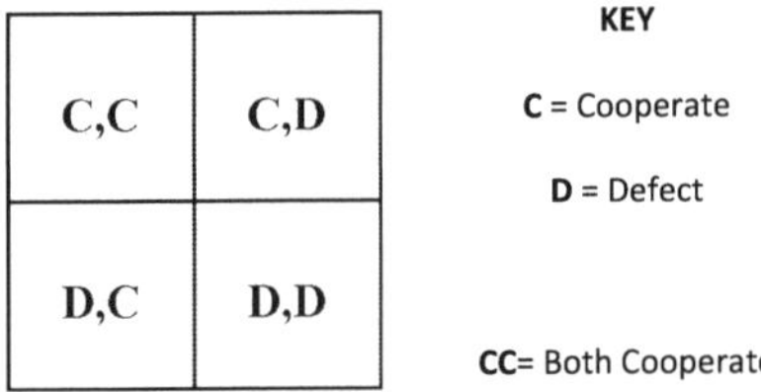

Figure 3.1: Prisoner's Dilemma

The game of Prisoner's Dilemma (Figure 3.1, above) is generally explained with reference to a fictional situation involving two partners-in-crime who are faced with a choice between confessing the crime, informing on their partner or keeping quiet in the face of police interrogation. Steven Kuhn offers one such situation:

> Tanya and Cinque have been arrested for robbing the Hibernia Savings Bank and placed in separate isolation cells. Both care much more about their personal freedom than about the welfare of their accomplice. A clever prosecutor makes the following offer to each.

---

[502] Donnelly. 2000, p.13.
[503] Donnelly. 2000, p.19; p.20.

122

"You may choose to confess or remain silent. If you confess and your accomplice re-mains silent I will drop all charges against you and use your testimony to ensure that your accomplice does serious time. Likewise, if your accomplice confesses while you remain silent, they will go free while you do the time. If you both confess I get two convictions, but I'll see to it that you both get early parole. If you both remain silent, I'll have to settle for token sentences on firearms possession charges. If you wish to con-fess, you must leave a note with the jailer before my return tomorrow morning."[504]

Placing a 'years of punishment' figure on Kuhn's situation – 4 years for the non-cooperating party if the other cooperates, 2 years parole if both cooperate with the police and 1 year if neither cooperate – Figure 3.2 (below) emerges.

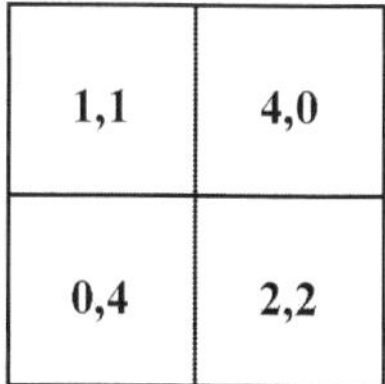

Figure 3.2: Prisoner's Dilemma with payoffs

Assuming a rational prisoner interested in minimising the period which they will spend in prison, the dilemma becomes clear. For Prisoner One, the ranking of strate-gies would be:

$$DC > CC > DD > CD$$

- or -

0 years in prison > 1 year in prison > 2 years in prison > 4 years in prison

Rationally and logically, then, Prisoner One should choose to admit his crime and inform on his fellow prisoner (that is, he should defect) and attempt to secure the ideal sentence that is, in fact, no sentence at all. However, the equally rational Pris-

---

[504] Steven Kuhn. 2003. *Stanford Encyclopedia of Philosophy (Fall 2003): Prisoner's Dilemma.* [10 May 2007] http://tinyurl.com/2qjpmu.

oner Two has been offered the same options by Kuhn's clever prosecutor and, rationally, will also favour admitting his crime and informing on his colleague (defecting). The dilemma emerges, then, as the two prisoners both choose to admit their crime, defect from their partner and yet, in doing so, find their sentence will be not the best outcome (no prison time) nor even the second best outcome (1 year in prison) but rather the second worst outcome: 2 years in prison.[505] In a situation where the prisoners cannot communicate and cannot be sure about the decision of their co-accused, the only logical course of action is one that – if chosen by both prisoners – will ensure a less than optimal situation for both. Cooperation, in such a situation, is not a rational choice for the prisoners and, thus, Kuhn's depiction of a clever prosecutor is more than accurate.

Realism and the Prisoner's Dilemma

Prisoner's Dilemma can be understood as realism by the assumptions that the game makes about the actors playing the game. The assumptions about the prisoners in the game are just as straightforward as Mearsheimer's or Waltz's and, as has been shown, the implications of the assumptions for the strategies and actions of the prisoners in the game are much more complex. The basic realist assumption of the Prisoner's Dilemma is that the actors are rational and strategic thinkers, with the additional assumption that there is no enforceable cooperation within the game. The first of these is a direct allusion to the neorealist and offensive realist schools while the second is, in its own way, an allusion to international systemic anarchy. In this section these two basic assumptions will be considered in turn in the context of the Prisoner's Dilemma to further outline the reasons why Donnelly's argument that the game is realist is valid.

The assumption of rationality and strategic thinking is key to understanding Prisoner's Dilemma the game as well as the dilemma of the game – the player's rational choice leading to a non-optimal situation – itself. Indeed, assuming anything other than strict rationality on the part of either prisoner reduces the utility of the game for the explanation of strategic decision making by either. Robert Wright makes just this

---

[505] Kuhn. 2003.

124

point in his 2000 book, *Non Zero: The Logic of Human Destiny* where he describes the perfect rationality demanded of the players as "irresistible logic", yet a logic that leads necessarily to a less than optimal outcome for the players of the game.[506] In the assumption of rationality, too, is found a core offensive realist contention. As noted earlier with regard to offensive realism, this rationality is not necessarily a "realist only" position; it remains, however, a common realist position and one that points to the inherent realism of the Prisoner's Dilemma.

With regards to the lack of enforceable cooperation within the Prisoner's Dilemma game, this, too, depicts a realist understanding of international politics. Unlike some theorists who consider that institutions or constructed supra-state adjudicators have a marked influence on the cooperation of state actors within the international system, strict realists reject such positions. Instead, it is argued that such institutions can only incentivise and reward certain behaviours within the international realm – and even then only with the direct assent of the states which endow them with limited sovereignty. In the final analysis states will take the action that best suits their own interests (survival being the base interest, of course) and will pay little regard to the wishes of incentives on offer from an institution. In the case of the Prisoner's Dilemma game, this feature of realist anarchy is outlined in the manner in which the players are separated by the prosecutor and – in such a position – can only rely on their own selfish motives to 'survive' this interaction under 'prosecutorial anarchy'. There is no institution that can encourage cooperation and no arbiter that can reward certain behaviour that is 'right' in the eyes of the wider system. There exist only players, choices and anarchy and no rational and compelling reason for the former to make choices with any cooperative behaviour in mind.

As well, the Prisoner's Dilemma places the players in a position where full and complete trust is impossible to assume, at least on behalf of each of the prisoners.[507] One imagines that while committing the crime for which they are being detained there existed some level of trust between the co-conspirators. After all, it seems unlikely that one of the two assumed rational actors would knowingly engage in a criminal pursuit with potentially significant personal costs without being sure that their partner would

---

[506] Wright. 2000, p.341.
[507] The game implies that the prosecutor – who sets the 'rules' of the encounter – can be trusted.

also be taking that same risk. However, having been caught and presented with the same decision matrix as their partner and knowing their partner is as selfish as they themselves are, the prisoner cannot afford to trust their partner to remain silent. Indeed, even if the prisoner felt confident at some level that their partner-in-crime could be trusted to remain silent, the best decision to make would be to speak up and walk away from detention with no punishment at all (the CD or DC eventuality). The logic, as Wright put it, is irresistible; thus, there can be no possibility of trust of either player by either player in the Prisoner's Dilemma.

Under realist anarchy the same is evidenced. For realists there can be no well-founded trust among states under anarchy. While cooperation is not impossible (the CC quadrant of the Prisoner's Dilemma does not rule out the possibility of both players cooperating) it is difficult to imagine, short-term and selfishly pursued. Altruism is non-existent and every interaction comes at a price. As well, realists are acutely aware of the relative gains which states pursue under anarchy. Like the prisoner choosing to defect with the knowledge that it may well put him in a position whereby he is punished more than he would be by cooperating and yet also aware that dual-defection has a lower cost than cooperating with a defecting opponent, realists hold that states under anarchy weigh the relative gains of an interaction and may even decide to suffer a temporary 'loss' as long as a rival does not suffer a relatively bigger 'win' at the same time. The inherent lack of trust and the awareness of relative gains in player power evidenced in the Prisoner's Dilemma indicate once again that at its heart the game is a useful realist model of political interactions under conditions of anarchy. Donnelly's argument, then, that the Prisoner's Dilemma is a "striking realist paradigm" is one that is well made and, when considered in light of the features of the game outlined above, entirely convincing.[508]

Explaining Cooperation: The Iterated Prisoner's Dilemma

Realists do not expect cooperation under anarchy, save for short periods of self-interested and selfish cooperation where states might work to a temporarily common goal. Yet within the international system there exist many examples of cooperation

---

[508] Donnelly. 2000, p.19.

between states which, while sometimes short in time or negligible in its implications, is oftentimes long standing and significant in its effects on the wider system. Explaining such cooperation through the realist lens can provokes a significant problem for realists and the Prisoner's Dilemma, like other realist approaches, is similarly burdened. The game theory approach, though, answers in a manner that reflects the reality of international interactions and proposes the Iterated Prisoner's Dilemma as a potential solution to this theoretical stumbling block.

The Iterated Prisoner's Dilemma suggests a realist situation in which the implications of the anarchical system – the lack of trust, the lack of cooperation – can be overcome. Assuming not a pair of prisoners in a single game but the same pair playing the same game over and over, game theorists such as Robert Axelrod and Robert Keohane have been able to demonstrate the emergence of cooperation under a strikingly realist anarchy. The sole difference between the Prisoner's Dilemma game outlined in Figures 3.1 and 3.2 is that at the completion of one game another game begins. Thus players, though still unable to communicate throughout the game, have a new piece of information with which to make their decision in each but the first round: the actions of the player in the round or rounds before. Thus, a player can learn whether their co-accused is someone who will defect or cooperate, act selfishly or act in the 'common good' of both accused. So significant is this new information for the two prisoners that the 'anarchy' of the Prisoner's Dilemma is almost overcome. The optimal strategy as discovered through competitions between various algorithms is cooperation in the first round and then a mirroring of the other player's previous move. This strategy, known as 'Tit-for-Tat', has proved consistently superior under testing and suggests to Axelrod and others that cooperation under anarchy is possible once trust and information is shared.

Yet while the motivation to cooperate in an iterated Prisoner's Dilemma might emerge and may well prove the best strategy over time, it needs to be assessed in the light of the international political system and the payoffs that exist in that sphere. Whether in the times of Thucydides and the great armies of the Peloponnesian Wars or in the modern era of thermonuclear weapons, the worst result is not a number of years in prison but the potential destruction of the state itself. Consider a map where the second and third quadrants offer not 4 years in prison but annihilation of the state (see Figure 3.3, overleaf).

Large Absolute Gain but No Relative Gain for Both States	Destruction, Large Relative Gain
Large Relative Gain, Destruction	Small Absolute Gain but No Relative Gain for Both States

Figure 3.3: Prisoner's Dilemma in the International System

With the payoffs now outlined in terms familiar to the realist, it is easy to see why cooperation may not emerge in the international state system despite the success of 'Tit-for-Tat' in Axelrod's Prisoner's Dilemma competitions. No longer dealing in abstractions or with small and survivable punishments such as a four year stay in prison, states are choosing whether to trust their survival to the cooperation of a rival when the payoff is at best an absolute gain matched by their rival. Indeed, when the survival of the state is on the line as in lower-left and upper-right quadrants and when the state is sure that there will be no relative gain or loss to their state if survival is assured, then they can only rationally choose to defect (lower right quadrant) and to do so repeatedly. With the stakes of the Prisoner's Dilemma game raised to those of the states that 'play' international politics, the only strategy under the anarchy of the system is to defect, maintaining the relative strength of the state and living to 'play' another day.

Anarchy, then, within the game of Prisoner's Dilemma, drives players towards strategies that are necessarily conflicting, less than optimal in most cases and which seem, on reflection, to be paradoxical and even nonsensical. Yet the anarchy of the Prisoner's Dilemma exhibits traits that are common to other realist theories. Like offensive realism, there is an assumption of rational and logical decision making among the actors. As in classical realism there is the assumption of self-interest on the part

128

of the players – indeed, the rationality and the self-interest of the player go hand-in-hand in speaking to the strategies necessary to compete in the game. Further, as in neorealism, there is the assumption that the nature of the system and the constraints on the player cannot be mitigated; that is, the neorealist assumption of ongoing and unescapable anarchy is analogous with the Prisoner's Dilemma and its inescapable rules and payoffs. Certainly, then, Donnelly can be considered correct in his conclusion that the Prisoner's Dilemma game mirrors realism and is a realist approach all of its own. The same selfishness, the same lack of trust between actors, the same expected competition and the same recognition of the salience of relative gains in a 'game' where an actor's survival is on the line make Prisoner's Dilemma a realist theory which not only clearly outlines the sometimes paradoxical choices of political actors but also the ubiquitousness of anarchy even in the simplest political games.

Neoclassical Realism: Filling the Waltzian Gap

It has previously been noted that some cite Kenneth Waltz and his neorealism as the premier and most influential of the realists in the post-World War Two era. Waltz's work was revitalising and reinvigorating for the realist paradigm in a period where it had fallen under increasingly heavy attack from alternate approaches within the discipline. Yet while Waltz's neorealist agenda breathed new life into an analysis millennia old, it left some theorists wondering if he had in fact moved from a theory that explained political outcomes and foreign policy choices by states (classical realism) to one that focussed on the political outcomes within the international system alone. Many felt that Waltz's neorealism lacked adequate explanation for state choices, that is, that Waltz did not offer a 'theory of foreign policy' to sit alongside his 'theory of international politics'. Some, like John Mearsheimer, developed their own more elaborate theories; others, however, worked to address this gap and, in their own words, sought to refine, but not refute, Waltz. Drawing on the neorealist focus on the importance of structure in the assessment of international politics while not forgetting the graceful theories of Morgenthau and Carr, these theorists were labelled "neoclassical realists" and their approach would form yet another arm in the wider paradigm of realism.[509]

---

[509] Gideon Rose. 1998. 'Neoclassical Realism and Theories of Foreign Policy.' *World Politics* 51(1): 144-172, p.146.

Counting among their number both academics, such as Randall Schweller and William Wohlforth, and high-profile commentators such as *Newsweek*'s Fareed Zakaria, neoclassical realists are among the best known of the international relations commentariat. Their work appeals to the traditional realists who considered the focus on systemic explanations for state behaviour unnecessary and also to neorealists who found Waltz's work of great benefit but still felt that a theory of foreign policy was necessary. In establishing another realist approach to the analysis of international relations, the neoclassicalists offered a compromise that offensive realists refused and that Waltz argued was unnecessary yet which was embraced for what was claimed to be a fuller and richer explanation for international events and state behaviour. This section examines three neoclassical essays in turn, drawing out their common arguments and assumptions and – in concluding – establishing the role and nature of anarchy within the neoclassical realist tradition. Victor Cha's 'Abandonment, Entrapment, and Neoclassical Realism in Asia' offers a focussed assessment of international relations between Japan, Korea and the United States and finds in the neoclassical position greater explanatory utility than the competing offensive or 'balance of threat' realist models.[510] Thomas Christensen's 'Perceptions and alliances in Europe, 1865-1940' turns from modern Asia to the European theatre between the wars of German unification the opening acts of World War Two, arguing that a more coherent approach to international relations can exist outside of the standard realist-liberal dichotomy.[511] Finally this section will consider Gideon Rose's neoclassical review essay, 'Neoclassical Realism and Theories of Foreign Policy' to draw out the themes offered by Cha and Christensen and summarise the neoclassical approach.

Victor Cha – Abandonment, Entrapment, and Neoclassical Realism in Asia: The United States, Japan and Korea

Academic, commentator and policymaker, Victor Cha takes embodies a typical neoclassical realist position which hovers between university-based theoretician and practical policy advisor. Holding both the Chair in Asian Studies at Georgetown Uni-

---

[510] Victor Cha. 2000. 'Abandonment, Entrapment, and Neoclassical Realism in Asia: The United States, Japan, and Korea.' *International Studies Quarterly* 44(2): 261-291.
[511] Thomas Christensen. 1997. 'Perceptions and Alliances in Europe, 1865-1940.' *International Organization* 51(1): 65-97.

versity and the position of Director for Asian Affairs in the United States National Security Council, Cha is in a position to assess both literature and intelligence and apply his experience in theory and practice in developing arguments on international affairs in the Asian region.[512] Notable for his notion of 'hawk engagement' by the United States with North Korea – a somewhat paradoxical notion, yet one that scholars such as Robert Jervis consider valuable as the superpower faces a weaker but nuclear armed regime – Cha is an East Asian area specialist with interest in the theories underlying the analysis of that region.[513] While well known as a conservative within the administration of President George W Bush, Cha continues to offer "dispassionate analysis", allowing for "open, honest and candid" assessments of international affairs. It is perhaps this dispassionate approach that attracted Cha to seek a path between the classical realists and neorealists on the one hand and the liberal internationalists and constructivists on the other in 'Abandonment, Entrapment, and Neoclassical Realism in Asia', turning instead to the approach suggested in the title and providing an explanation for foreign policy in East Asia that would serve as the foundation of more extensive works to follow.[514]

In 'Abandonment, Entrapment, and Neoclassical Realism in Asia' Cha promotes his neoclassical position by first critiquing the existing realist logic on the East Asian region and finding it lacking and, secondly, suggests that the neoclassical perspective is better able to explain the evolving US-Japanese-Korean relationship. The historical record, he argues, supports the standard realist prediction that in periods of low external threat states like Japan and Korea will not seek close security partnerships.[515] Yet in periods of high external threats to both Japan and Korea where realists would expect an alliance to emerge, the historical record fails to support the realist position; indeed, Cha emphasises that it is clear that "high levels of threat do *not* produce strong bilateral cooperation".[516] Further, Cha argues that explaining the international

---

[512] The White House. 2007. *Victor Cha: Director for Asian Affairs, National Security Council* [4 June 2007] http://tinyurl.com/2rmp2k.

[513] Claire Lui. 2006. *Victor Cha '83, NSC's Asian Affairs Expert* [4 June 2007] http://tinyurl.com/2uykxd.

[514] Victor Cha. 1999. *Alignment Despite Antagonism: The United States-Korea-Japan Security Triangle.* Palo Alto: Stanford University Press; Victor Cha. 2003. *Nuclear North Korea? A Debate on Strategies of Engagement.* New York: Columbia University Press.

[515] Cha. 2000, p.262.

[516] Cha. 2000, p.262.

relations of the East Asian region with regards to externalities and capabilities alone, that is, to ignore the role of national political cultures and historical tensions, leaves realists lacking significant explanatory power for the shifts and shapes of Asia-Pacific relations.[517] Thus, in order to overcome the lack of explanatory power offered by structural and externally focused realism for the East Asian region, Cha introduces his neoclassical realist position which, he argues, offers a better means by which to understand the realities of the region.

Cha nominates a "quasi-alliance" model which not only considers the external threats and powerful states in the foreign policy calculations of relatively minor powers like Korea and Japan but also the critical role played by historical anger in the relationship between the two smaller powers.[518] A methodology common to other theoretical positions – including the emerging constructivist theories, for example – what moves Cha's analysis to a neoclassicalist position is his concentration on the *perceptions* by states of the external threats and international system in which they exist as causal factors in determining alliance behaviour.[519] This is a critical difference to the other realisms considered within this chapter: unlike Mearsheimer's offensive realism, this infers a reduced level of rationality on the part of states in assessing its security environment; unlike the Prisoner's Dilemma, this stance infers consideration of factors outside of those central to the achievement of a relative gain. Neoclassicalists like Cha bridge the gap between the externally focussed structuralists and the human nature focussed biological realists by considering both the threats and system external to the state and the reactions and perceptions of the state powers to those externalities. Indeed, Cha's choice of the somewhat triangulated Korean-Japan-United States alliance provides some clear examples of neoclassical assessments in practice.

Cha argues that his quasi-alliance neoclassical model:

> ...highlight[s] a neoclassical realist notion of threat and the interconnections of alliance and adversarial strategies in a manner not readily addressed by balance of threat theories.[520]

---

[517] Cha. 2000, p.262.
[518] Cha. 2000, pp.262-263.
[519] Cha. 2000, p.263.
[520] Cha. 2000, p.264.

Presenting what he terms the "puzzle" of Korean-Japanese engagement in East Asia, Cha offers a timeline of strained relations between two otherwise close partners of their "patron" power, the United States.[521] In the two decades following the end of the long occupation of Korea by Japanese forces Cha notes the relationship between the two states was strained, defined by claims of compensation on the part of the Koreans and a general refusal to engage in talks by both sides.[522] The normalisation of relations between the two in 1965 saw an alliance blossom, culminating in a security alliance of sorts through a clause in a 1969 US-Japan military base treaty.[523] Relations soured again in the first half of the 1970s as the "Korea clause" of the military treaty was reneged by Japan in an effort to seek closer ties with the North Korean regime.[524] Yet three years of strained relations were followed by a longer period of cooperation as Japan and Korea sought close defence and diplomatic ties, only to be brought to an end in 1979 with Korea "openly proclaiming itself anti-Japanese".[525] A turbulently dynamic relationship, so complex and multifaceted, Japan and South Korea offer the neoclassical realist the chance to demonstrate just how perceptions and internal state dynamics can affect state choice and foreign policy behaviour.

Where structural or offensive realists focus on the rational balancing of threats by states in explaining and predicting the behaviour of states, Cha presents the relationship between Korea and Japan in relation to their partner and ally, the United States. Though both are states, both face the same proximate (North Korea) and continental (China) threats and though both are allied with the United States, Cha argues the strictly functional and rational assessment of alliances and the international situation in East Asia is tempered by feelings and perceptions. In the case of Korea it is a fear of abandonment while for the Japanese it is a fear of entrapment within the trilateral security relationship.[526] Where structural realism would reject such perceptions with its rational and objective assessment of international relations, neoclassical realism notes the importance of such perceptions for understanding the movements of states

---

[521] Cha. 2000, pp.264-265.

[522] Cha. 2000, p.264.

[523] Cha. 2000, p.264. See also Hideya Kurata. 2000. *Dialogue and Deterrence: The 1970s as Prototype.* Paper presented at the North Korea Policy After the Perry Report Workshop, Sigur Centre for Asian Studies, George Washington University, Washington, DC, USA.

[524] Cha. 200, p.264.

[525] Cha. 2000, p.264

[526] Cha. 2000, pp.270-271.

and, in the specific case presented by Cha, the behaviour of South Korea and Japan.[527]

A second example of the role of perceptions of international relations have on the behaviour of states is offered by Cha in the shape of Japanese and South Korean relations in the post-Cold War 1990s. Cha notes:

> Realists would argue that substantial improvements in Japan-ROK political and security cooperation in the post- Cold War era are a direct result of DPRK threats. However, this proposition is incorrect. The level of aggregate threat posed by the North in the 1990s is actually *lower* than during the Cold War.[528]

As a result of this lower external threat a realist would assume the likelihood of cooperation between Korea and Japan would decrease, the threat of a DPRK invasion of the South Korean state having fallen away.[529] Yet instead, the relationship in the post-Cold War period between the two powers became closer still despite the lack of a clear external threat provoking the states into cooperation.[530] The neoclassical model Cha presents with his "quasi-alliance" argument, however, does explain this cooperation with reference to the policies of the United States, the larger ally of both states. As he argues, the East Asian states recognise that in a post-Cold War environment the policy of the United States to its smaller partners in Asia "can change virtually overnight with a change of administration in Washington".[531] Furthermore, as the disappearance of Cold War bipolarity has made balancing the Soviet/Russian threat in East Asia less salient, the chance of US withdrawal from the region and from previously binding defence alliances with Korea and Japan increases as rivals emerge in the new multipolar security environment.[532] Thus, neoclassicalists recognise the likelihood that Korean and Japanese perceptions and feelings about the security situation in East Asia represent significant explanatory features of the East Asian system, features that

---

[527] Cha. 2000, p.264.
[528] Cha. 2000, p.283. Emphasis in the quotation is in Cha's original.
[529] Cha. 2000, p.283.
[530] Cha. 2000, p.283. See also Glen Hook, Julie Gibson, Christopher Hughes and Hugo Dobson. 2005. *Japan's international relations: politics, economics and security*. 2nd edition. Oxford: Routledge, pp.257-268.
[531] Cha. 2000, p.284.
[532] Cha. 2000, p.284.

134

structural, offensive and classical realists cannot and do not recognise in their analysis.

Thus, by examining the relationship between Japan, Korea and their ally, the United States, Cha is able to point to an example of an evolving and dynamic triangulated alliance that classical and structural realists cannot easily explain. Where realists suggest a rational assessment of East Asian security issues would see closer ties between Japan and Korea history proves otherwise. Likewise, where realists imagine periods of strained relations would continue history instead presents periods of closer relations between the two Asian states. Explaining the ebbs and flows in the alliance between Japan and Korea requires that the historical context and also the role of an uninvolved and non-threatening power, the United States, be considered and, to do so, Cha must turn to the neoclassical position. With neoclassicalism, Cha finds he is able to consider the *actual* and *historically informed* realities, that is, the *constructed* realities of state units rather than only the assumed rational and objective reality that the states *should* consider in establishing a foreign policy position. Cha speaks to the utility of the neoclassical position in concluding:

> In order to understand one of the most idiosyncratic, purportedly "non-theorizable" relationships in Asia, a specified use of alliance theory that appreciates the causal impact of structural forces but filters these through perceptions and a more differentiated understanding of the substructural units is more productive than either cultural or acultural approaches.[533]

His article was not the first area study to endorse the neoclassical perspective and neither is the technique restricted to state relations after World War Two. Indeed, one can turn to Thomas Christensen and his study of 19th and 20th century study of alliances in Europe to demonstrate just how perceptions of the international system mattered to statesmen just as much as the likely objective truth about that same situation.

---

[533] Cha. 2000, p.287.

Thomas Christensen – Perceptions and Alliances in Europe, 1865-1940

At first glance, Princeton's Thomas Christensen would seem a strange author of an article assessing pre-World War Two alliances in Europe.[534] After all, the man who in 2007 served as US Deputy Secretary of State for East Asian Affairs dealing primarily in foreign policy matters concerning China and Taiwan and has a substantial publication record focused on the region.[535] Yet a closer look at Christensen's research suggests that – as with the research of Mark Beeson, for example – he has found parallels between the two disparate geopolitical regions.[536] In 'Perceptions and Alliances in Europe, 1865-1940' Christensen applies a realist approach but argues that the balance of power and the "relative efficacy of offense and defense" alone are not enough to explain and account for the actions and alliance building strategies of European powers in post-Crimean War, pre-World War II period.[537] Instead, Christensen suggests that "we must include in our analysis the perceptions and misperceptions of both [these] realist variables", a hallmark of the neoclassical realist position.[538]

Christensen is clear from the outset as to the implications of his neoclassicalism:

> Even if leaders think in terms consistent with realist assumptions, in complex multipolar environments they will often misread either the distribution of capabilities in the system and/or the efficacy of military offensives and defensives. This will lead to policies that

---

[534] Christensen. 1997.

[535] Department of State. 2006. *Thomas J. Christensen: Biography.* [8 June 2007] http://tinyurl.com/2c55m4. A selection of Christensen's East Asian/Asia Pacific works includes Thomas Christensen. 1992. 'Threats, Assurances, and the Last Chance for Peace: The Lesson's of Mao's Korean War Telegrams.' *International Security* 17(1): 122-154; Thomas Christensen. 1996. *Useful Adversaries: Grand Strategy, Domestic Mobilization, and Sino-American Conflict, 1947-1958.* Princeton: Princeton University Press; Thomas Christensen. 1999. 'China, the US-Japan Alliance, and the Security Dilemma in East Asia.' *International Security* 23(4): 49-80; Thomas Christensen. 2002. 'The Contemporary Security Dilemma: Deterring a Taiwan Conflict.' *The Washington Quarterly* 25(4): 7-21; Thomas Christensen and Michael Glosny. 2003. 'Sources in Stability in US-China Security Relations.' In *Strategic Asia 2003-04: Fragility and Crisis*, edited by Richard Ellings, Aaron Friedberg and Michael Wills. Washington DC: National Bureau of Asian Research, pp.53-80.

[536] Mark Beeson. 2005. 'Rethinking regionalism: Europe and East Asia in comparative historical perspective.' *Journal of European Public Policy* 12(6): 969-985.

[537] Christensen. 1997, pp.65-66.

[538] Christensen. 1997, p.65.

may be driven by concerns about power and security but that may still seem at odds with the predictions of both balance-of-power and security dilemma theories.[539]

More bluntly, Christensen is suggesting that by considering the perceptions of actors as well as the base 'facts' of the international political and military situation can and should, indeed, be *expected* to render strict classical realist predictions of behaviour wrong.[540] Christensen offers a number of examples in support of this contention, turning briefly to the failure of structural realist theories to explain different routes to pan-continental war in 1914 and 1939 before considering, in turn, the Austro-Prussian War, the Franco-Prussian War and the two major conflicts of the first half of the twentieth-century: World War One and World War Two.[541] Each confirms for Christensen the significance of the expectations, biases, intuitions, perception and misperception of state leaders in explaining state behaviour, actor choices and politico-military events in an international context and, considering each in turn, the neoclassical assumptions implicit in this argument are immediately evident.

In depicting the weakness of existing realist approaches, Christensen posits the differing European power structures before both World War One and World War Two, the former with its entangling alliances checking the power of rival states, the latter a continent of 'buck passers' seeking another to protect all from a rising German threat.[542] Yet despite such disparate structures, notes Christensen, in both cases a system-wide war emerged in which all European powers were engaged.[543] How, then, can a balance-of-power assessment lending great weight to international structures explain how such differing structures lead to such similar outcomes? For Christensen the answer is simple: it cannot. Rather he suggests that by 'grafting' a "a nonstructural variable – leaders' perceptions about the relative efficacy of offensive or defensive doctrines – onto Kenneth Waltz's structural theory" it is possible to predict which distributions of power were likely to lead to conflict and which would remain

---

[539] Christensen. 1997, p.66.

[540] Christensen also alludes to the link between the realist theories and the decision making processes of the leaders of states implying that there is something quite rational about considering politics from the realist perspective.

[541] Christensen. 1997, p.67; pp.70-76; pp.76-81; pp.82-83; pp.83-92.

[542] Christensen. 1997, p.67.

[543] Christensen. 1997, p.67. Note here that 'system-wide' for Christensen refers only to the European system of states and powers though, particularly in relation to World War Two, it would not be wrong to conclude that the war was 'system-wide' in the most global sense.

more stable.[544] It is this methodology that Christensen and co-author Jack Snyder outlined in a 1990 article which the author uses in his neoclassical assessment of the major conflicts of the post-Crimea period in European history.[545]

Consider the Austro-Prussian war that led largely to the balance of power that would dominate Europe in the late-nineteenth and early-twentieth centuries. Christensen rejects arguments such as those of James Morrow which seek to explain the failure of France and Austria to ally against Prussia with reference to the domestic political situation under Napoleonic rule.[546] Instead he maintains that the international perspective remains the most relevant but that the perceptions of Napoleon and his advisors – all of whom felt that Austria remained the most powerful of the German states – led to the failure of the French to ally with the Austrians against a rising Prussian threat.[547] Christensen illustrates this misperception of the balance of power by pointing to the shockwaves that spread through foreign policy elites upon the Prussian victory at Königgrätz in July 1866 which led Austria to sue for peace following the massive casualties inflicted upon them by a numerically-inferior Prussian force.[548] So distorted was the perception of Austrian power that Christensen notes that both European officer corps and European governments demanded an answer to the same questions: "how did this happen?"[549] A combination of this misperception of Austrian superiority and a firm belief that warfare had become an exercise in attrition was, for Christensen, the reason why a balance of power assessment or a focus on international structure alone could not explain international behaviour before and during the Austro-Prussian conflict.[550]

---

[544] Christensen. 1997, p.67.

[545] Thomas Christensen and Jack Snyder. 1990. 'Chain gangs and passed bucks: Predicting alliance patters in multipolarity.' *International Organization* 44(2): 137-168.

[546] Christensen. 1997, pp.70-71. See also James Morrow. 1993. 'Arms versus allies: Trade-offs in the search for security.' *International Organization* 47(2): 207-233.

[547] Christensen. 1997, p.71.

[548] Geoffrey Wawro lists 24,000 Austrian soldiers dead or wounded and 20,000 more captured compared to just 9,000 Prussian casualties. According to Wawro, the Prussian victory at Königgrätz "was a breathtaking accomplishment that utterly destroyed Austrian morale". See Geoffrey Wawro. 1998. *The Austro-Prussian War: Austria's War with Prussia and Italy in 1866*. Cambridge: Cambridge University Press, p.274.

[549] Christensen. 1997, p.72.

[550] Christensen. 1997, pp.73-76.

The Franco-Prussian War (1870-1871) again saw a French and Austrian alliance fail to emerge despite the common threat from a Prussia under the leadership of Otto von Bismarck. Again, misperception of the actual balance of power in Europe on behalf of France and Austria, as well as a misplaced confidence in the likely shape the war would take, led to a failure for the states involved to act as strict classical or structural realists would expect they should.[551] On two points in particular were such misperceptions evident: French overconfidence in its ability to defeat Prussia quickly if French forces moved first and the Austrian belief that France would be able to win both quickly and alone, particularly in the early battles.[552] The former led Napoleon to brag to the Austrian ambassador on the eve of the war, "the winner will be the one who can be ready first", the French leader seemingly blind to the advances in Prussian weaponry and tactics and pre-Austro-Prussian reforms to its arrangements for general staff.[553] The latter saw a hesitant Austria refuse to mobilise against the enemy who had previously left the Austrians bloodied and beaten at Königgrätz. Of course, the Russian threat to Austria's east remained a consideration in Vienna's mind but Christensen notes that even Russia suffered from an overestimation of French strength, this driving closer ties by Russia with the Prussian empire.[554] Austria, perhaps sensibly, refused a formal alliance with the French following their early losses in the field sure as they were that such an alliance would lead to two "chain gangs" on the continent sure to face each other in a devastating pan-European war.[555] Some clarity of perception, then, on the part of Austrians, though one that would only stave off such a conflict until the second decade of the new century.

With regards to World War One Christensen argues, "both beliefs about the offense-defense balance and the balance of power affected the security policies of the major powers".[556] The alliances that tied state to state across Europe in the years before the war were a result of a widespread belief in an offensive military posture as the most effective war-fighting strategy, a belief that naturally suggested strong allies ready to

---

[551] Christensen. 1997, p.77. Note that, once again, Christensen rejects turning to domestic causes for the behaviour of states in and around the Franco-Prussian War.
[552] Christensen. 1997, p.77.
[553] Christensen. 1997, p.78.
[554] Christensen. 1997, pp.80-81.
[555] Christensen. 1997, p.81.
[556] Christensen. 1997, p.82.

mobilise quickly were essential.[557] Yet as Richard Hephner recalls, World War One saw the "nightmarish conditions" associated with trench warfare and a prolonged, defensive struggle against a fortified enemy.[558] Christensen argues that the major European powers so underestimated the efficacy of a defensive war that they were financially and militarily unprepared for such a long pan-continental conflict.[559] Thus, where realism predicated rational states assessing the European political reality and balancing power through alliances to avoid a rival's success, instead a tangled web of alliances based on misperception were held to have caused Europe to enter a conflict the likes of which had never been experienced in the continent's long and bloodied history.

Again, and with regards to World War Two, Christensen notes that it is only by considering the misperceptions of actors that realism can truly explain the pre-war preparations of Britain, France and the Soviet Union. The former was so sure that the more powerful German army would falter, or at least be somewhat slowed, in its advance by the defensive fortifications of the French Maginot Line that they sought a "not very vigorous" alliance with frontline France.[560] France's own belief in the likelihood of a long war of attrition – a sort of Great War Part II – led to its investment in fortified defences and discussions with Great Britain as to what strategies might play out in the "crucial" third year of the struggle.[561] So deep rooted were these French perceptions of German battle strategy that even during the so-called 'Phony War', being the months after German forces overran Poland with its devastatingly effective *blitzkrieg* tactics, Paris continued to prepare for a long and drawn-out conflict with their neighbour. Even the power that Christensen nominates as one of only two "true poles in the system", the Soviet Union, Christensen argues that Stalin and his general staff overestimated both the efficacy of the French defences and also the power of the French state as a whole.[562] Where neoclassicalists and structural realists see states acting out of the ordinary, Christensen's neoclassicalism allows him to pinpoint the

---

[557] Christensen. 1997, p.82.
[558] Richard Hephner. 1997. *Where Youth and Laughter Go: The Experience of Trench Warfare from Petersburg to the Western Front.* MA Thesis, Virginia Polytechnic Institute and State University, p.56.
[559] Christensen. 1997, p.82.
[560] Christensen. 1997, p.84.
[561] Christensen. 1997, p.90.
[562] Christensen. 1997, p.91.

human factors that led to continental conflict – a neoclassicalism that is endorsed in the overarching review of the approach offered by Gideon Rose in 'Neoclassical Realism and Foreign Policy'.

Gideon Rose – Neoclassical Realism and Foreign Policy

A fixture at the influential US think-tank Council on Foreign Relations and Managing Editor of the high-profile journal *Foreign Affairs*, Gideon Rose is amongst the better known international relations academicians working in the United States today. Previously assistant editor of the then-newly established, politically right-of-centre foreign affairs journal *The National Interest*, Rose has also served on the editorial board of *The Public Interest* before moving to *Foreign Affairs* in the year 2000. Educated at Harvard, Rose served on the faculty at both Columbia and Princeton after serving on President Clinton's National Security Council as Associate Director for Near East and South Asian Affairs between 1994 and 1995. A regular contributor to publications such as *The New York Times, Foreign Affairs, Public Affairs, International Security* and the author, editor or contributor to thirty-three books, Rose is a prolific publisher in a highly competitive publishing environment. Yet across his extensive list of publications it is a single paper – 'Neoclassical Realism and Foreign Policy' – that has emerged as his most often cited piece.[563] The reason for this is clear: in less than thirty pages Rose reviews five neoclassical texts and – from them – extracts the essence of the neoclassical position that was seeing structural realism significantly challenged from another realist perspective for the first time in more than a decade.

Rose opens 'Neoclassical Realism and Foreign Policy' by placing it both within and aside the intra-disciplinary debates between Waltzian structural realists and the neo-liberalists, offensive realists and defensive realists.[564] In his review of works by Brown, Christensen, Schweller, William Wohlforth and Zakaria – all of which fall

---

[563] Rose. 1998. Google Scholar returns more than twice as many citations as Rose's second most commonly cited work being the post-9/11 book, *How Did This Happen? Terrorism and the New War.* See Gideon Rose and James Hoge (eds.). 2001. *How Did This Happen? Terrorism and the New War.* New York: Harper Collins.

[564] Rose. 1998, pp.144-146. Notably Rose does not consider the constructivist challenge to neorealism.

beneath the theoretical umbrella of neoclassical realism – Rose finds a fourth contra-neorealist position, one he explains thus:

Neoclassical realists argue that relative material power establishes the basic parameters of a country's foreign policy; they note, in Thucydides' formula, that "the strong do what they can and the weak suffer what they must." Yet they point out that there is no immediate or perfect transmission belt linking material capabilities to foreign policy behavior. Foreign policy choices are made by actual political leaders and elites, and so it is their perceptions of relative power that matter, not simply relative quantities of physical resources or forces in being.[565]

While classical and structural realists have always been prepared to predict what will eventually happen within the international system while, at the same time, remaining clear not to set a particular date for said event to occur, Rose notes that neoclassical realists overcome the difficulties of short- and medium-term prediction in political systems.[566] As Cha and Christensen have both been shown to contend previously, the perceptions and biases of the leadership of states makes a difference to the assessment of the balance of power that – while significant in its implications for actors – is not of sole importance when assessing competing international political strategies.

Rose contends that the neoclassical realists, with their "understanding [of] the links between power and policy" demand the "close examination of the contexts within which foreign policies are formulated and implemented", a position which distinguishes the neoclassicalists from the classical and structural realists.[567] Yet Rose does not argue that this makes the neoclassicalist position any less realist; indeed, he states that neoclassicalists – unlike those theorists that consider domestic politics to have a significant effect on the international behaviour of states – assume that "relative material power vis-à-vis the rest of the international system" remains the single most dominant factor in explaining the choices of states in the international system.[568] He cites Zakaria in support of this contention, stating:

---

[565] Rose. 1998, pp.146-147.
[566] Rose. 1998, p.147.
[567] Rose. 1998, p.148.
[568] Rose. 1998, p.150.

142

<blockquote>
A good theory of foreign policy…should first ask what effect the international system has on national behaviour, because the most powerful generalisable characteristic of a state in international relations is its relative position in the international system.[569]
</blockquote>

Yet despite what is a fairly standard structural realist claim, the neoclassicalists reject the power-seeking calculus of Waltz and even Mearsheimer in favour of assessing states that seek to "respond to the uncertainties of international anarchy by seeking to control and shape their external environment".[570] The end result, then, is that neoclassical realists hold a position somewhat between the strict structural realists and the Wendtian constructivists where they agree that there exists an assessable distribution of power in a political system, they agree that such a distribution can be measured and mapped, they agree that this is the dominant factor in explaining state choices and actor behaviour, yet also agree that consideration must be paid to the interpretation of this balance of power and the perceptions and misperceptions of states in assessing it.[571]

Having located neoclassical realism in the spectrum of international relations theories, Rose turns to four examples that distinguishes the approach from its realist rivals: explaining the rise and fall of great powers in the international system; the significance of perception and misperception by states; the significance of the state as an institution in assessing international behaviour; and the methodology employed by the neoclassicalists, itself a significantly more broad and complex undertaking than standard classical realist assessments of the balance of power.[572] This section will consider each of these four in turn and note the parallels with both the work of Cha and Christensen, as well as the other neoclassical realists considered by Rose.

The rise and fall of great powers, itself implying a measure of relative power between actors in a system, is where Rose finds the first distinctive realist traits of the neoclassicalists. Nominating two earlier movements within realism as focused primarily on relative power and foreign policy, Rose suggests that the work of Zakaria, Wohlforth and Christensen lead the neoclassical movement in a third wave.[573] Consider the

---

[569] Rose. 1998, p.151.
[570] Rose. 1998, p.152.
[571] Rose. 1998, pp.152-153.
[572] Rose. 1998, pp.155-168.
[573] Rose. 1998, pp.156-157.

arguments of Christensen, says Rose, who argues that "shifting distributions of power in the international system" drove the Cold War policies of China and the US, or Wohlforth's contention that "state behavior [is an] adaptation to external constraints conditioned by changes in relative power".[574] In such cases it is possible to see one of the central tenets of neoclassicism – assessing the relative distribution of power in a system as opposed to a simpler neorealist assessment of 'unipolar', 'bipolar' or 'multipolar' systems – emerging across the perspective. Add to this the innovative assessment of the causes of World War Two by Randall Schweller, with a focus on an international "pecking order" rather than a crazed German dictator driving conflict in Europe, and the neoclassical focus on relative power is clearly differentiated from both classical and neorealist perspectives as well as standard historical explanations for conflict in the international political system.[575]

If attention to the distribution of power in a system is the third in a wave of structural realist approaches then the second trait Rose considers – perception and misperception – is distinctly neoclassical. Rose makes a similar point to both Cha and Christensen, though rather more succinctly:

> Neoclassical realists, in contrast, argue that the notion of a smoothly functioning mechanical transmission belt is inaccurate and misleading. The international distribution of power can drive countries' behaviour only by influencing the decisions of flesh and blood officials, they point out, and would-be analysts of foreign policy thus have no alternative but to explore in detail how each country's policymakers actually understand their situation.[576]

Considering the Cold War and the twin superpowers, the US and the USSR, Rose suggests that the neoclassicalists highlight the perceptions of actors as well as their manifest capabilities. The American understanding of the Soviet threat during the Cold War were not so much a function of the actual material threat but rather of the perception of US policymakers of Soviet power which was remarkably overstated on behalf of the United States.[577] Events such as the collapse of the USSR – considered across the board as an almost unprecedented "shock" to the modern international sys-

---

[574] Rose. 1998, p.157.
[575] Rose. 1998, p.157.
[576] Rose. 1998, p.158.
[577] Rose. 1998, pp.159-160.

144

tem – provoke in states a "perceptual shock", realigning the material capabilities with the dominant political perception.[578] Such shocks of perception must, argue neo-classicalists, be taken into account when considering explanations of international state behaviour.

Rose next differentiates the neoclassicalists by their reference to the apparatus of the state in operationalising the available national power capabilities. Again rejecting standard structuralist assessments of state power, the neoclassicalists explicitly refer to the access a state's leadership has to that power.[579] Rose argued, "national leaders may not have easy access to a country's total material power resources" and, thus, assessment of the international balance alone is of little independent utility.[580] A parallel might be drawn to a confrontation between two individuals armed with a loaded revolver but where one of the individuals lacks the physical coordination to pull the trigger. While their offensive weapons capability is the same, one of the two obviously maintains the ability to operationalise this capability while the other does not. It is only by considering the opportunities for international political actors to exercise their material capabilities that the power of a state can be correctly assessed, argue the neoclassicalists, and this, says Rose, "brings [neoclassical] analysis significantly closer to the real world without abandoning the [realist] paradigm's core concepts and assumptions".[581]

Finally Rose turns to the methodology of the neoclassicalists, his fourth and final point of departure for this corner of Elman's "big tent" of theoretical realism.[582] Here Rose distinguishes between preceding realist analysis of international affairs and the emerging neoclassicalist perspective, writing:

> A distinct methodological perspective flows from neoclassical realism's theoretical argument: analysts wanting to understand any particular case needs to do justice to the full complexity of the causal chain linking relative material power and foreign policy outputs... Neoclassical realists therefore think that neither spare game-theoretic modelling nor pure "thick description" are good approaches to foreign policy analysis. They

---

[578] Rose. 1998, pp.160-161.
[579] Rose. 1998, p.161.
[580] Rose. 1998, p.161.
[581] Rose. 1998, p.168.
[582] Elman. 1996, p.26.

favour beginning intellectually at the systemic level but then taking care to trace precisely how, in actual cases, relative power is translated and operationalised into the behaviour of state actors.[583]

The neoclassicalists, then, acknowledge the complexities of international interaction amongst states, or at least to an extent that structural and strict classical realists do not. As a result neoclassical scholars favour regionalist approaches to international relations, eschewing the universalist bent of Waltzian structuralists, a position that sees their claims questioned by those who would suggest a pan-regional algorithm for assessing and predicting international relations exists.[584] The focus on individual situations, national and even regional differentiation and the specifics of state access to power leads some to question whether neoclassicalism is even a theory of foreign policy at all. Rose suggests that "hard-line positivists and historians" might be among those that suggest that "the lack of precise predictions generated by neoclassical realism [and] the stress it places on detailed historical analysis" give rise to something less than a social science.[585] Rose counters this, however, by returning to the positivist's own international relations theory mentor, Kenneth Waltz, and reminding readers that a neoclassical theory of international relations identifies the links between various international factors, prioritises the relationships between these factors and suggests how changes in one factor can lead to changes in others.[586] Thus, by a positivists own standards, the methodology of the neoclassicalists is theoretically and methodologically valid, if different from competing perspectives within the realist paradigm. What has not changed, however, is the foundational assumption of anarchy which remains a constant cornerstone for the neoclassicalists.

These four distinguishing features, then, for Rose, identify the neoclassical realist position from the more common neorealist or classical realist stance. A focus on relative power aligns the neoclassicalists with other realists but, when combined with an assessment of the perceptions and misperceptions of states leaders and policymakers, provides a new direction for realist theory. Coupled with concentration on the ability of the state to exercise power (as opposed to its raw material capabilities) and a

---

[583] Rose. 1998, pp.165-166.
[584] Rose. 1998, pp.166-167.
[585] Rose. 1998, p.167.
[586] Rose. 1998, p.167. See also Waltz. 1979, pp.8-10.

146

methodology that further separates it from standard realist considerations of international relations and Rose is correct to conclude that the perspective offers a "judicious appraisal" of state behaviour in the international system.[587] Further, Rose is correct in highlighting the link neoclassicalists draw between the international actions of a state and the domestic situation that state enjoys. While not going so far as to privilege the domestic over the international – a move that would see neoclassical realism struggle to maintain the latter half of that qualification – the neoclassicalists recognise the significance of the domestic in explaining the international, as Wohlforth notes when stating:

> Any realist discussion of international change must combine the domestic and international levels of analysis. A [purely structural] realist explanation cannot offer a comprehensive account of precisely why a given state's domestic political, social, and economic institutions decline in comparison to those of competing powers.[588]

The neoclassical approach, then, goes some way to weakening the grasp of the structuralists on the assessment of the international system at the dawn of the 21st century; what the approach does not offer, however, is a new understanding of the nature of that system which remains, as in all other realist approaches thus far identified, confirmedly anarchic.

Conclusion: Anarchy in Neoclassical Realism

Chan, Christensen and Rose outline a realist approach that questions some fundamental assumptions of the major realist approaches thus far examined in this book. Neoclassicalists challenge realist accounts that privilege the relative power of states without considering how such power is raised or applied. They continue to assess the state as the central and most important actor in international relations making them realist, but delve also into the domestic structure of the state and the minds of the strategists who would lead the state. Neoclassicalists are critical, too, of the neorealists focus on the structure of the international system in explaining the emergence of international conflict and the behaviour of states more generally. What the neoclassicalists do not question, however, and which places them most certainly within the wider realist

---

[587] Rose. 1998, p.172.
[588] In Rose. 1998, p.170. See also Rose. 1998, cf.51.

paradigm, is the nature of the international system itself. Like the classicalists, structuralists, offensive realists and game theorists before them, the neoclassicalists assume that the international system is anarchic.

For the neoclassicalists there is no need to assume a fundamentally different nature for the international political system in order to explain state behaviour within it. While seeking improvements over the existing realist approaches and a more nuanced assessment of the international reality though the integration of individual and domestic level factors in their analysis, the neoclassicalists remain firmly rooted to the notion of an anarchic system. Indeed, the neoclassicalists offer only a different interpretation of the effects and strength of international anarchy on the state actors that exists beneath it. Writes Rose:

> [N]eoclassical realists assume that states respond to the uncertainties of international anarchy by seeking to control and shape their external environment. Regardless of the myriad ways that states may define their interests, this school argues, they are likely to want more rather than less external influence, and pursue such influence to the extent that they are able to do so.[589]

Like the offensive realism of John Mearsheimer where anarchy is significant and influential and the "benign" anarchy of defensive realism, the neoclassicalists simply put a new spin on the nature of the system that the paradigm has held on to since the discipline's birth.[590]

Conclusion

This chapter concludes a three chapter exploration and explication of realist thought in international relations. From the ancient diplomacy recorded in the histories of Thucydides through Machiavelli, Hobbes, Carr and Morgenthau, the structuralist theoretical revolution under Waltz and, in this chapter, the offensive realism of John Mearsheimer, the game theory approach typified in the Prisoner's Dilemma and the neoclassicalism of Cha, Christensen and Rose, it is clear that the discipline's domi-

---

[589] Rose. 1998, p.152.
[590] The differences between the various 'realisms' on this point is discussed in Rose. 1998, pp.149-152.

nant paradigm is indeed, in Elman's words, "a big tent".[591] Realists question all manner of assumptions about the international system and differ on fundamental matters including the significance of the balance of power, what is important in assessing the power of states, what drives states to conflict and the possibilities for peace in a world that has experienced system-wide war after system-wide war. If there is a realist who claims that structure is important there will be another that will say the effects of structure are overemphasised. For every biological realist claiming that war begins in the nature of man there will be a neorealist pushing the nature of the system as the root cause of conflict. Yet on one point all realists agree, maintaining a pan-paradigmatic belief as firm in the minds of the modern game theorist as the ancient Greek historian: the international system is anarchic.

Yet anarchy is not the sole possible structure for the state of nature. Indeed, it will be argued that not only do other systemic configurations exist but that one may prove significantly more relevant to an international system composed of a myriad of state, institutional, corporate and individual actors all involved in innumerable global, political, industrial, military and economic interactions each day. An international system that is not anarchic would, in turn, call for a theory that recognises the implications of such a system and leaving realism and its anarcho-centric analysis aside. With the following chapter – The Limitations of Anarchy – this book opens Part Two of its research by considering just what sort of system international political relations exist within, examining the alternatives and concluding which best describes the international environment. Arguing that there is an alternative conception of the nature of the system which can describe and account for the international interactions that have shaped international relations in the past, the fourth chapter of this book puts a name to the system and lays the foundations for an argument and explication of a new method of analysis in international relations. Indeed, the Chapter that follows proposes an alternative method of analysis replacing the anarchy premise of realist international relations theory with a theoretical premise that has the potential to be more analytically and theoretically fruitful and of greater explanative utility.

---

[591] Elman. 1996, p.26.

THE LIMITATIONS OF ANARCHY

As seen throughout the previous three chapters the consistent assumption across all of realism is one of systemic anarchy. While the implications of this assumption vary somewhat between diverse strains of the realist paradigm, the foundational nature of anarchy is central to the realist approach to international relations. Yet, like all assumptions in any theory of international affairs, the realist assumption of anarchy is just that: an assumption. In the construction of a realist theory anarchy is a premise selected for its contribution to theoretical parsimony; that is, realists choose to base their approach on a foundation of anarchy knowing it is not an exact representation of reality but a way by which to simplify reality so that the theory is of some utility to the analyst of international politics. Yet with realists facing some difficulties in explaining events in the international system and with realist predictions of major developments in international relations regularly failing, it is wise to question whether the assumption of anarchy in the name of parsimony comes at too high a cost. If the cost, measured in terms of the utility of the anarchy-based theory in describing reality, is too high then this founding notion must be rejected in favour of an alternate understanding of the nature of the international system, one that better reflects the reality that is international politics.

This chapter is presented in three parts in an effort to establish the precise goals of a theory of international relations such as realism, the role of anarchy in realism's attempt towards theoretical parsimony and to estimate the costs to theoretical utility of the assumption of anarchy in realism. The first part of this chapter, titled 'What is a Theory?', clarifies the notion of 'theory' in the context of international relations, identifies the necessary and significant elements of a theory, the goals of a theory and introduces a cartographical analogy to illustrate the potential costs of parsimony to analytical and theoretical utility. The second part of this chapter, 'The Assumption of Anarchy and the Quest for Realist Parsimony', considers the realist theorists and approaches that the previous chapters have discussed and highlights the ways in which anarchy is employed as a parsimonious assumption in each case. Finally, the third part of this chapter, 'Establishing the Cost of the Assumption of Anarchy', uses three case studies from the twentieth century – the outbreak of World War One, the Fall of the Soviet Union and the post-Cold War integration of Europe – to demonstrate that this pursuit of parsimony comes at too high a cost to theoretical and analytical utility. In concluding the chapter, a case will be made for the rejection of anarchy as a foundation for international relations theory, opening the door to an improved approach based on the assumption of a complex international system.

What is a Theory?

Before considering the place of anarchy in a realist theory of international relations it is appropriate to explore what a theory in the discipline of international relations, and indeed the wider social sciences, is. Doing so allows us to benchmark the utility of realism in describing, explaining and predicting international politics and the level of impact that the assumption of anarchy within realist thought has on this theoretical and analytical utility. Towards this end, this first part of the chapter will achieve the following ends: first, the notion and definition of 'theory', generally, in the social sciences and then in international relations specifically, will be detailed; second, the elements and goals of a theory of international relations will be explained and examples from prominent realists offered in support of the conclusions made; third, this chapter will offer a revealing analogy between theorising international relations and the role and tasks of the cartographer in an effort to illuminate the problems that can potentially emerge from theorists privileging the pursuit of parsimony in their theories; fourth and finally, the costs of seeking such parsimony in a theory will be detailed and it will be argued that the best international political theory is that which finds the best balance between reality and representation of reality.[592] In concluding this part of the chapter, it will be argued that a theory of international politics that achieves parsimony at the cost of analytical utility is a theory that is of little use to the analyst of international affairs.

---

[592] As will be made clear in later portions of this chapter, the theoretical-cartographical analogy was employed in a conference paper presented in January 2008. I am grateful for the comments and criticisms of participants at the 3rd Graduate Conference in Political Science in Memory of Yitzhak Rabin, Hebrew University, Jerusalem, Israel.

Defining 'Theory'

Like other terms which exist in both academic and popular discourse, the word 'theory' is often employed in different contexts and various definitions of the term exist in common English discourse. Consider, for example, the context of the term in the movie *Pearl Harbor*:

> - Sir, I believe they're going to hit us where it'll hurt the most, Pearl Harbor.
> - *It's 4,000 miles from Japan to Pearl, that's a long distance to steam a navy, Captain! Your theory is based on what?*
> - Well, it's what I would do.

In this context, as in much popular discourse, the term 'theory' in this exchange is synonymous with 'guess' or 'intuition'. Like the television detective who promotes his 'theory of the crime' based on 'gut instinct' alone, the term in this context suggests that theories are intuitively inspired, somewhat removed from the assessment of facts and represent a single person's take on the events and world around them. Elsewhere in popular discourse is found a dyadic relationship between what is considered 'theory' and its polar opposite, 'practice'. Variously attributed to Albert Einstein, Jan van de Snepscheut and Yogi Berra, the observation that "in theory there is no difference between theory and practice, but in practice there is" demonstrates this admirably. In this context, theory is supposed to be something outside of the real commenting upon what can be sensed and experienced – but with possibly no impact upon it. This popular conception of a theory being an inspired guess and distinct from the reality it describes might be explained by the history of the term itself.

Bertrand Russell traces the history of the term 'theory' to Orphism where, citing FM Cornford, he claims it meant a religiously inspired "passionate sympathetic contemplation".[593] Followers of Pythagoras embraced the term but added an intellectual and mathematical basis to the contemplation of the world. As Russell explains, the Pythagoreans ensured the term would take on a modern scientific meaning but that "for all those who were inspired by Pythagoras, [theory] retained an element of ecstatic revelation".[594] It is little wonder then that the popular conception of theory is related

---

[593] Russell. 1993, p.52.
[594] Russell. 1993, p.52.

to inspired guessing and leaps of logic unavailable to the average person for, as Russell continues:

> ...to those who have experienced the intoxicating delight of sudden understanding that mathematics gives, from time to time, to those who love it, the Pythagorean view will seem completely natural **even if untrue**. It might seem that the empirical philosopher is the slave of his material, but that the pure mathematician, like the musician, is a free creator of his world of ordered beauty.[595]

The modern and scientific meaning that Russell alludes to is much removed from both popular, Pythagorean and Orphic interpretations of theory. Indeed, not only are the links between practice and theory clear and necessary but guessing and estimation play little part in defining a scientific theory.

Theory, then, suffers from bearing a variety of definitions and being established as everything from akin to truth in the case of scientific theorems to akin to a 'best guess' in the case of the term when popularly employed. Russel's explanation as to the history and etymology of the word 'theory' goes some way to explaining the confusion between popular and scientific use of the term. The confusion in defining the term generally, however, is reflected in the discipline of international relations itself. Realists and non-realists have recognised the multiple meanings attached to the term within the international relations literature and attempted to clarify the term in their own work even as others continue to muddy the definitional waters by confusing the term with other concepts such as 'model', 'law' and 'paradigm'. Turning to this literature and it is easy to see the various definitions of theory in play.

'Theory' in International Relations

Stephen Walt once noted that the discipline of international relations was concerned with one world but many theories.[596] One might extend this point to note that not only are there many theories but also different definitions of what a theory in international relations is. Walt notes the link between a theory of international relations and the

---

[595] Russell. 1993, p.53. Emphasis added.
[596] Stephen Walt. 1998. 'International Relations: One World, Many Theories.' *Foreign Policy* (110): 29-46.

international political reality calling the relationship "inescapable".[597] Yet it would be Walt's one-time teacher and fellow realist Kenneth Waltz who would provide an influential analysis of the different meanings attributed to theory and explicate best the confusion surrounding the term in *Theory of International Politics*.[598] Here Waltz laid out in a short opening chapter both the looseness in which the word 'theory' was used in international relations and also its confusion with sometimes related, but certainly different, concepts.[599] Waltz offers, and these next paragraphs will consider, the terms 'law' and 'model 'as often used as synonyms for theory in international politics.[600] To this we can add one more, 'paradigm', and by considering each of these three in succession and distinguishing each from the others we can determine, as Waltz did, the correct meaning of 'theory' in the context of the international relations literature.

Waltz opens by juxtaposing the term 'theory' with the term 'law'. He claims that while the definition of theory might be in doubt – and this is already clear from the discussion above – the definition of law is widely agreed upon.[601] He argues that:

> [l]aws establish relations between variables, variables being concepts that can take different values. If *a*, then *b*, where *a* stands for one or more independent variables and *b* stands for the dependent variable: in form, this is a statement of a law.[602]

Waltz argues that some scholars in international relations often consider theories to be "collections of sets of laws pertaining to a particular behaviour or phenomenon".[603] The difference between laws and theories, then, is simply a matter of quantity and not one of type.[604] The attempt to make 'law' more or less synonymous with 'theory' is supported by a notion of theories emerging by theorists who simply collect related laws.[605] A collection of laws, though, is not a theory; as Waltz would later point out, theories must *explain* laws and not group laws on related themes to-

---

[597] Walt. 1998, p.29.
[598] Waltz. 1979.
[599] Waltz. 1979, Chapter One.
[600] Waltz. 1979, p.1; p.7.
[601] Waltz. 1979, p.1.
[602] Waltz. 1979, p.1.
[603] Waltz. 1979, p.2.
[604] Waltz. 1979, p.2.
[605] Waltz. 1979, p.2.

gether.[606] Theories cannot be discovered by induction as laws are, rather "theoretical notions can only be invented, not discovered".[607]

Similarly, Waltz notes confusion in the employment of the term 'model' as a synonym for 'theory'. Within the literature the term 'model' is used in two different ways: as a synonym for theory and as a representation of reality arising from a theory.[608] The problem Waltz finds in describing a 'model' as a 'theory' is the former's attempt to represent reality as closely as is possible whereas the latter is "distinct from the reality it explains".[609] He likens the aim of the model-as-theory scholars as akin to the amateur model airplane enthusiast:

> A model airplane should look like a real airplane...Some political scientists write of theoretical models as though they were the model airplane sort...they first criticise the state-centric model of international politics because it has supposedly become further and further removed from reality. Then they try and make models that mirror reality ever more fully. If their efforts were to succeed, the model and the real world would become one and the same.[610]

The problem with appropriating the term 'theory' for this ever closer modelling of reality is that it makes no attempt to explain the reality, as a theory does, and instead only seeks to represent it. While theories are tested by their ability to explain experiences in reality, theory cannot arise from the depiction of experience by the modeller. As Waltz argues, it is impossible to understand international political phenomena before contriving the means for explaining the phenomena to which we are witness.[611]

The word 'paradigm', too, is often employed as a synonym for 'theory' within the international relations literature. Consider, for example, Stanley Hoffman's opening contribution to Crawford and Jarvis' collection of essays, *International Relations* –

---

[606] Waltz. 1979, p.5.
[607] Waltz. 1979, p.5.
[608] Waltz. 1979, p.7.
[609] Waltz. 1979, p.7.
[610] Waltz. 1979, p.7. The model airplane was also an analogy embraced by Sidney Verba in an earlier article. See Sidney Verba. 1964. 'Simulation, Reality and Theory in International Relations.' *World Politics* 16(4): 490-519, p.502.
[611] Waltz. 1979, p.7.

Still An American Social Science?[612] Hoffman's comments on the realist paradigm are, at times, such that the word 'paradigm' can be substituted with 'theory' without at all affecting his point.[613] Elsewhere, though, Hoffman presents the term in its proper context where it is used to describe an overall, largely consistent approach to the problem of theorising international relations. Thus, we can speak of a realist paradigm that encompasses all of the theories founded on the assumptions of state-centricity and systemic anarchy, but we must do so recognising that the realist paradigm is not a theory itself. As R. Stephen Warner argued, a paradigm is not a theory but a meta-narrative or "a 'gestalt', a way of seeing the world, a representation, picture, or narrative of the fundamental properties of reality".[614] Thus, theories are developed which fit into a certain paradigm rather than paradigms being theories themselves or theories about theories.

If an international relations theory is not a law, a model or a paradigm, and if it is not an estimate, a guess or a gut-feeling, how can a theory within the discipline be defined? Returning to Waltz, he states a theory is "not the occurrence seen and the association recorded, but is instead the explanation of them".[615] Reflective of the world, though not an exact model of it, a theory is constructed through the simplification of reality into an order wherein phenomena are arranged to be mutually dependent.[616] Further to this, Waltz adds that a theory:

> ...connects otherwise disparate facts; it shows how changes in some of the phenomena necessarily entails changes in others. To form a theory requires envisioning a pattern where none is visible to the naked eye...Simplifications lay bare the essential elements in play and indicate the necessary relations of cause and interdependency – or suggest where to look for them.[617]

A theory, then, is a simplification of the real world that partly describes but, more importantly, *explains* the observable world by drawing links and expounding the rela-

---

[612] Stanley Hoffman. 2001. 'An American Social Science: International Relations.' In *International Relations – Still An American Social Science?*, edited by R Crawford & D Jarvis. New York: SUNY Press, pp.27-52.
[613] For example, Hoffman. 2001, p.40.
[614] R. Stephen Warner. 1997. 'A Paradigm is Not a Theory: Reply to Lechner.' *The American Journal of Sociology* 103(1): 192-198, p.193.
[615] Waltz. 1979, p.9.
[616] Waltz. 1979, p.9; p.10.
[617] Waltz. 1979, pp.9-10.

tionships between elements in the system under examination. The key to a theory is not its representation of phenomena but the explanations for the phenomena it represents. Reductive in nature, parsimonious in goal and fundamentally explanatory, theories in international relations are the foundation on which all international analysis is built. In the paragraphs that follow we will consider the elements and goals of a theory of international relations in greater detail.

Elements of a Theory of International Relations

The first step in developing a theory of international relations is defining and differentiating the phenomena or system which is being theorised. This is true not only of theories of international relations but of all theories. Consider, for example, how Pythagoras' Theorem defines its realm (right-angled triangles) or how the cosmological Theory of the Big Bang limits its considerable realm (activity at the universe level). Both do what international relations theorists must for, as has been argued,

> ...in order to have a theory, you'll have to have a subject matter, because you can't have a theory about everything...The first question is, how can you think of international politics as a domain in its own right, as something that you could possibly have a theory about?[618]

Within the realist tradition specifically and, indeed, across all of international relations generally, the domain of international politics is defined as politics that exists between states and under conditions of anarchy. The international is differentiated from the non-international by systemic anarchy; domestic politics, in contrast, is organised hierarchically. It is this anarchic structure that, for realists, makes it possible to have a theory of international politics at all.[619] Without a bounded realm, environment or system, it is impossible to claim that a theory of international relations exists.

Having defined and differentiated the system to be theorised, it is next necessary to define what the essential elements of that system are. For theorists of international relations, these elements can vary, particularly between paradigms. Most theorists of international relations include nation-states as essential elements in their theories and

---

[618] Waltz. 2003.
[619] Waltz. 2003.

158

some limit themselves to states alone. Others, though, extend their theories to encompass international institutions, such as the United Nations, regional bodies, such as the European Union, and non-state actors, including corporations, terrorist groups and non-governmental organisations. Others, too, theorise international politics with regards to elements such as socio-economic class, race and gender, though these theories are less-mainstream than realist, liberalist and even constructivist approaches. Some theorists include certain capabilities of states and actors as elements of their theories, for example, military capability, nuclear weaponry and financial power. However, while all theories limit the elements they include for the sake of theoretical parsimony, all theories also make no claim to be *exactly* representative of the international political system. As noted previously, theories can only reflect part of reality and will never offer an exact facsimile of the observable world and, thus, the elements the theorist chooses to focus on define not the system but the theorist's representation of the system.

Finally, having defined the system to be theorised and establishing the most significant elements of the system to be assessed by the theory, the theorist must define the relationship between the elements. These relationships can be in the shape of strict laws (if a, then b) or laws with a certain probability attached (if a, then b with probability x). The relationships between the elements are sometimes expressed in terms which personify or attribute motivations to the elements. For example, some realist theories suggest that states in a system are competitive while others argue that elements in the system are interdependent.[620] Other theories highlight the relationships between smaller or weaker state elements and larger, great powers. A theorist of international relations seeks "law-like regularities" within the system and, finding them, describes how they explain the relationships between the elements identified by the theory.[621] These three steps – defining the system, defining the elements of the system and the defining the relationships between the elements – are found in all theories of international relations as the following three examples drawn from the realist paradigm attest.

---

[620] Mearsheimer. 2006a, p.112.
[621] Waltz. 1979, p.116.

The realism of the Prisoner's Dilemma (outlined in the third chapter) is clear in bounding the system, identifying the elements and the relationships between them. Indeed, the mathematical logic and reductionist approach that sees the number of actors reduced to just two makes this perhaps the most parsimonious of the realist approaches in this regard. The 'system' in the Prisoner's Dilemma is defined as two separate prison cells. Though there is obviously a world outside of the cells that world is of no influence on the game itself and is thus discounted. The significant elements of the system are not nation-states but the two players. Only the players have any impact on the game and while, again, there are obviously other actors in the real world – their jailers, for instance – they are not significant elements in the game. Finally, the game clearly identifies the relationship between the elements: self-interested, equivalent in power, distrustful, rational but acting on limited information. In this realist game the system, the number of significant elements and the relationships between the elements are extremely simplified and certainly a very parsimonious representation of politics between states. Other realist approaches are equally parsimonious but closer to representing the reality of inter-state relations.

In a 2006 interview, John Mearsheimer outlined Waltzian neorealism thus:

> Waltz says that his theory is built on two simple assumptions: (1) the system is anarchic, and (2) states seek to survive. He explicitly says that he does not assume that states are rational actors.[622]

Yet while these two assumptions might define neorealism, they do not completely define the system Waltz is theorising. In *Theory of International Politics*, however, Waltz is clear in defining the subject of his theory as the anarchical system. He differentiates the international politic from the domestic politic by reference to the structure of the political system: the former and focus is anarchic, the latter hierarchic. The elements of a neorealist theory are nation-states alone. While not denying that there are other actors that operate at the international level and under the anarchic conditions that bind states, neorealists limit the elements of the system that they analyse to states. The relationship between the elements is alluded to by Mearsheimer's recollection in that Waltz argues that the states in the system seek survival; more signifi-

---

[622] Mearsheimer. 2006a, p.112.

160

cantly, though, the states seek survival *from* other states, implying an interdependence and competitiveness between the elements of the system. Yet turning to a third example, that of Mearsheimer's offensive realist theory, we find that layers of complexity can and are added to the parsimony of Waltz and the Prisoner's Dilemma.

John Mearsheimer defines the base assumptions of his theory of international politics thus:

> My theory is based on five assumptions: (1) the system is anarchic, (2) all great powers have some offensive military capability, (3) states can never be certain about other states' intentions, (4) states seek to survive, and (5) great powers are rational actors or strategic calculators.[623]

Mearsheimer, like Waltz, has constructed a theory where the international realm is defined by its anarchic nature and differentiated from the hierarchic politics of intrastate politics in the same manner. He defines the most significant elements in the system similarly to Waltz but notes there are 'state' elements and 'great powers'. While all great powers are states, Mearsheimer distinguishes between those functionally similar but politically and militarily insignificant small states and the great powers of the international system.[624] Again, Mearsheimer is not denying that other elements exist in the system but, for the purposes of theorising international relations, it is not necessary to focus attention upon them.[625] As to the relationships between the elements, Mearsheimer mimics Waltz but adds a significant qualifier: states and great powers are rational actors in the system.[626] This differentiates the neorealism of Waltz – which is without a theory of foreign policy for the elements – from the offensive realism of Mearsheimer while remaining under the broader paradigmatic umbrella of realism.

Thus, in the Prisoner's Dilemma, Waltzian structural realism and in Mearsheimer's offensive realism, we find three examples of realist theories that clearly define the system, the elements in the system and the relationships between them. Each is

---

[623] Mearsheimer. 2006a, p.112.

[624] Mearsheimer is not alone in focussing on 'great powers' as distinct elements in a theory of international relations. See also Doran and Parsons. 1980.

[625] See, for example, Mearsheimer. 1994.

[626] Mearsheimer. 2006a, p.112.

somewhat similar to others, the reason is of course they are all part of the wider realist paradigm, yet each is different in the ways in which they depict international politics. What each of these and all other theories of international relations share in common besides their theoretical structure, though, are the goals of the theory. These goals – simply stated but generally difficult to achieve – are defined and expounded in the paragraphs that follow.

Goals of a Theory of International Relations

Whatever the paradigm and whatever the internal assumptions of the individual theory, each theory of international relations seeks similar goals. These goals can be expressed in three simple words: *describe, explain* and *predict*. While theorists disagree as to which is the most important of these and, sometimes, whether all of them are necessary at all, the best theories of international relations, as measured by the theory's utility to the analyst and scholar, seek to satisfy all three.

A good theory of international relations should, at the least, describe the international political environment. It might do so by representing the entire system, a part of that system or even a single decision making structure within the system. An example of the former can be found in Morgenthau's classical realism and then in the neoclassical realism that would later emerge. In both cases the large swathes of international politics are described and theories of foreign policy expounded to support the description. Neorealist approaches, as well as offensive and defensive realist approaches, tend to describe smaller sections of the international politic, focussing almost exclusively on the role, behaviour and choices of nation-states to the exclusion of all other international actors. Yet other realist theories and approaches only consider specific situations in international politics and, while offering a description of those specific events, describe not much more than the limited decision making environment. A clear example here arises in the game theoretic approaches that exist in the realist tradition. While there has been some extrapolation and iteration of Prisoner's Dilemma games that claim to describe politics in the international sphere, in essence each game is an abstract depiction and description of a single international engagement. Whatever the scale of the description and without heed to the abstractness of the representation, each theory's first aim is to describe the international system under study.

The second aim and, for realists like Waltz, the most significant aim of any theory of international politics, is to explain international politics. It is useful here to reflect on a sports analogy to illustrate the difference between these first two aims: to present a description of a football game is to present it live-to-air on television but it is the commentary team that provides the explanation of the game. A theory must explain the interactions that define international politics lest it fall to the same level of utility as a soundless broadcast of a football match where, despite the image being presented to the viewer, all analysis, supporting data and team strategy remains a secret. While not all will agree with Waltz's characterisation of explanation as the most significant aim of international relations theory, all theories must offer some explanation of international phenomena, if only by virtue of the construction of the theory which must offer an explanation of the nature of the relationships between elements in the system. Examples of such explanations within realist theory would include references to the "balance of power" amongst nation-states, references to the nature of humans in classical realism and references to the trustworthiness (or lack of) amongst players in a game of Prisoner's Dilemma. In every case the theory outlines an explanation for phenomena based on its description of the system and, so the theorist hopes, allows the analyst and scholar to understand the world outside of the necessarily limited theoretical depiction.

The third aim of theory – and what makes it relevant not only to analysts and scholars but to practitioners of international relations – is prediction. Through reference to the links established between the elements of the theory's system and with regard to the explanations offered for phenomena in the system it can be possible for the person employing the theory to make predictions about future phenomena in the system. Such predictions range from the specific to the vague but any theory, by virtue of its description and explanation of international relations, is capable of being operationalised in order to provide measureable predictions. Within the literature there are numerous examples of realist theorists making predictions, though in recent years it is perhaps the offensive realist Mearsheimer who posits the most reaching – and perhaps the most wrong. In 'Back to the Future: Instability in Europe after the Cold

War' Mearsheimer argued for four potential futures for a post-Cold War Europe, extrapolating his predictions from his strict, offensive standpoint.[627] Unfortunately for Mearsheimer each of his predictions proved poor guides to post-Cold War realities in Europe with even his 'most likely' future (managed nuclear weapons proliferation across the continent) failing to even approximately match the post-1991 European geopolitical landscape.[628] In the case of 'Back to the Future', the predictions extrapolated from the theory would seem to raise problems for the offensive realist approach though, and this is significant, Mearsheimer's mistakes need not invalidate all realism or even all offensive realist approaches within the wider paradigm.

Finally, it is important to note, however, that of the three broad goals of a theory – description, explanation and prediction – it is the second that is most important. As the realist Waltz himself has argued:

> [T]heory is a simple instrument which you hope to be able to use in order to understand and explain the real world. The emphasis is on explanation, not on prediction. Prediction is nice. If you can predict, fine. But the key requirement: if a theory is not able to explain what's going on, then it's not theory, or it's a worthless theory. It's not a theory at all.[629]

As a result, Mearsheimer's failure to predict accurately does not invalidate the offensive realist approach or competing realist approaches to international relations. Whilst accurate prediction remains a future goal of any theorist, explanation is a far more significant and relevant yardstick by which to evaluate international relations theory.

Guiding the theorist towards all of these goals, though, is a single task that the theorist must hold central in constructing, developing and evaluating their theoretical advances. The parts of a theory – the system, the elements and the relations between them - and the goals of the theory, description, explanation and prediction, all demand that the theorist seek one thing: parsimony. The theorist of international affairs cannot present international relations as it *actually* is any more than the artist can present in a painting the reality he observes or the photographer can extrapolate from a

---

[627] Mearsheimer. 1990a.

[628] Dylan Kissane. 2007b. 'Offensive Realism and Central & Eastern Europe after the Cold War.' *CEU Political Science Journal* 2(4): 381-402.

[629] Waltz. 2003.

single frame the complexities of a real-world situation. Whatever the description of international affairs, the theorist must seek parsimony; whatever the explanations offered, the theorist should aim for parsimony. Yet parsimony in theory is also a risk. When theorists simplify the real world they run the risk of *over*simplifying the real world at a cost to explanations and predictions extrapolated from their work. While parsimony is necessary it is therefore also hazardous and, in this vein, this book draws an analogy between the theorists of international relations and the cartographer in order to demonstrate both the necessity and the pitfalls of seeking theoretical parsimony in international politics.

The Cartographical Analogy

Like the theorist of international relations, the cartographer faces a similar challenge. A maker of maps must produce a representation of reality that is of practical utility for the user who wishes to understand the world around them. Mapping is inherently a subjective and exclusionary practice as the cartographer decides which elements of the world are significant enough to be included, which can safely be ignored and which elements of the landscape are most central to the planar representation.[630] In a similar way, when an international relations theorist describes a new theory it is necessary to define the elements which are essential to understanding the complexities of an international political system, explain why other elements have been excluded and justify why those decisions were made. Thus, the cartographer's challenge is analogous to that of the theorist of international politics and the goals of the cartographer are much the same, also.

Like the theorist, the first task of the cartographer is to describe the environment that is under study.[631] Whether they consist of hastily scribbled squiggles on the back of an envelope, heavily contoured representations of local topography or high-tech

---

[630] Anne-Marie Slaughter, Andrew Tulumello and Stepan Wood. 1998. 'International Law and International Relations Theory: A New Generation of Interdisciplinary Scholarship.' The American Journal of International Law 92(3): 367-397, p.369.

[631] These ideas were first considered by the author in Dylan Kissane. 2008a. *On the Problems in and the Possibilities for Mapping International Chaos*. Paper presented at the 3rd Annual Graduate Conference in Political Science in Memory of Yitzhak Rabin, Hebrew University, Jerusalem, Israel, 17 January 2008. The author is grateful for the comments and criticisms received from workshop colleagues and academic staff at the Hebrew University.

handheld GPS depictions of highway systems, maps are an essential part of everyday life. Maps serve an essential purpose by breaking down a complex three-dimensional world to a simpler, two-dimensional representation of that world's most significant features. Like a theory of international relations, maps do not depict a perfect reality but rather offer a parsimonious depiction of the environment so as to aid the traveller, the businessperson or the scholar. The cartographer who wishes to map the international realm chooses a manner of projection and identifies geographic features, political boundaries and lines of longitude and latitude which he adds to his representation of the political world.[632] Thus:

> [t]he person who seeks to describe to a friend a cross-city route would mention major landmarks, suggested streets and any false turn that is likely to lead his friend astray. In either case the map-maker chooses to exclude largely irrelevant elements of the landscape in favour of the essential items by which the landscape can be determined. Thus, even a city-scale map would likely exclude the potholes on Main Street and a depiction of political boundaries on paper is likely to discard all notions of elevation safe in the knowledge that a boundary is a boundary, whether at 2000 metres or sea level.[633]

As a result, the descriptions of the environment offered by cartographers vary in scale and detail in a similar way that, for example, Morgenthau's global-scale realism varies in scale and detail from the Prisoner's Dilemma.

The second goal of the cartographer is to explain the environment they have described. This is not the same as explaining the reasons for the environment being the way it is: the map maker needs not identify processes of plate tectonics or histories of urban planning any more than the international political theorist need give a history of post-Westphalia nation-states or historical claims to territory by states. Rather the cartographer explains the environment with reference to the relative location of elements within it, for example, a building adjacent to a crossroads, a train line parallel to a highway or a one way street passing through a built up area. Like the theorist of international relations, the cartographer must identify the relationships between the elements in the environment that is modelled so as to provide utility for the person who would use the map as a tool by which to navigate the terrain. Though the rela-

---

[632] Tangentially, maps as political objects are considered in Arthur Klinghoffer. 2006. *The Power of Projections: How Maps Reflect Global Politics and History*. Westport, CT: Greenwood.
[633] Kissane. 2008a, p.6.

166

tionships are depicted visually, as opposed to the theorist who must use language and logic, the goal of the map maker remains the same as the theorist in that – if the goal of explanation is not fulfilled – the map is of very little use at all.

The third and final goal of the cartographer is prediction. In the same way that analysts and scholars can extrapolate predictions from theories of international relations, the user of a map can make certain predictions about the mapped environment from the chart the cartographer presents. Thus, for example, a person looking at a map can predict the best route to take to arrive at building A or devise a train journey between points B and C with reference to a map of rail routes. Also, just as the utility of a theory of international relations for a policymaker can be judged on the validity of the predictions it offers, so too the quality of a map and the work of the cartographer can be judged by considering the utility it offers for the person who wishes to make their way across the mapped environment. Thus, for example, a map which identifies a road as one-way south is likely to be of less utility when the road is, in fact, one-way north. Again, scale is all important here as a map that is useful for navigating a short distance in a city may not be useful for the person who wishes to travel a long way through the same city or even further afield. Yet, like the analyst of international affairs choosing a theory with which to analyse a political environment, the user of a map must first make sure that the environment defined by the map actually matches where they would wish to explore. Maps, like theories, are necessarily limited in their descriptive and explanative scope.

Yet another parallel between cartography and theory making lies in the parsimony that both the theorist and the cartographer seek. Like the theorist, the map maker's skill is representing a complex environment simply, subjectively choosing the most significant elements of the environment and excluding all that does not add to the fundamental understanding of the end user. As a result, the map maker can take a complex urban crossroad and reduce it to a simple '+', perhaps only noting the names of the streets that intersect. In doing so, the cartographer has deliberately excluded all other elements that exist in and around that crossroad: the advertising on the billboards, the names and numbers on the buildings, the markings on the road, the signs that warn of potholes and the traffic signals that determine the legality and legitimacy of a driver's entry into the crossroad. Every one of these things could prove significant for the user of the map yet all are excluded: the map maker does not seek to represent reality perfectly but to provide a parsimonious representation of the most significant features of that reality. In seeking parsimony the map maker excludes most of the environment and his decisions are judged right or wrong by the utility of the end product in describing, explaining and predicting the mapped reality.

The Costs of Cartographical and Theoretical Parsimony

It is obvious, then, that the parsimony of the cartographer comes at a 'cost' of representing reality. A map, of course, cannot represent reality perfectly and its depiction can only ever be a simplification of a complex reality. Even a photograph – perfect in its representation of an observable moment – cannot truly depict the world lacking, as it does, the possibility of depicting the wind or the weather or of translating movement within the frame of the picture. But a map, unlike a photograph, makes no claims to being 'truth'; rather the map makes a point of its parsimony but also realises that this parsimony comes at a cost. In the paragraphs that follow the costs of this parsimony as well as the folly of *not* seeking parsimony in producing a map will be explored before the same assessment is made of the pursuit of parsimony in international relations theory. In concluding this section it will be clear that there are some costs that arise from the search for parsimony that are too high to bear, whether or not the pursuer is making maps or writing grand theories of international affairs.

A map which seeks parsimony above all else is of little use to anyone approaching the environment with little or no knowledge of the area. The utility of the map – like the utility of a theory of international politics – is far more important than its parsimony. Consider the example below (Figure 4.1, overleaf) of a map taken from the Analogue Art Project and depicting Brooklyn, New York.

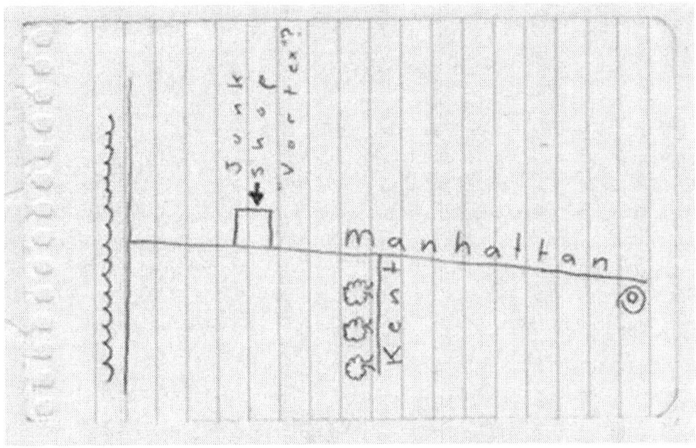

Figure 4.1: Brooklyn 'Mud Map'[634]

So parsimonious is this map that only two roads, a single store, some trees and the river are included in depicting a borough that is home to 2.5 million people. The map includes no scale and a person moving right to left on 'Manhattan' has limited information by which to find the 'Junk Shop' building. Not only are insignificant elements of the environment excluded (as they are in all maps) but also other elements that would allow a person to identify the exact location of the 'Junk Shop' are excluded. Indeed, all a user knows for sure is that the 'Junk Shop' is located on 'Manhattan' between 'Kent' and the river and not the exact location or the relative size of the building sought. A person unfamiliar with the area who would use this map to explore Brooklyn would find little utility in the obvious parsimony.

However, a map which fails to pursue parsimony and draws too many unnecessary connections between insignificant elements of the environment is no better than the map in Figure 4.1 (above). Indeed, by neglecting parsimony and attempting to include all elements of the environment in the cartographical depiction, the map maker has failed; not in describing or predicting the environment but in explaining clearly the elements that are significant for the map user. No matter the potentially significant impact that small elements such as potholes, children's crossings and kerbside

---

[634] Analogue Art Map. 2006. *Brooklyn Mud Map*. [20 February 2008] http://tinyurl.com/3x42jv.

parking ranks may hold for the map user, there is little utility in including all in a map. Consider:

> The person who seeks to describe to a friend a cross-city route would mention major landmarks, suggested streets and any false turn that is likely to lead his friend astray. In either case the map-maker chooses to exclude largely irrelevant elements of the landscape in favour of the essential items by which the landscape can be determined. Thus, even a city-scale map would likely exclude the potholes on Main Street...Yet any driver will be aware that potholes are potentially very dangerous obstacles to a vehicle and, similarly, any customs agent is aware of the significance of the geography surrounding a nation's border; why, then, can such features be ignored by the mapmaker?[635]

The answer, of course, is that the map maker should not include that which does not add to the explanation of phenomena in the system being mapped. The cartographer must make decisions which lead to cartographical parsimony else he presents nothing more than a photograph of the city: perfect in depicting a single moment but of little utility for finding one's way through the streets. The map maker must therefore balance his efforts between the ultra-simple mud-map and ultra-inclusive map of everything.

For the theorist of international relations parsimony is also a key to constructing a useful theory. Also like the cartographer, avoiding parsimony leads to a situation where the end theoretical result is of little use to any analyst or scholar. As Waltz reminds us, there are innumerable factors present within the international system and a theory that attempts to include them all is not a theory at all.[636] To avoid including the unnecessary Waltz argues that the theorist must take one of four courses: isolation, abstraction, aggregation or idealisation.[637] The first forces the theorist to seek parsimony by focussing on only a small part of the wider system, allowing the chosen elements to remain static while all else is allowed to change. The second, more analogous to the mapmaker, seeks parsimony by constructing a theory by excluding certain elements altogether to the benefit of the included elements. The third, aggregation, "requires lumping disparate elements together according to criteria derived from a theoretical purpose".[638] The fourth, idealisation, requires the theorist to as-

---

[635] Kissane. 2008, p.6.
[636] Waltz. 1979, p.10.
[637] Waltz. 1979, p.10.
[638] Waltz. 1979, p.10.

sume that theoretical perfection has been attained despite the fact, and knowledge by the theorist, that this is impossible. Theories of international relations that offer meat for Occam's Razor are of little use to the analyst and parsimony remains a key to achieving the three goals of description, explanation and prediction.

Yet, like the map maker, too much parsimony leads to problems for international theorists, too. Looking at three realist examples – the classical realism of Morgenthau, the structural realism of Waltz and the offensive realism of Mearsheimer – allows the problems that arise through the pursuit of parsimony in realist international relations theory to be explored. In each case these theorists simplify the system under study, choosing to exclude actors and elements that they have deemed to be relatively insignificant. Yet in each case, too, such simplifications render the theory either unable or inadequate to describe, explain and predict major events in the international system. While each of these realist approaches is different in their assumptions about international politics and the actors that engage in international politics, there are two assumptions, both made for reasons of theoretical parsimony, that are common to all three: a focus on nation-states and the assumption of systemic anarchy. In the paragraphs that follow it will be shown how in each case these two and other assumptions made in the pursuit of parsimony ultimately come at a cost to theoretical utility.

Morgenthau's realism seeks parsimony through a series of assumptions the classical realist makes about the international political system. His second principle of political realism (state interests are defined in terms of power) is one of these assumptions as it denies all other motivations for states acting in pursuit of their interests.[639] This presents a problem for explaining some state actions which appear altruistic, an example being the international efforts against South Africa's apartheid policy. While it is possible to reduce all international political behaviour, even altruistic behaviour, "to individual rewards and interest explanations", in reality it seems more likely that something else is motivating the actions of states.[640] As Audie Klotz argues:

---

[639] Morgenthau. 1993, p.5.
[640] Audie Klotz. 1995. *Norms in International Relations: The Struggle Against Apartheid*. New York: Cornell University Press, p.13.

In practice, actions are motivated by a complex combination of self-interest (the reciprocity relationship ensures our receiving gifts in the future), self-affirmation (we all like to feel good about ourselves), and group interest (we like to make our friends happy).[641]

Actions taken by states to fulfil the last of these motivations fall outside of Morgenthau's theoretical calculations. So too do most of the actions taken by non-state actors as Morgenthau, like other classical realists, simplifies international relations by focussing on what he holds to be the most significant political actors, the nation-states. He further simplifies international relations by outlining where the power of a state lies, excluding elements which would become known as 'soft power' in later years.[642] Finally, Morgenthau seeks parsimony by assuming that international politics takes place under conditions of anarchy and argued that it was this anarchy that allowed, though did not cause, conflict in the international system.[643]

In Waltz's work the parsimony is more pronounced. Indeed, Waltzian theory has been reduced by some to only two assumptions: the system is anarchic and that states seek to survive.[644] Again, any other motivations for state action must be subsumed beneath this notion of survival which, admittedly, is a little easier for the analyst to achieve than with Morgenthau's interest-based action. Indeed, for neorealists, all state actions – joining a coalition, fighting a war, sending foreign aid – are elements in a wider strategy of survival. This parsimonious explanation, however, is problematic when considering actions that states take that effectively *decrease* their chances of survival as an independent international actor. Examples include the ceding of sovereignty to international organisations, voluntarily divorcing the state of its own central banking policy and making decisions in times of crisis that to any rational observer would seem to be devastating to the survival chances of the state, Germany's two-front strategy in World War Two being a prime example of the latter.[645] Similarly to

---

[641] Klotz. 1995, p.13.

[642] Morgenthau. 1993, pp.124-165. On soft power see Nye. 1990; Nye. 2002; Nye. 2004.

[643] James Speer lyrically suggested that Morgenthau had "identified the ecology of international politics as one of anarchy". Keith Shimko agrees, stating that "although anarchy was an important part of international life in Morgenthau's analysis, he did not stress the *explanatory* power of anarchy" (emphasis added). See James Speer. 1968. 'Hans Morgenthau and the World State.' *World Politics* 20(2): 207-227, p.223; Keith Shimko. 1992. 'Realism, Neorealism, and American Liberalism.' *The Review of Politics* 54(2): 281-301, p.293.

[644] Mearsheimer. 2006a, p.112.

[645] Edward Shils and Morris Janowitz. 1948. 'Cohesion and Disintegration in the Wehrmacht in World War II.' *The Public Opinion Quarterly* 12(2): 280-315, p.302; McCormick. 2002, p.10.

Morgenthau, Waltz's state-centric and anarchy-centric assessment of the international political realm leaves his theory open to criticisms of excessive parsimony. Indeed, in the wake of the Cold War, some researchers, including Richard Lebow and Paul Schroeder, pronounced that realist approaches such as Waltz's were fatally flawed, prompting Waltz to reply in his own defence that the fundamentals of the system had not changed.[646] Perhaps; but Waltz's super-simplification of international politics leaves his theory open to charges of ignoring reality and ignoring the utility of his realism for the analyst, too.

Turn to Mearsheimer's offensive realism and a relatively less parsimonious realist approach is found, at least in comparison to Waltz. Mearsheimer himself reduces his theory to a set of five premises: the system is anarchic; all great powers have some offensive military capability; states can never be certain about other states' intentions; states seek to survive; and great powers are rational actors or strategic calculators.[647] Like Waltz, the same objections to states motivated by survival exist but his focus on the military capability of states is also problematic. By focussing on the military capabilities of states there is a real chance – one evidenced in Mearsheimer's own work – that hypotheses and predictions based on the theory will emerge that are divorced from reality.[648] Mearsheimer's focus on states and great powers, which are also states, and their military capabilities are also parsimonious moves but one that has been criticised for limiting the theory's utility as:

> ...by limiting analysis to state actors, to nuclear strategy, to great powers and by assuming that states would choose the 'rational' path – all of which are demanded by a realism founded upon anarchy – the smaller, sub-national but significantly influential events that would result in all of Mearsheimer's scenarios failing to eventuate are effectively ignored.[649]

But also like his predecessors, Mearsheimer's reliance on an assumption of anarchy, while parsimonious, also leaves his approach open to attacks on its utility. The anarchy that drives the search for military capabilities and results in the security competi-

---

[646] Lebow. 1994; Schroeder. 1994; Waltz. 2000, pp.5-6.
[647] Mearsheimer. 2006a, p.112.
[648] See Mearsheimer. 1990a. For a critique of Mearsheimer's offensive realism as expressed in that article see Kissane. 2007b.
[649] Kissane. 2007b, p.398.

tion and dilemmas of offensive realism is not of much use in explaining why states would join together in a continental wide European Union. Neither is Mearsheimer's assumption of anarchy of much utility in explaining the continued cooperation by states in alliances such as NATO when, according to his offensive realist dogma, such an alliance should have folded in the same way its opponent alliance, the Warsaw Pact, did. Once again, the parsimony of realism has come at a cost to explaining the actual events in the international system.

Conclusion: From Theory, Through Parsimony, To Utility

This section has defined what a theory is, how it is distinguished from 'laws', 'models' and 'paradigms' and noted how the realist approaches thus far considered in the book can all be considered theories of IR. It has established the necessary elements of a theory of IR, the goals of IR theory and explained how good theory must deliver both utility and parsimony. Drawing on an analogous cartographical example, this section has outlined the costs of parsimony in depicting the real world and explained how similar costs exist for theories of IR. Specifically, it has considered the theoretical approaches of Morgenthau, Waltz and Mearsheimer and argued that, in each case, the pursuit of parsimony by each theorist has resulted in significant limitations in the utility of their approach in explaining major events in the international system. While it is acknowledged that no theory can necessarily explain every event in a complex political system, these three popular approaches have failed to explain major events such as regional alliances, the collapse of empires and the outbreak of systemic war. As a result, it has argued that the best theory is that which balances these costs against the utility of the theory. The question becomes, then, in assessing realist theory, has parsimony been achieved at a too-high cost to theoretical and explanatory utility?

The Assumption of Anarchy and the Quest for Realist Parsimony

In a 1999 article, Jeffrey Legro and Andrew Moravcsik outlined the many assumptions of realism and those who self-identify as realists in modern international relations.[650] Despite their differences, though, Jack Donnelly and, indeed, this book have argued that there is at least one assumption about the international system that all realists hold in common, namely, anarchy.[651] However, like other common assumptions amongst realists, such as state-centricity or power balancing state strategies, it is one that is made in the realist's theoretical quest for parsimony. While mentioned in relation to the assessment of Morgenthau's, Waltz's and Mearsheimer's theories above, this section will take a detailed look at the role anarchy plays as a tool of parsimony in each of the theorists and realist approaches considered thus far in this book. Each of the nine realist approaches will be considered in historical order and the means by which each approach uses anarchy to provide a simpler depiction of the international reality will be outlined. In concluding this section it will be argued that every realist approach uses anarchy as a tool of theoretical parsimony, opening the proverbial door to the section that follows which will assess the cost of this parsimony on theoretical and explanatory utility.

Thucydides

This book has identified five theorists as prototypical classical realists: the historian Thucydides, the political theorists Machiavelli and Hobbes, the former diplomat Carr and the scholar Morgenthau. It is Thucydides whose work emerged first and his *History of the Peloponnesian War* that was the focus of this book's assessment of his theoretical contribution in the first chapter of this book.[652] While the role of anarchy in this history is clear, the role anarchy plays as an element in simplifying the international reality is less so.[653] Reference to the Melian Dialogue, however, and a comparison of the contrasting Melian and Athenian positions reveals just how anarchy, or at least its implications, is a parsimonious move on behalf of the Greek historian.[654] The position of the citizens of Melos on the nature of international relations is reminiscent of modern idealism: appeals to justice, inter-state discussion and debate are all elements which the Melians return to in attempting to persuade the Athenian envoys to

---

[650] Legro and Moravcsik. 1999.
[651] Donnelly. 2000, pp.81-103.
[652] Thucydides. 1998.
[653] See discussion in The first chapter of this book for the place of anarchy in Thucydides' canonical work.
[654] See Thucydides. 1998, pp.167-176.

spare their island from harm.[655] As the Athenians would comment, the Melian's position on international society suggested they were "the only men who deem the future to be more certain than the present, and regard things unseen as already realised...in fond anticipation", the envoys clearly suggesting, with Thucydidean endorsement, that their understanding of the international system was flawed.[656]

In contrast, the Athenians presented what Thucydides alludes to via his account of their victory as the correct interpretation of the nature of the international system. The Athenian asserted that both sides,

> ...know that in discussions of human affairs the question of justice only enters where there is an equal power to enforce it, and that the powerful exact what they can, and the weak grant what they must...[657]

This pronouncement is not only a stipulation as to the nature of anarchy but a direct explication of theoretical parsimony. Unlike the alternative and idealistic conception of the international offered by the Melians, the Athenian position reduces the complexities of international relations to three elements: powerful actors, weak actors and a systemic structure that allows the former to exact from the latter what it chooses. The assumption of anarchy in the Thucydidean history simplifies the international environment to the point where only power (not explicitly defined) is the determining factor for explaining international behaviour. Thucydides, through his sympathetic retelling of the Athenian struggle in the ancient world, endorses this notion of anarchy and the parsimonious effect it has for explaining and predicting the victors and the vanquished across the geopolitical landscape of Greece.

Machiavelli

Machiavelli also uses the assumption of anarchy as a tool of parsimony. The Italian political theorist, most notably in his work *The Prince*, describes the international realm of European affairs to be one of competition, consistent warfare and inter-royal disputes. Like Thucydides, he divides the world of states into two groups: the pre-

---

[655] Thucydides. 1998, pp.168-169.
[656] Thucydides. 1998, p.176.
[657] Thucydides. 1998, p.168.

pared and the unprepared. And, like Thucydides, the former are the rational and successful in Machiavelli's work, the latter fodder for a prepared Prince's army.[658] Machiavelli's anarchy, too, is reminiscent of that of Thucydides. He describes a system of 'self-sufficiency' where his aggressive advice to his Prince is the only logical choice.[659] Indeed, only a system other than the self-sufficient anarchy that Machiavelli describes would open the possibility of alternate strategies for states and Princes. However, under Machiavellian anarchy, only his strategies of deception, cunning and consistent refusal to rely on others for assistance are potentially successful strategies for states and Princes and further, by reducing the complexities of pan-European politics to a world of self-sufficient anarchy, Machiavelli has mirrored Thucydides in yet another way: his pursuit of parsimony.

Machiavelli employs the notion of an anarchic European system where each Prince must be self-sufficient in order to simplify the options on offer to the Prince who seeks to maintain control of his territory and population. In doing so, Machiavelli limits the possibility for explaining alliances between states of which there were many at the time of his writing *The Prince*.[660] Further, while providing a simple canvas for Machiavelli to paint his Princely strategies, he admits he cannot account for the nature of fortune and chance in determining outcomes in the European sphere. Indeed, in the closing passages of *The Prince* Machiavelli admits that he considers "it to be true that Fortune is the arbiter of one half of our actions".[661] This admission and the rationale that accompanies it is proof positive that Machiavelli knew he was offering not a close depiction of the nature of inter-state relations but a simpler, anarchic version which could not account for the role of small, non-state and non-human nature causes for action. In contrast to the strict instructions to state rulers in previous chapters, in these final passages Machiavelli writes:

> In the case of two cautious men, we also see that one reaches his goal while the other does not. And likewise, two men prosper equally employing two different means, one

---

[658] Machiavelli. 2005, pp.38-39.

[659] Machiavelli. 2005, p.38.

[660] Machiavelli made reference in *The Prince* to alliances between states but warned against them, particularly in the case of weaker states seeking a stronger partner. See Jesse Reeves. 1941. 'The Interrelation of the Domestic and Foreign Policies of a Nation.' *Annals of the American Academy of Political and Social Science* 218: 1-8, p.1.

[661] Machiavelli. 2005, p.84.

being cautious and the other impetuous...two men acting differently can reach the same result; and of two men acting identically, one reaches his goal and the other does not.[662]

The difference between the outcomes can only be explained by fortune or chance, neither of which is held to play a part in the strictly anarchical realm where Machiavelli urges Princes to take rational positions of strength in the face of assured opposition by other Princes in the system. Though he recognises the complexities brought about by chance in the system, Machiavelli is unable to account for them with his parsimonious theory. He has thus produced a simple theory of interstate relations but one that even he himself admits cannot account for "one half of our actions" in interstate affairs.[663]

Hobbes

Thomas Hobbes, too, introduces an anarchic international system as a tool of theoretical parsimony. His claim that under anarchy there is "no power able to overawe...all" and that this, in turn, leads to competition between actors that then ensures a life that is "solitary, poore, nasty, brutish, and short" is clearly a parsimonious construct: his "state of nature" an philosophical exercise rather than a depiction of reality.[664] As Ed Miller notes:

> The theoretical state of nature is, thus, very important. But it is only theoretical. In spite of its advantages of freedom and equality, we do not, nor can we, actually live in such a state, at least not for long.[665]

Bertrand Russell agrees, noting that the anarchy that Hobbes describes can always account for the "ferocity and destructiveness of war" in the international system.[666] Yet it is more difficult to account for international cooperation under Hobbesian anarchy. The evolution of domestic cooperation, of course, lies at the heart of Hobbes' *Leviathan* but international cooperation is suggested to be impossible in a world

---

[662] Machiavelli. 2005, p.85.
[663] Machiavelli. 2005, p.84.
[664] Hobbes. 2002, pp.56-57.
[665] Ed Miller. 1996. *Questions that Matter: An Invitation to Philosophy.* 4th edition. New York: McGraw-Hill, p.510.
[666] Russell. 1993, p.541.

where only three motivations – competition, diffidence and glory – drive international action.[667]

Yet Hobbes' international anarchy, like his realist predecessors, is simply a tool by which to simplify the observable world. Hobbes rejects the possibility of international cooperation despite the fact that he embraces such cooperation at the domestic level. His theory cannot account for the international cooperation that does occur and did occur at the time he wrote his canon. His theory ignores the complexities of the coloniser-colonised relationship in favour of a strong-weak dichotomy; his theory rejects international altruism as unnatural and impossible; his approach reduces the international system to a number of competing actors in a hostile environment where winners survive and losers do not. The limitations of the approach are readily apparent and his theory came under sharp criticism from John Locke, who argued that Hobbes' aggressive 'state of nature' was not at all a depiction of reality:

> It is often asked as a mighty objection, where are, or éver were, there any men in such a state of Nature?...[I]t is not every compact that puts an end to the state of Nature between men, but only this one of agreeing together mutually to enter into one community, and make one body politic; other promises and compacts men may make one with another, and yet still be in the state of Nature. The promises and bargains for truck, etc., between the two men in Soldania, in or between a Swiss and an Indian, in the woods of America, are binding to them, though they are perfectly in a state of Nature in reference to one another for truth, and keeping of faith belongs to men as men, and not as members of society.[668]

Locke here suggests what this book does: Hobbes' depiction of anarchy in the form of his 'state of nature' over-simplifies the reality of human interaction. The competitive, untrusting, aggressive 'state of nature' Hobbes describes does not reflect the more complex world where Native Americans and Swiss citizens can maintain trust and cooperate without recourse to the overwhelming power. Hobbes has indeed achieved parsimony but he has done so at a price.

---

[667] Hobbes. 2002, p.56.

[668] John Locke. 2005. *Two Treatises of Government*. [25 February 2008] http://tinyurl.com/2rytcw, p.6.

Carr

For EH Carr, anarchy is described as setting the system in a state of inescapable "potential war".[669] This systemic structure drives the foreign policies of states and empires, forcing them to arm themselves militarily and economically against other states.[670] The constant need to secure defences and the fear that other states will attack are a direct result of an anarchy where states maintain a hunger for power.[671] Yet in Carr's realism, too, we find that anarchy is again employed as a tool of parsimony, depicting a world of constant security competition despite Carr's admission that, from time to time, states do indeed act altruistically.[672] Carr's rejection of what he terms international idealism and utopianism, being the sorts of conceptions of the system that produced the failure that was the League of Nations, in favour of an anarchy is clearly a step towards simplifying international relations. The dangers of anarchy that Carr expounds allow him to focus on the military power and, to a lesser extent, the economic power of the state for, under anarchy, what other sort of state power can be significant enough to ensure the survival of the state? Anarchy facilitates Carr's focus on such elements of national power but this simpler conception of the system also leaves his approach open to attack.

How, for example, would Carr account for the successes of international organisations such as the United Nations?[673] This international body is an example of an institution that has endorsed and achieved peaceful change in the international system, something that Carr rejects as a possibility in international affairs.[674] Indeed, under Carr's anarchy, notions of a "world legislature" and a "world court" are discarded as "purely utopian and muddle-headed" yet, in the United Nations General Assembly and bodies such as the International Court of Justice and the International Criminal Court, the world has arguably made embryonic steps towards both.[675] Under the anarchy Carr describes it is argued that states are unlikely to submit to international trea-

---

[669] Carr. 2001, p.102.

[670] Carr. 2001, pp.102-106.

[671] Carr. 2001, pp.104-105.

[672] Carr. 2001, pp.144-145.

[673] The author notes that the United Nations has been responsible for many international failures. Not recognising the obvious successes of the institution, though, would be short-sighted.

[674] Carr. 2001, p.202.

[675] Carr. 2001, p.202.

ties and – should they choose to do so – will not feel themselves bound to them when their national interest is at stake.[676] Yet in the more complex world of international law nation-states regularly submit themselves to treaties and, in the case of some treaties, pay penalties for acting contrary to the treaty's decree. Far from international anarchy and the lack of an arbiter leading to a drop in respect for international treaties, many states in the modern international system willingly submit to treaties and feel bound by their interstate agreements. Carr's anarchy, while simplifying the system and providing a base on which to theorise international relations, proves to be very different from the realities of international life.

Morgenthau

Anarchy plays an important role in Hans Morgenthau's realism and, again, it serves as a tool to simplify international relations for theoretical reasons. Morgenthau argues that the international system is decentralised and, as a result, states must fend for themselves in an amoral, unpoliced, largely law-free system.[677] Morgenthau's theory simplifies the international system to the point where states are the only significant actors, international governance does not exist and is unlikely to exist, states balance the power in the system by forming alliances and cooperation between states is inevitably short.[678] Yet, like Carr, the observable reality is very different to the world of competition and power balancing that Morgenthau presents in his theory.

Consider, for example, Morgenthau's argument that the nature of international politics means that alliances between states can only ever be short term. In Chapter 12 of *Politics among Nations* Morgenthau states:

> ...alliances are typically of temporary duration and most prevalent in wartime...the interests for which the war was waged is bound to yield, once victory is won and the peace treaties are signed, to the traditionally separate and frequently incompatible interests of the individual nations.[679]

---

[676] Carr. 2001, p.176.

[677] Morgenthau. 1993, pp.254-255.

[678] Morgenthau specifies that national loyalties will always overcome international loyalties and – for that reason – no international police force could ever exist, at least in a permanent form. See Morgenthau. 1993, p.297.

[679] Morgenthau. 1993, p.201.

Under the anarchy Morgenthau describes allies must always be careful as today's friend might be tomorrow's enemy and, in this, he echoes Machiavelli.[680] He further explains that the alliances that last longest are narrowly constructed and serving a very specific common interest.[681] Yet the reality of the twentieth century saw a broadly constructed military and security alliance in the shape of the North Atlantic Treaty Organisation (NATO) survive the fall of its rival and *raison d'être*, the Soviet Union, go on to prosper as a security pact facing no real opposition in the post-Cold War world and to co-opt some of its former foes. NATO stands as a strong counter-example to the anarchic world Morgenthau's theory paints: if cooperation is temporary under anarchy, how can the NATO alliance in the post-Cold War world be explained? If states seek to balance the power of an anarchic system, why do smaller, weaker states seek to join an alliance with the world's sole superpower? Morgenthau's anarchic backdrop makes international relations easier to understand but his parsimony belies the reality in the international system which is rather more complex. Like his realist forebears, Morgenthau has employed anarchy to allow for a simpler description of international reality – and also like his forebears he would not be the last to do so.

Waltz

Kenneth Waltz's realism took a paradigm that had highlighted the evils of human nature and sought to make the realist approach a scientific one. Unlike his predecessors, though, Waltz explicitly identified the international system as anarchic and suggested that this systemic anarchy was what drove state and actor behaviour in the international realm. Anarchy is the means by which Waltz distinguishes the international from the domestic but it also a depiction of the international that is parsimonious. While Waltz is sure to make clear that his "theory is not an edifice of truth and not a reproduction of reality", it is a depiction of reality, albeit on a simpler scale.[682] Once he assumes anarchy as a systemic structure Waltz need only add a second premise – that states seek to survive – to found his theory of structural realism.[683] Yet almost

---

[680] Morgenthau. 1993, pp.200-201.
[681] Morgenthau. 1993, p.201.
[682] Waltz. 1979, p.8.
[683] Mearsheimer. 2006a, p.112.

from the time he published *Theory of International Politics* Waltz's theory was criticised for its parsimony, specifically its presentation of a hierarchic domestic/anarchic international dichotomy.

As John Ruggie argues, Waltz's assumption of anarchy means that he misses a "dimension of change" in his explanation of international relations.[684] Ruggie points to the transition between medieval times and the present and notes that Waltz's assumption of international anarchy is not useful in explaining this evolution.[685] Neither is Waltzian anarchy – under which states are inherently competitive – any more useful than its classical cousin for understanding much of the cooperation in the post-Cold War period. Richard Lebow notes the failure of structural realism to explain and account for the collapse of the Soviet Union and the withdrawal of a superpower from the global stage.[686] Indeed, Lebow notes that in the post-Cold War system:

> International relations among the developed democracies have taken on many of the characteristics of relationships in domestic societies. An increasing number of states have begun to acknowledge the necessity of regulating their political and economic intercourse through rules, norms and agreements. As in domestic relations, this high degree of compliance is motivated by enlightened self-interest.[687]

In contrast, structural realist anarchy is presented as unchanging, Waltz going so far as reject any change in the anarchic structure at all and suggesting that the evolution in state relations that Lebow points to is simply a 'within-system change' that occurs "all the time".[688] Of course, the reason Waltz must make this argument is that his theory collapses when the foundation of anarchy is removed. Waltz himself has admitted that "if the conditions of a theory has changed, the theory no longer applies" and a change of the shape and magnitude that Lebow suggests has taken place then Waltz's approach is essentially finished.[689] Parsimonious as the Waltzian assumption of anarchy is for differentiating the domestic and the international, cannot fully account for the changes that are clearly emerging in a post-bipolar world.

---

[684] Ruggie. 1986, p.148.
[685] Ruggie. 1986, pp.141-148.
[686] Lebow. 1994.
[687] Lebow. 1994, p.277.
[688] Waltz. 2000, p.5.
[689] Waltz. 2000, p.5.

Mearsheimer

Anarchy is similarly foundational in the offensive realism of John Mearsheimer. Indeed, Mearsheimer's first assumption about the international system is that it is a anarchic, perhaps reflecting the impact that the structural approach of Waltz had had on the discipline by the time he came to construct the offensive theory of realism.[690] Also in line with structural realism is the offensive realist's use of anarchy as a tool for making a complex international system easier to understand. On this point there is little debate, indeed other theorists have commented that his strict adherence to systemic anarchy is part of what helps him to sharpen the theoretical issues dividing realism and Institutionalist theories.[691] Yet these same theorists also identify the failures that this commitment to anarchy by the offensive realists present when considering the actual and observable international system. In particular, offensive realism and its reliance on a conception of the system as competitive and anarchic fails to account for peaceful transformations, states surrendering sovereignty to institutions and those same institutions playing a role in establishing the interests of the states in the system.

Robert Keohane and Lisa Martin, for example, point to Mearsheimer's anarchy as blinding him to the significance of the politico-economic factors in the international system as opposed to the military factors which are often the focus of his research.[692] As well, Keohane and Martin argue that the competitive anarchy that Mearsheimer paints under which alliances and cooperation between states is limited and transient does not match the observable reality and, further, the implication that such cooperation is easy to come by when state interests merge is also unsupported.[693] Transformations in inter-state relations (such as from Cold War division to more inclusive European integration since the Cold War) are similarly poorly accounted for under Mearsheimer's anarchy.[694] As one theorist argued in relation to Mearsheimer's 1990 article 'Back to the Future':

---

[690] Mearsheimer. 2006a, p.112.
[691] Keohane and Martin. 1995, p.39.
[692] Keohane and Martin. 1995, pp.43-44.
[693] Keohane and Martin. 1995, p.50.
[694] Kissane. 2007b.

184

In terms of nuclear proliferation, the post-Cold War strategic environment in Europe has been distinguished not by its instability and inherent dangers, as Mearsheimer imagined, but by a stability, economic growth and peace that characterises the European Union today. To be blunt, when it came to the post-Cold War reality of Central, Eastern and Western Europe, realists like John Mearsheimer got it almost completely wrong.[695]

Thus, the critic can construct a list of failures that flow from the decision by Mearsheimer to simplify the international system by assuming it is anarchic. Such a list would include the theory's failure to reflect the international reality when it comes to international economic interactions, instances of interstate alliance, cooperation between international actors, the ease of forming coalitions in the international system, regional integration efforts and stability under conditions of multipolarity. The link between Mearsheimer's pursuit of theoretical parsimony through the assumption of anarchy and his consequent failure to describe, explain or predict international politics with any great utility is, as with his fellow realists, again clear.

Prisoner's Dilemma

The realism of the Prisoner's Dilemma is nothing if not parsimonious. The reduction of a world of states, institutions, norms, rules and calculations to a simple two-player game or, in some of the literature, an iterated two-player game is parsimonious in the extreme.[696] Anarchy in the Prisoner's Dilemma is witnessed in the lack of an arbiter to referee the players, the salience of relative gains in determining best strategies, the lack of complete information available to each player and a reality wherein neither player can be sure of what their one-time ally will choose to do. The two-by-two grid that is the pictorial representation of the game represents anarchy by, ironically, failing to include any reference to it. By this it is meant that anarchy is implicit in the game and the rules that guide the interaction of the players necessitate an anarchic background. Yet this anarchy and the game itself is a significant simplification of the international system and the interactions between actors present in it. Indeed, in the case of the Prisoner's Dilemma, perhaps more than the other realist approaches thus

---

[695] Kissane. 2007b

[696] Axelrod. 1980a; Axelrod. 1980b; Orkin. 1987.

far identified, the use of anarchy as a tool of parsimony is clear and its drawbacks most obvious.

Though some realists claim that international politics is but "the Prisoner's Dilemma iterated for many moves", international politics is in fact far more complex than this view would allow.[697] The reduction of complex international manoeuvring such as dyadic arms races and disarmament to mere iterations of a game under anarchy belies the significant external factors far removed from trustworthiness, second-guessing opponents and the lack of an overarching power.[698] Cooperation is proven to be circumstantial, limited and prone to dissention under the anarchy of the Prisoner's Dilemma yet the real world offers countless examples of states cooperating even when acting on incomplete information. As well, there are a number of examples where states have cooperated with other states long after it has provided any tangible relative gain. Consider the Soviet Union-German non-aggression pact that was maintained by the Soviets right up until the day that German forces invaded in 1941 and in spite of clear German recruitment campaigns for what would become Operation Barbarossa. Indeed, the Soviets, via the German-Soviet Trade Agreement, continued to supply the Germans with grain, fuel oil, cotton and iron though intelligence sources within Germany were warning the Soviet leadership of German plans to invade. The anarchy of the Prisoner's Dilemma seems incapable of explaining this continued cooperation by the Soviets in the face of incomplete but compelling information that it was not in the national interest to do so. While the Prisoner's Dilemma game offers a simpler view of international relations, it is again one that might be described as *overly* parsimonious.

---

[697] Axelrod. 1980a, p.3.

[698] Snyder, for example, is one theorist who suggests that arms races and disarmament efforts can be considered as practical examples of the Prisoner's Dilemma in action. However, as John Borrie has argued, it is possible in real world disarmament negotiations for states to effectively change the payoffs for each actor *during the game* so as to push a rival or urge an ally to move in a certain way. See Glenn Snyder. 1971. '"Prisoner's Dilemma" and "Chicken" Models in International Politics.' *International Studies Quarterly* 15(1): 66-103, p.68; John Borrie. 2006. 'Cooperation and Defection in the Conference on Disarmament.' In *Thinking Outside the Box in Multilateral Disarmament and Arms Control Negotiations*, edited by J Borrie & V Randin. Geneva: United Nations Institute for Disarmament Research, pp.89-108.

Neoclassical Realism

The final realist approach this book has considered is neoclassical realism. Previously this book has described this part of the realist paradigm as filling the gap Waltz left in the realist approach.[699] The differences between the neoclassicalists, the classicalists and the structuralists lies more in their conception of the interests, motivations and expected behaviours of states rather than their conception of the nature of anarchy. That said, the significance of anarchy is somewhat different to the structuralists in that it is not a central defining feature but – in the spirit of the offensive and defensive realists – a background reality on which the drama of international politics is played out. Similar to the anarchy of the classical realists, though, the neoclassical anarchy expounded by Cha, Christenson and Rose simplifies the international environment and does not truly reflect the international reality.

Neoclassical realists reject the power calculations of a Mearsheimer or a Waltz rightly recognising the uncertainties of inter-state relations. It is strange, then, that the founding assumption of anarchy common to Waltz and Mearsheimer is maintained, particularly in light of the obvious elements of certainty it lends to the assessment of international politics. While the neoclassical realists place much of the uncertainty in the system at the level of the state they reject the possibility of uncertainty being a part or at the heart of the system itself. In essence, the neoclassical approach rejects the 'billiard ball' construct of international relations with its bound and certain system and predictable actors and instead offers an equally bound and certain system with less predictable actors; anarchy remains and is no more complex or exact than the neoclassicalist's paradigmatic predecessors. Problems remain in explaining long periods of broadly sustained peace, the integration of previously hostile states into a union so strong that violent conflict between members and security alliances that endure in the face of no significant threat, leaving states to bandwagon instead of balance. Anomalies like these – at least anomalies for the neoclassicalists – cannot be explained with reference to an anarchic system of the style with which they base their analysis of the system. Cooperation between competitors, especially long term cooperation, remains a problem despite the allowances made by neoclassicalists with regards to uncertainties at the unit level.

---

[699] See Anarchy in Offensive Realism, Game Theory and Neo-Classical Realism.

Conclusion: Anarchy in Realism as a Tool of Parsimony

Whether in Thucydidean histories or political game theory, classical approaches to the system or more recent structural theories, mid-millennial political philosophy or interwar realist reflection, anarchy has been consistently employed by theorists across the realist paradigm as a tool by which to simplify a complex world of political interactions. By assuming an anarchic background to international affairs realists can then focus on the significant elements of the system they identify and seek to provide explanations for the interactions between them. Yet in every realist approach assessed above, the assumption of anarchy necessarily involves a simplification which leaves the theory that is built upon this assumption open to criticism. Theories which assume a competitive anarchy, for example, are of less utility in explaining cooperation, particularly long term cooperation and continent-wide integration. Alliances like NATO in the post-Cold War period were expected to crumble under conditions of realist anarchy and yet they prosper. Anarchy begets distrust amongst states yet examples of states refusing to lose faith in allies even when confronted with evidence of deceit abound. It is clear, then, that the assumption of anarchy allows for a more parsimonious depiction of international relations but that with parsimony arise problems in terms of theoretical utility. A cost resulting from this parsimonious assumption can then be assumed and, in the third part of this chapter case studies are provided by which the extent of this cost can truly be measured.

Establishing the Cost of the Assumption of Anarchy

The previous part of this chapter suggested that there is a cost to theoretical utility associated with the assumption of anarchy by realists. This part of the paper will present three case studies by which the extent of this cost will be outlined and assessed. In choosing the case studies care has been taken to consider major events in the international system, namely the outbreak of World War One, the fall of the Soviet Union and the integration of Europe in the shape of European Union. Each of these events or processes have had a significant impact on the entire international system, be it through extended conflict (World War One), a shift from stable bipolarity to unipolarity and, later, multipolarity (Soviet Union) or pan-continental political and economic integration of nearly 15% of the world's nation-states after centuries of war (European Union). Each will be considered in turn using a common framework: first, a broad historical introduction to the event or process will be offered; second, the realist explanation for the event or process and the role of anarchy will be presented; third, the problems with the realist explanation will be identified; fourth and lastly, for each case study the clear link between the problems in the realist explanation and the assumption of anarchy will be identified. In concluding this part of the chapter it will apparent that the cost to theoretical utility of pursuing parsimony through the assumption of anarchy is simply too much for the discipline to bear.

The Outbreak of World War One[700]

Otto von Bismarck was said to have remarked that if there is ever another war in Europe, it would come out of 'some damn fool thing in the Balkans'. He would be proved horribly right as the assassination of an Austrian Archduke in Sarajevo gave way to a conflict that would engulf much of the world and sound the death knell for a world system dominated by European empires. From such 'damned fool' beginnings, the conflict which would become known as the Great War plunged a continent into a modern conflict from the Caucasus to the English Channel. As a war that sprung from political assassination, World War One was unprecedented in scale. As James Joll and Gordon Martel recall:

> The murder of prominent people – kings, presidents, leading politicians – had been for some three decades a familiar technique used by groups and individuals anxious to draw attention to what they believed to be national or social injustices, but no previous assassination in living memory had provoked a major international crisis, as the killing of the archduke was to do.[701]

Archduke Franz Ferdinand's death led Austria to declare war on Serbia, Russia to rush to Serbia's aid, Germany to mobilise and within a few short weeks countries from the Southern Ocean to the North Sea to send troops into battle in the European

---

[700] Some parts of this section are directly extracted from a longer, case specific article that was written and published in the course of the author's PhD research. See Kissane. 2006.

[701] James Joll and Gordon Martel. 2006. *The Origins of the First World War*. New York: Pearson, p.13.

theatre. Unsurprisingly, the realists with their focus on conflict, states and military strength have found the outbreak of the war a fruitful case for examination.

For realists, the outbreak of war is usually explained in terms of the great powers of Europe. Conventional realist accounts would include, for example, Austrian Chief-of-Staff Conrad von Hötzendorff's pronouncement that "...the First World War came about inevitably and irresistibly as the result of the motive forces in the lives of states...like a thunderstorm that must by nature discharge itself".[702] Such accounts often rely on interpretations of the Grand Alliances that dominated European relations at the time of the outbreak of war in the Balkans. The most common sees Austria-Hungary drawn into conflict with Serbia; Russia mobilizing to assist Serbia; Germany moving to support Austria; France, bound by treaty to Russia, moving to counter Germany; and Britain moving to support neutral Belgium and, in some interpretations, France. As historian Richard Lebow notes, reasons for the inevitability of war in the anarchic system of the early 20th century range from "social Darwinism, [to] nationalism, the alliance structure, and shifts in the balance of power".[703] Essentially, then, the realists depict the outbreak of war in 1914 as analogous to a falling house of cards or the bouncing of billiard balls across a table. A realist explanation for the outbreak of the war is little more than a series of 'if x then y, if y then z' ad infinitum.

The problems with such an explanation are clear. Such accounts attach causal significance to these large factors – the alliances, the balancing – and little, if any, attention is paid to events or factors at the individual level of analysis. Thus, the importance of the Triple Entente is highlighted while local terrorist operations in Serbia are marginalised; the Germany/Austria-Hungary pact is brought to the fore while the interpretation by individuals of their responsibilities under such a pact are often left unexamined.[704] While the scale of the conflict had never been seen before (and, in some ways, has not been seen since), it would seem that international relations analysts

---

[702] In Lebow. 2000a, p.2.

[703] Lebow. 2000b, p.592. Other realist explanations point to the notion of the 'cult of the offensive' that infected European politics at the time. See Stephen van Evera. 1984. 'The Cult of the Offensive and the Origins of the First World War.' *International Security* 9(1): 58-107.

[704] Jack Levy attempts to counter the common claim that alliances lead to war in Jack Levy. 1981. 'Alliance Formation and War Behavior: An Analysis of the Great Powers, 1495-1975.' *The Journal of Conflict Resolution* 25(4): 581-613.

190

have taken it upon themselves to also consider only the grand interactions that, in an anarchic realm, are the only ones that are held to matter anyway.[705] Thus, it is clear that the standard explanation for the beginning of the First World War is mainly concerned with Great Power Politics, entangling alliances, and a feeling of inevitability. In the anarchic systems on which realist theories are based where conflict is usually seen to be inevitable this is nothing more than what is to be expected.[706]

The realist depictions of the outbreak of the war fail to engage with the numerous and potentially significant sub-state issues and individual-level factors that contributed to the opening of the Great War in Sarajevo. For example, consider the assassination of Archduke Franz Ferdinand of Austria-Hungary in Sarajevo on the 28th of June 1914. The Archduke was only in Sarajevo for reasons of protocol, having arrived in Bosnia with the main mission of overseeing troop movements in the region.[707] He travelled with his wife in an open car and – after surviving one unsuccessful assassination attempt in the morning – died in a successful second attempt just before midday. But what of this second attempt? History holds that it was only a wrong turn by a confused chauffeur that put the Archduke and his wife anywhere near the assassin who eventually killed them. It seems in one sense, then, that the lives of millions in World War One could really have hung on the driving skills of a single man.[708]

---

[705] There remain exceptions, of course. Bruce Russett lists many factors as contributing to the outbreak of World War One but the smaller, immediate events that spin out of control are labelled only 'surprises' and not 'real' causes. In doing so, Russett implies that such small matters have some importance in the beginning of the war but he does not attribute cause to them as one might in a chaotic system. See Bruce Russett. 1962. 'Cause, Surprise, and No Escape.' *The Journal of Politics* 24 (1): 3-22, pp.7-9.

[706] Waltz. 1979; Mearsheimer. 1994.

[707] Michael Duffy. 2006. *Who's Who: Archduke Franz Ferdinand.* [14 April 2006] http://tinyurl.com/3csxza.

[708] Indeed, such questions haunt security scholars. Consider this from an editorial in *International Security*: "Though distant in time, the disaster of 1914 continues to haunt the contemporary security debate. In the nuclear age, the images that remain from the summer of 1914 – the escalation from an isolated event in a far corner of Europe to global war, the apparent loss of control of the situation by key decision-makers, the crowding out of diplomacy by military exigencies, the awful, protracted, often senseless slaughter on the battlefield – raise troubling doubts about our ability to forever conduct affairs of state safely in an international environment plagued by the ever present risk of thermonuclear war". Such escalation, or feedback, and the 'apparent' loss of control can be interpreted as signposts of a chaotic system. International Security. 1984. 'The Great War and the Nuclear Age: Sarajevo after Seventy Years.' *International Security* 9(1): 3-5, p.3.

Consider, too, not only this single event but also all of the others that were involved in putting the Archduke in Bosnia that day. Firstly, had his closer-to-the-throne relative not died, it would have been unlikely that the Ferdinand would have even been sent to Bosnia to review the troop exercises. Indeed, when he was born it seemed that there was little chance that Franz would ever be close to being heir to the throne, let alone be groomed for the crown, as he was when he died.[709] Secondly, had his political views not been so widely misinterpreted outside of his own empire, it would seem that he would be an unlikely target for the Black Hand group.[710] Thirdly, had he not chosen to visit Sarajevo on the feast of St Vitus, a day on which the local Serbians traditionally take part in patriotic observances, the Archduke might not have been targeted at all.[711] Fourthly, as the Archduke's wife, Sophie, was not accorded the respect in Austria-Hungary a woman in her position would normally expect (owing to her parentage and 'station' in life at the time they were married), then Ferdinand would not have had to leave Austria-Hungary in order to fete her in public for their anniversary.[712] Whereas at home it would not be normal for the heir to parade with his wife in public, in Bosnia, far from home, it was completely acceptable. Thus, to celebrate their anniversary, the couple set to the streets of Sarajevo together, an action that might not have occurred had the Archduke been able to parade his wife in Vienna.

---

[709] Samuel Williamson's history of Ferdinand's rise to the position of heir, along with the increased policy role that he played in the Austria-Hungary Empire, is instructive on this point. See Samuel Williamson. 1974. 'Influence, Power, and the Policy Process: The Case of Franz Ferdinand, 1906-1914.' *The Historical Journal* 17 (2): 417-434.

[710] Historian John Langdon describes the Archduke as a "misunderstood statesman" and argues that most in the monarchy were "thoroughly wrong in their evaluations of Ferdinand". See John Langdon. 1986. 'Emerging From Fischer's Shadow: Recent Examinations of the Crisis of July 1914.' *The History Teacher* 20 (1): 67-68.

[711] The entry of the Archduke to the region on St Vitus' Day was interpreted as an insult to the Serbs. See Michael Neiburg. 2004. *Warfare and Society in Europe: 1898 to the Present.* New York: Routledge, p.27. Also, though she finishes with placing the blame for the outbreak of war on Germany, Bernadotte Schmitt does note the significance of St Vitus' Day in Serbia and in motivating the Black Hand. Bernadotte Schmitt. 1952. 'The Origins of the War of 1914.' *The Journal of Modern History* 24 (1): 69-74, p.71. Other authors who allude to the significance of this day for nationalist Serbians – both historically and in more recent times – include: Fred Singleton. 1989. *A Short History of the Yugoslav Peoples.* Cambridge: Cambridge University Press, p.47; Michael Sells. 1996. *The Bridge Betrayed: Religion and Genocide in Bosnia.* Berkeley: University of California Press, pp.44-45.

[712] On the nature of Ferdinand and Sophie's particular style of marriage, known as morganatic, see discussion in David DeVoss. 2006. *Searching for Gavrilo Princip.* [17 April 2006] http://tinyurl.com/2jnswv.

A realist theorist is essentially blind to such sub-state level interactions and affairs as their assumption of anarchy forces them to focus on states and state actions to the neglect of sub-state actors and individual circumstance. While it is obvious from the examples above that there are any number of sub-state interactions, social mores and individual circumstances, personal skill sets and even dumb luck that played a hand in the assassination of Ferdinand on that day in Sarajevo every one of them is ignored in a anarchy-based realist explanation of the outbreak of the Great War. A few small changes in the historical, cultural, or social realities of the time would have seen either a completely different series of events lead up to the war or, perhaps and more interestingly, the war not occur at all. While the realists may have approximated the international system with their anarchic assumption, a case such as this clearly demonstrates the cost of this simple approximation. Ignorance of the sub-state interactions that determined the opening of World War One suggests that the cost is significant, indeed.

The End of the Cold War and the Collapse of the Soviet Union[713]

Following the devastation of World War Two the global political system slipped into what would become known as the Cold War. Distinctive from the wars that came before it in that it didn't see direct armed conflict between the primary powers of the day, the USSR and the USA, the Cold War defined half a century of global politics and set military, strategic and political opinion for decades. While some saw it as a battle of ideologies, others saw it as a "great crisis" and a "military standoff" that would have led to a 'hot' war had it not been for the wisdom and guidance of experienced foreign policy advisors.[714] Yet the end of the Cold War, to paraphrase Andersson and Ulvaeus, ended with a whimper and not with a shout and left many realists wondering what it was they had missed in their analysis of the superpower politics of the late-20th century. The long conflict that defined the second half of the century,

---

[713] Some parts of this section are directly extracted from a longer, case specific article that was written and published in the course of the author's PhD research. See Kissane. 2007b.

[714] Robert Cooper. 2004. *The Breaking of Nations: Order and Chaos in the Twenty-First Century.* New York :Grove Press, p.14; Andrew Bacevich. 2005. *The New American Militarism: How Americans Are Seduced by War.* [22 October 2007] http://tinyurl.com/2lnsta; Walter Hixson. 1997. *Parting the Curtain: Propaganda, Culture, and the Cold War, 1945-1961.* New York: St. Martin's Press.

and the lifetime of many contemporary realists, would end without the destruction of global warfare and surprise many in the international relations discipline who, almost to a person, failed to predict what was unravelling in front of them.

A realist explanation for the fall of the Berlin Wall and the collapse of the Soviet Union as a superpower was hard to come by when it occurred but has emerged in time. Though failing to predict the collapse of America's rival, the realists countered by pointing to the elements of the Soviet regime that surely led to the disintegration of the USSR and the failure of the Eastern rival in the global East-West geopolitical competition. William Wohlforth outlines a typical realist explanation for the end of the Cold War, stating:

> The Cold War was caused by the rise of Soviet power and the fear this caused in the West. The end of the Cold War was caused by the relative decline in Soviet power and the reassurance this gave the West. Stalin, Khrushchev, and Brezhnev may have had many reasons for competing with the United States, ranging from genuine fear to ideological conviction, but a necessary condition for competition was their perception that they had the *capability* to do so. Gorbachev may have had numerous reasons for seeking to withdraw from the rivalry with the United States, but a necessary precondition was the perception of *reduced capability* to continue competing.[715]

Further, Wohlforth argues that, despite the claims of liberalists and neo-liberalists, the end of the Cold War did not invalidate the realist position.[716] Instead, Wohlforth notes that the end of the Cold War exposes one of the weaknesses of realist prediction being that the end of the Cold War "was merely a single data point" and that "even if it is inconsistent with realism it is insufficient to falsify it, because international relations theories are capable only of predicting patterns of behaviour".[717] This failure of realism to predict 'single data points' in the international system, while not invalidating the approach, does suggest a weakness, one that might be overcome by considering the role that anarchy has played in determining the realist approach.

As in the case of the outbreak of World War One, realist accounts of the end of the Cold War and the geopolitical landscape that emerged in Europe rely on theories

---

[715] Wohlforth. 1994, p.96.
[716] Wohlforth. 1994, p.92.
[717] Wohlforth. 1994, p.92.

founded on anarchy which minimise or completely discount the impact of sub-state events on the wider system. Yet what if the ordering principle is not what realists and others assume it to be? Could this not be the reason, as opposed to the liberal institutionalist counter arguments outlined above, that the realist predictions for post-Cold War Central and Eastern Europe such as Mearsheimer's proved so wrong? As the axiomatic principle professed jointly by classical and structural realists alike, if it is proved to be dysfunctional then it follows that there exists a significant possibility that predictions based on such an axiom are also wrong. In analogical terms, if one states that that in mathematics $2 + 2$ and 2^2 are both equal to four and, therefore, $2x = x^2$ in every situation will surely make errors as integers other then 2 are tested. An error in calculation does not necessarily imply an error in a foundational axiom; however, where there *is* an error in a foundational axiom errors in predictions based upon this axiom are sure to emerge. In the case of the pessimistic predictions of realists for post-Cold War Central and Eastern Europe, this is exactly what this book holds to have occurred. An error as basic as the arithmetic allegory offered herein is to blame for Mearsheimer's errors, the error being, specifically, presenting the international system as anarchic.

The generally peaceful transition from socialist superpower domination of Russia and Eastern Europe to liberal capitalist democracy (or limited democracy in the case of Russia) could not be predicted when basing analysis upon a competitive, anarchic international system. The move by Russia to take over the Soviet Union's seat on the United Nations Security Council and maintain a powerful role in global security – an act that was deemed contrary to international law by Yehuda Blum in the *European Journal of International Law* – went unchallenged by other states in the system despite the fact that it delivered a relative gain in power to a competitor and despite the fact that it offered a weak state a role disparate to its actual strength.[718] Under anarchy realists expect competition between states yet the post-Soviet bloc, with the exception, perhaps, of elements of the former Yugoslavia and border regions of Georgia, have existed in relative cooperation since 1991. Under anarchy realists expected nuclear proliferation to become a problem in Europe, either exploding in a post-Cold War security dilemma or being managed by the Soviet Union and the United

---

[718] Yehuda Blum. 1992. 'Russia Takes Over the Soviet Union's Seat at the United Nations.' *European Journal of International Law* 3(2): 354-361.

States.[719] Yet the post-Cold War world saw only limited proliferation and all of it far from the East-West battleground in Central and Eastern Europe. An exclusive focus on states in anarchy blind the realists to strong local pressures in European states against further proliferation of nuclear weapons and fails to take into account the wishes of newly-independent populations.[720]

Once again, the realist foundation of anarchy and the consequent focus on interactions between states and associated ignorance of sub-state events sees the theory fail to explain events as they actually occurred. While parsimonious in their depictions of the world, the reality is far more complex than anarchy-based realism will allow. As a result, potentially significant events, public feelings and driving forces are not considered and the parsimonious representation is found to lack explanatory utility. Realist analysts considering the Cold War world in the late 1980's or predicting the future of a post-Cold War world in the early 1990's offered depictions, explanations and predictions which would be proved far from the observable reality. Indeed, Realists, secure in their models of a stable, peaceful and bipolar Europe, were especially astonished by the fall of, first, the Berlin Wall and, second, the superpower that constructed it. One need only look at the academic press in the weeks and months prior to the Cold War's end to recognize that few realists thought the end of the half-century long conflict was nigh. Major journals published dozens of articles on Soviet doctrine and nuclear balancing, yet barely a handful of these articles dared to question that the established European order may by more fallible and have less traction than common realist notions would admit. As with the case of the outbreak of World War One, anarchy and the other realist assumptions that followed it have proved a liability for the analyst of international affairs.

---

[719] Mearsheimer. 1990a.

[720] Consider the Robin Wood group in Germany, the Romanian Physicians for the Prevention of Nuclear War, Ukrainian Physicians for the Prevention of Nuclear War or IPPNW Georgia – all of who protest against nuclear proliferation in Central and Eastern Europe in the post-Cold War period.

196

The European Union and Regional Integration[721]

John McCormick writes that:

> [t]he creation of the European Union will go down in history as one of the most remarkable achievements of the twentieth century. In the space of just forty years – less than two generations – Europeans fought two appalling wars among themselves, finally appreciated the dangers of nationalism and the futility of violence, and sat down to design a system that would make it inconceivable that they would ever take up arms against each other again.[722]

From the European Coal and Steel Community (ECSC) which brought about the political reconciliation of France and Germany and laid the basis for the economic integration of Western Europe, through the Treaty of Rome which established the European Economic Community (EEC) to the Maastricht Treaty which established the European Union (EU), the recent history of Europe has been one of continued and extensive economic and political integration.[723] Former rival states, including states that had made war on each for centuries in the past, built not only regional economic institutions but also an international parliament and a supra-state decision making body in the form of the European Commission. While in practical terms the integration of the continent has long been an aim of prominent Europeans including Charlemagne, Napoleon and Hitler, the post-World War Two integration of the continent from Britain and Ireland in the west all the way to the Russian border in the east is the first time that this integration has been achieved peacefully and with the consent of the people. Europe now sits as the most striking example of regional political integration on the planet and its success serves as an example to other regional integration efforts worldwide.[724]

---

[721] Some parts of this section are directly extracted from a longer, case specific article that was written and published in the course of the author's PhD research. See Kissane. 2007b.

[722] McCormick. 2002, p.xi.

[723] McCormick. 2002, pp.56-83; John Gillingham. 2003. *European Integration 1950-2003: Superstate or New Market Economy?* New York: Cambridge University Press, p.4.

[724] Percy Mistry considers the case of the African Union and notes, "In June 2000 African leaders went a step further in declaring their intention to achieve full economic and political union; they changed the name of the Organization for African Unity into the African Union, in premature mimicry of the European Union." See Percy Mistry. 2000. 'Africa's Record of Regional Co-Operation and Integration.' *African Affairs* 99(4): 553-573, p.561.

Realists have had difficulty explaining the post-World War Two integration of Europe and the development of the institutions that now are part of the European Union. In 1990, for example, John Mearsheimer lampooned analysts who imagined "a new age of peace in Europe" and argued that "the prospects for major crises and war in Europe are likely to increase markedly".[725] Kenneth Waltz relied on his structural approach to predict the demise of NATO in a no longer divided Europe, arguing that "NATO's days are not numbered, but its years are".[726] More specifically, Waltz explained that "once the new Germany finds its feet, it will no more want to be constrained by the United States acting through NATO than by any other state".[727] Further he argues that he:

> ...has used structural theory to peer into the future, to ask what seem to be the strong likelihoods among the unknowns that abound. One of them is that, over time, unbalanced power will be checked by the responses of the weaker who will, rightly or not, feel put upon.[728]

Stephen Walt mirrored Waltz on the future of NATO in the light of European integration efforts arguing that NATO was growing increasingly fragile.[729] More broadly, though, realists reject the idea that any alliance between states can be permanent as interstate alliances are issue specific. As a general rule realists remained generally pessimistic about the likelihood of peaceful integration and democratic transitions of the post-Socialist states of Central and Eastern Europe.[730]

Yet the observable reality emerged as so different from what these realists expected that it seems almost as if the realists were describing a different continent altogether. The major wars and crises that offensive realism expected never eventuated.[731] As historian Richard Hellie notes, the final days of the Cold War and of the Soviet Union

---

[725] Mearsheimer. 1990a, p.5; p.6.

[726] Kenneth Waltz. 1993. 'The Emerging Structure of International Politics.' *International Security* 18(2): 44-79, p.76.

[727] Waltz. 1993, p.76.

[728] Waltz. 1993, p.79.

[729] Stephen Walt. 1999. 'The Ties that Fray: Why Europe and America are Drifting Apart.' *The National Interest* 54: 3-11, pp.10-11.

[730] An excellent overview of realist predictions can be found in Robert Lieber. 2003. *Are Realists Realistic about Foreign Policy?* Paper presented at the Annual Meeting of the American Political Science Association, Philadelphia, 28-31 August 2003, pp.1-16.

[731] Kissane. 2007b, pp.386-387.

mirrored those of the Russian Empire itself in 1917: both "collapsed almost without a whimper".[732] Waltz's structural realist argument that concluded that the NATO alliance was only years away from devastation proved to be false: some 15 years after Waltz's article was published NATO not only continues to exist but has expanded to encompass many of the former socialist states that the alliance was formed to oppose. Far from the narrowly defined interest-based alliance that realists depict and depicted, NATO, according Robert Hunter, has:

> ...evolved over the years into a deep-rooted institution with a commitment to democratic values and practices that, along with its unique, integrated military structure, sustains it even at times when its members' short-term strategic calculations diverge.[733]

The fragility of NATO after the end of the Cold War Walt described seems misplaced, particularly in the wake of the 11 September 2001 terrorist attacks in the United States that saw Article 5 of the treaty (the collective security article) activated for the first time. Further, even with continued political and economic integration in Europe leading some to conclude that the EU was balancing against the United States, the US-centric alliance remains fundamental to European security.[734] Furthermore, the pooling and voluntary secession of sovereignty by states to a superstate international institution is firmly contrary to realist assumptions. While international institutions and alliances are common elements of the international system even for realists, an institution of the style and type of the EU went unpredicted and largely unexplained.

The role of anarchy in these realist missteps is obvious. Where realists assume an anarchy where states weigh relative gains and an unlikely future it forces them to assume that states are inherently competitive. Thus, faced with a continent of some three dozen nation-states, scarce resources and a history of violent conflict, the realist naturally assumes that the 'natural order' will be maintained and competition will be the rule. The unpredictability of anarchy also forces realists to consider alliances between states to be temporary, situation specific mergers of common, selfish interests.

---

[732] Richard Hellie. 2005. 'The Structure of Russian Imperial History.' *History and Theory* 44(4): 1-22, p.8.

[733] Robert Hunter. 2004. 'A Forward-Looking Partnership.' *Foreign Affairs* 83(5): 14-18, p.14.

[734] Keohane. 2002, pp.760-761.

The integration of Europe, however, offers a clear example of such anarchy-based realist explanations and predictions failing. The parsimony that anarchy offers the theorist directly assists in the failure of the realists to explain one of the most significant international changes in inter-state relations. Where anarchy should provoke competition Europe proves that cooperation can persist and grow. Where anarchy should see actors hold tight to their sovereignty, states in the EU willingly ceded aspects of their sovereignty to a supranational actor. The integration of Europe stands in contrast to the anarchical systems described by realists. Once again, anarchy has contributed to a failure of realism and the cost in terms of theoretical and explanatory utility is high.

Conclusion: The Problems with Parsimony

Each of these case studies demonstrates that the assumption of anarchy by realists has – for significant events in the international system – rendered the paradigm unable to offer accurate descriptions, explanations or predictions as a theory is expected to do. The outbreak of the First World War is explained by realists with reference only to states and their actions, ignorant of the sub-state factors that made the assassination in Sarajevo possible in the first place. The collapse of the Soviet Union went unpredicted and the geopolitical landscape that emerged in its wake was far from what the realists imagined it might be. The long term peace in Europe and the integration that has seen dozens of states work to harmonise economic and political interests in a super-state institution is hard if not impossible to credibly explain with reference to realist anarchy, the competition expected failing to emerge in any real way. Anarchy, then, seems to have led realists astray. While certainly offering a parsimonious representation of international reality, the theories are of reduced utility for the analyst when even events of the magnitude of a system changing conflict, the collapse of a superpower and the outbreak of peace on a continent previously ravaged by war fail to be explained or predicted. The continued reliance on the assumption of anarchy by realists results in a theoretical approach that is of decreasing utility for understanding international politics.

Conclusion

This chapter opened by defining what a theory of international relations should be. The necessary elements of a theory of international politics were outlined, the goals of a theory were presented and a cartographical analogy which highlights the role of theory as a tool of parsimony was introduced. The chapter then considered the role of anarchy in each of the realist approaches thus far considered by the book. This part of the chapter highlighted the similarities between the anarchies presented in the work of realist theorists from the ancient world to the twenty-first century, in particular the ways each theorist uses anarchy as tool of theoretical parsimony. Having identified the role of anarchy in the realist pursuit of parsimony, a third part of the chapter considered three case studies of significant international political events: the outbreak of World War One, the end of the Cold War and the collapse of the Soviet Union, and the regional integration of Europe in the shape of the EU. In each case the failure of realists to properly describe, explain and predict these events and the events that would follow was traced back to the assumption of anarchy in the realists whose explanations were considered. Anarchy, then, while offering a parsimonious representation of reality, leads to theory that lacks the utility to describe even major events in the international system. It seems clear, then, that a better basis for international relations must be found and, in the chapter that follows, this book will offer a basis and a theory founded on it that may provide such an alternative to the paradigm that has dominated the discipline for decades.

A THEORY OF COMPLEXITY

The realist reliance on anarchy and the construction of theories of international politics where states act within it has been argued to be insufficient to describe and explain the reality of international relations. Major events at the international and regional level which have had significant impacts including the outbreak of World War One, the collapse of the Soviet Union and the integration of Europe all point to failures in the realist paradigm to explain important elements of international politicking. Other critiques of realism have pointed to problems with the theory's focus on states over institutions, assumptions of power balancing over band-wagoning and sustained focus on military power in the face of the challenge of incorporating notions of soft power. Yet the critique offered within this book is not focussed on what might be considered secondary assumptions by scholars working within the realist paradigm; rather it has highlighted the consistent foundation of realist approaches on the assumption of an anarchic system and criticised this theoretical foundation for the misrepresentations and poor explanations realists draw from their anarchy-based approaches. What is needed, then, is an alternative approach based on a systemic approach that better reflects the reality of international relations and allows the theorist to draw more accurate conclusions and offer more credible explanations for events within the international system.

The first chapter of this book presented the classical realist perspective that was and that continues to be one of the dominant streams of international political theory. From the histories of Thucydides and his famed Melian dialogue and Machiavelli's strictly amoral advice to Italian princes, Hobbes depiction of an anarchical state of nature and Carr's inter-war argument to Morgenthau's six principles of political realism, classical realists all share a common conception of the basic nature of the international system: anarchy. The second chapter of the book considered the structural realism that emerged as a critique of the classical position. Waltz's neorealism brought an anarchically structured international politic to the forefront of international political theory, centralising the assumption of anarchy as a key to theorising international affairs. The third chapter considered various realist approaches and, again, concluded that each assumed an anarchic international environment at its theoretical foundation. Whether Mearsheimer's offensive realism or the neo-classical realism of Cha, Christensen and Rose, where the assumption of anarchy is explicit, or in the implicit anarchy of the simple Prisoner's Dilemma game, these realist approaches also made the structure of international relations key to understanding world politics. Finally, in the fourth chapter, this book outlined three significant events in recent international politics that were poorly explained by realists from across the paradigmatic spectrum. These events and the failure of realists of any persuasion to account for them with their anarchy-based approaches led to the conclusion that an alternative approach must be offered by which to assess, describe and explain international relations and it is to this task that this fifth and final chapter in the book now turns.

This chapter will be presented in two parts, each with sub-sections that present in detail this alternative approach to theorising international relations. The first part – 'First Principles' – outlines the basis of this alternative approach and presents the major elements of international politics as understood by this alternative approach. Beginning by defining the subject of the theory in terms of what exactly international relations *is*, this first section continues by defining the key elements of the international system, the goals of these elements, their motivations for action and a justification for the significant departure that this alternative approach takes from traditional international analysis. Closing out this first part is a detailed explanation of the nature of the relationship between the identified elements of the system and the structure of the system which, following from the previous chapters and in line with the argument of this book, is not an anarchic structure. Having outlined the components and interrelations of this alternative approach to international analysis, the second part of this chapter – 'Testing the Alternative Approach' – offers an assessment of the posited approach. By first drawing out hypotheses from the stated assumptions of the alternative approach and then testing them against both historical examples that realists have had difficulty explaining as well as examples described and explained by realists with ease, this final part of the chapter produces case after case from classic 'system level' events to smaller, sub-regional events to demonstrate the utility of this non-realist, non-anarchy based theory. In concluding the chapter it will be argued that pursuing and developing this alternative approach is likely to permit analysts to map and theorise the reality of international politics more closely and with greater success.

First Principles

As the mathematician builds his proofs upon axioms and the philosopher begins by seeking a basis for her philosophy, so too a theory of international relations begins by laying out its base principles and assumptions about that which is being theorised. This first part of the chapter, then, describes and explains the key assumptions behind this alternative theoretical approach, relying on the same methodology that was used in the preceding chapter to deconstruct the alternative realist approach. Thus, the first section in this part of the chapter defines the subject of this theory of international politics, the second section defines the elements of the system and their goals and motivations and a third defines the structure of the system and the relationships between the elements within it. At the conclusion of this part of the chapter an alternative approach to theorising international affairs will have been outlined and it will then be possible – in this chapter's second part – to assess this alternative approach for validity and utility.

Defining the Subject of the Theory

In the previous chapter it was argued that it is not possible to have a theory of international politics without first defining what is meant by 'international politics' itself. This point has been made previously by Waltz where, in a 2003 interview, he opined:

> First, in order to have a theory, you'll have to have a subject matter, because you can't have a theory about everything. The first question is, how can you think of international politics as a domain in its own right, as something that you could possibly have a theory about...You will have to figure out a way of defining it as an autonomous field of study.[735]

---

[735] Waltz. 2003.

This first section will offer two perspectives on this definition of an autonomous field of study: the common realist perspective and an alternative conception which forms a significant part of the alternative approach contained herein. In the case of the realist perspective of what constitutes 'international politics' examples will be drawn from the more than ten theorists and approaches this book has thus far considered, as well as drawing on complementary accounts elsewhere in the realist literature. The alternative conception will offer justifications instead of examples from within the wider international relations discipline. In concluding this section not only will a non-realist understanding of the notion of 'international politics' have been outlined but a definitional base constructed on which further elements of the theory can be constructed.

The Realist Perspective

Realists not only share a common assumption in the shape of international anarchy but also a notion of what constitutes international politics for the purposes of their theoretical approach. It is little surprise that realists – with their focus on states and state actions – define international politics as politics at the supra-state level. As a result, their theories of international politics often exclude intra-state events, domestic uprisings and individual actors from their analysis. Further, the focus on states often reduces large elements of international politics to mere extensions of states or mani-festations of states pursuing their interests. Thus, long-term alliances such as NATO with a permanent bureaucracy and a headquarters far from where the military alli-ance's power really lies is depicted by realists as an alliance of states pursuing a common, short term goal. The domain of state politics is, for realists, the domain of international politics as is demonstrated in the work of the realists themselves.

Andrew Dunne writes of a "brink" that must delineate international politics, that is, a limit to what can be considered international and what is not.[736] Donald Macintosh and Michael Hawes note that realists clearly describe this 'brink' in realism as being actions exterior to the state. They argue that, for realists, "political and diplomatic

---

[736] Andrew Dunne. 1996. *International Theory: To the Brink and Beyond.* Westport: Greenwood Publishing, p.3.

interactions between sovereign states constitute the core of international relations".[737] Waltz is a particularly good example of this 'supra state equals international politics' perspective, his *Man, the State, and War* clearly delineating three political levels: the individual, the state and its government with the third level, the supra-state realm, being the domain of international analyst and the only realm for international political theory.[738] EH Carr argued that the domain of international politics is a melange of "the business of soldiers" and "the business of diplomats", that is to say matters of war, peace and foreign policy at the inter-state level.[739] A review essay by Richard Snyder notes various definitions of 'international politics' among realist scholars: Morgenthau argues that the 'brink' is "political relations" between states, Charles Schleicher includes "all inter-state relations", Norman Padelford and George Lincoln limit international politics to "interactions of state policies" and Norman Palmer and Howard Perkins identify the subject of international relations as "concerned with the state system".[740] Despite the differences in emphasis that Snyder points to, all of these realists share the common conception of international politics as relating to the actions and interactions of states.

The realist conception of what constitutes international politics is, in a sense, both broad and narrow. It is broad in that state interactions by which realists define their field of study are numerous and encompass multiple levels of both engagement and seriousness. For realists a world war and a war between two neighbours are both part of international politics. A global trade treaty, a regional trade treaty and a free trade agreement between two allies are all part of what is included in 'international politics'. Diplomatic manoeuvring within an international institution or between state leaders at a press conference also fall within the scope of what realists consider international politics. Matters military, economic and diplomatic between states represent a broad spectrum of political interactions and provide fruitful fodder for realist analysts and theorists of international affairs. Yet the realist agenda is also narrow in that it limits what are considered significant interactions to those involving states. Events

---

[737] Donald Macintosh and Michael Hawes. 1992. 'The IOC and the World of Interdependence.' *Olympika: The International Journal of Olympic Studies* 1: 29-45, p.32.
[738] Waltz. 2003. See also Waltz. 2001.
[739] Carr. 2001, p.3.
[740] Richard Snyder. 1955. 'Toward Greater Order in the Study of International Politics.' *World Politics* 7(3): 461-478, p.463.

at a domestic level that spiral up into the international arena are not part of 'international politics', though the end result at the international level is. Groups that act outside of states or that interact with states without being states themselves can be problematic for realists as their actions fall outside of their narrowly construed 'international politics' arena and are usually not considered the most significant international actors. Indeed, this narrow definition of what constitutes international politics is the same as that which was offered in the previous chapter to help explain why realists have trouble explaining international events that emerge from domestic, intra-state realities, including the outbreak of World War One and the collapse of both the Berlin Wall and the Soviet Union.

Other criticisms of the narrowness of the realist perspective exist in the literature, most commonly from theorists of the liberalist perspective. The failure to engage with significant international institutions is highlighted by Keohane and Martin who argued:

> Realism's insistence that institutions have only marginal effects renders its account of institutional creation **incomplete and logically unsound**, and leaves it without a plausible account of the investments that states have made in such international institutions as the EU, NATO, GATT, and regional trading organizations.[741]

Citing Ronald Mitchell, they argue that treaties negotiated through international institutions independently influence an actor's behaviour, thus limiting the utility of realist approaches that narrow the realm of 'international politics' to state actions alone.[742] Significant criticism of the realist focus on extra-state relations also exists within the democratic peace literature. Democratic peace scholars such as Gilat Levy and Ronny Razin claim that it is "a well-established empirical observation" that liberal democracies do not fight wars with each other, mirroring the perspective of Michael Mousseau and Yuhang Shi who note "democratic nations very rarely engage each other in war, and this pattern is highly unlikely to be attributable to chance".[743] Levy, Razin, Mousseau and Shi all ascribe international political impact to domestic

---

[741] Keohane and Martin. 1995, p.47. Emphasis added.

[742] Keohane and Martin. 1995, p.48.

[743] Gilat Levy and Ronny Razin. 2004. 'It Takes Two: An Explanation for the Democratic Peace.' *Journal of the European Economic Association* 2(1): 1-29, p.1; Michael Mousseau and Yuhang Shi. 1999. 'A Test for Reverse Causality in the Democratic Peace Relationship.' *Journal of Peace Research* 36(6): 639-663, p.663.

political organisation. In effect, those scholars working towards the development of the democratic peace thesis offer a critique of the narrowness of the realist notion of what constitutes 'international politics'. While few will go as far as James Ray and claim that the "democratic peace research program does have the ability to 'falsify' realism", at the very least democratic peace theorists are challenging the limited imagination that realists demonstrate by defining the subject of their theories in the way that they do.[744]

As institutionalists like Keohane and Martin and democratic peace theorists such as Ray and his peers demonstrate, alternate understandings of what constitutes 'international politics' for the purposes of international relations theory both exist and have been used as the foundation for legitimate and extensive research in the discipline. Indeed, disciplinary historian Brian Schmidt has noted that the boundaries of international politics have been "a matter of consistent controversy" within the discipline for decades.[745] Thus, there is nothing new about expanding the notion of 'international politics' in theorising international relations, nor is there anything particularly questionable about it. Indeed, what constitutes 'international politics' within the discipline today reflects a fundamental spectrum ranging from the narrowest of realist conceptions through to the broadest conceptions that can be found in discussions of international politics in an age of economic and political globalisation. In the paragraphs that follow this book will define, explain and justify its own notion of the subject of its theory. It is one that – it should come as little surprise – is rather different from the one adopted by realists as their own.

The Perspective of the Alternative Approach

In the previous chapter it was argued that realists attempting to explain the outbreak of World War One and the collapse of the Soviet Union faced problems or offered weak explanations when limited to the consideration of states and state actions and motivations alone. Like the democratic peace theorists who suggest, at the very least,

---

[744] James Ray. 2003. 'A Lakatosian View of the Democratic Peace Research Program: Does it Falsify Realism (or Neorealism)?' In *Progress in International Relations Theory: Metrics and Methods of Scientific Change*, edited by M Elman & C Elman. MIT Press: Boston, pp.205-243, p.206.
[745] Schmidt. 2006, p.5.

a correlation between domestic events and international realities and the institutionalists who note that independent international organisations have a real and marked intervening effect on state actions and international events, the previous chapter of this
book suggested that events at the domestic level and institutions at the international
level can have a real and marked intervening effect on how international political reality is formed. Further, the previous chapter also suggested that events and realities
at an individual level, including such things as the familial relationships, personal experiences and everyday choices of individual people, can have a marked impact on
international politics. The feedback from individuals in historically-specific situations
can affect domestic governance, inter-state relations and have – in the case of the collapse of the Soviet Union and the outbreak of World War One – system wide effects
which resonate decades after a decision is made or action is taken. What is needed,
then, is a notion of what constitutes 'international politics' that better reflects the
complex nature of interactions between states, institutions, individuals and other international actors (terrorist groups, corporations and NGOs, for example) and moves
beyond the narrow confines of inter-state politics to which the realists limit their
analysis.

The perspective taken in this alternative approach is to include under the umbrella of
'international politics' *all political acts and actors and that effect politics above state
level.* To consider the elements of this definition of 'international politics' in turn,
look first to the idea of 'political acts'. An act that is defined as political consists of
"the application, reallocation, and legitimisation of power" and power, in turn, can be
defined as the ability to control or influence another actor. [746] Note that neither political acts nor power are defined in terms of the extent of their effect on other actors but
rather on whether there is an effect. Further, the application, reallocation and legitimisation of power need not be immediate to be a political act, that is, there is no temporal restriction on an international political action. An act may have immediate repercussions or the repercussions may take many years to manifest. Neither immediacy nor delay renders an act any more or less political or potentially any less significant in the analysis or theorising of international relations. As well, the *intent* of the
actor makes no difference to whether their acts are to be considered political: even if
an actor means for their action to have only a local or a limited impact on others it

---

[746] Amitai Etzioni. 2003. *What is Political?* [9 April 2008] http://tinyurl.com/5srzwz, p.1.

may be construed as an international political act if it has unintended repercussions on the supra-state system. Finally, the alternative approach's notion of a 'political actor' is simply defined as a unit that makes a political act with, of course, the same caveats as above being that there not necessarily need be any specific intent, immediacy or extensive impact on the part of the actor.

Such an understanding of what international politics is shares little similarity with the realist position. Certainly there is at least one common element – being the notion that politics is international when it takes place at the supra-state level – yet in all other elements there are significant differences. Whereas the realists place their main focus on a specific and small group of international political actors, the definition of 'international politics' offered in this alternative approach is significantly broader as to demand the inclusion and analysis of actors that realists generally exclude. The breadth of the definitions of 'international political act' and 'international political actor' draw terrorist groups, international institutions, non-governmental organisations, corporations and individuals into the assessable group of international actors and their particular actions and motivations become legitimate, and also necessary, elements for international political analysis. The qualifier 'all' is also significant for reasons that will be outlined completely later in this chapter; for the moment it is suffice to say that ignorance of even the smallest acts and actors may blind the theorist and the analyst to the potential feedback effects that such acts and actors can have on the wider system. Without a model that incorporates all such potentially powerful acts and actors the theorist is left, as the realists are, to explain major events with reference only to proximate factors.

Justification for this conception of international politics can be found within the literature or, more precisely, the non-realist literature of the discipline. As well as Keohane and Martin's institutionalist position and the work already cited within the democratic peace research program, scholars within the wider liberalist tradition have long called for a wider understanding of what is a part of international politics. Joseph Nye, for example, uses his soft power thesis to advance the notion that powerful actors in international relations are not limited to states and that a state's power should be measured both by the 'hard' power of its national capabilities and the 'soft' power of its domestic, non-governmental and corporate actors.[747] John McCormick notes that understandings of international politics must broaden to include regional actors such as the European Union, a body that maintains a level of control over member states and that can negotiate in international forums and enter into binding agreements on behalf of themselves and certain state actors.[748] Broadening the notion of what is included in 'international politics' has also been previously addressed by this author in relation to the interactions between major powers, interactions where "the European Union [standing] as a clear candidate for assessment" alongside states.[749] Nye, McCormick and other scholars agree that broadening the definition of what is considered 'international politics' offers opportunities for more accurate analysis whereas the limited, state focussed realist approach cannot.

Consider also the work of Richard Falk who, as Steve Smith writes, discusses a world order that "focuses not on social groups or states but on people" and notes that, for Falk, "the point of reference [for describing international political problems and solutions] is the individual".[750] Michael Mann, too, questions the focus on state-state relations as the sole elements of international politics, pointing to "transnational civil society" and "soft geopolitics" conducted by non-governmental organisations and motivated individuals as potentially significant elements in international politics.[751] Consider also Kal Holsti who argues in 'The coming chaos?' that sub-state groups have a real and measureable impact on events at the supra-state level and points to "coming difficulties and possible chaos" arising from sub-state realities such as drug dealing, judicial corruption, unrestrained population growth, transnational crime and deforestation.[752] Reading the work of scholars like Smith, Mann and Holsti makes clear that there are sub-state influences on international politics. Exclusion of those sub-state influences which, when considered in the light of the alternative definition of 'international politics' offered here must be considered international political acts by inter-

---

[747] See, among many others, Nye. 1990; Nye. 2002; Nye. 2004.

[748] McCormick. 2002, p .196.

[749] Dylan Kissane. 2008b. 'Forecasting the Storm: Power Cycle Theory and Conflict in the Major Power System.' *Europolis* 2: 10-43.

[750] Smith. 2001, pp.102-103.

[751] Michael Mann. 2001. 'Has globalization ended the rise and rise of the nation-state?' in *International Order and the Future of World Politics*, edited by T Paul & J Hall. Cambridge: Cambridge University Press, pp.237-261, p.254; p.260.

[752] Holsti. 1999, p.299.

national political actors, ensures that the analysis will always be insufficient. Indeed, the narrow interpretation of what is part of 'international politics' means that realists will continue to see as unlikely events such as the regional integration of Europe despite decades of political movement in that direction, will be unable to consider the collapse of superpowers even just months and weeks before the collapse occurs and will continue to rely on convoluted state-based explanations for events that clearly find cause at the sub-state and even individual level of political actions.

The beginning of an alternative outline of international relations theory thus must begin with a reassessment of what is being theorised. Acknowledging that the realist limitations to the subject of their theories is overly narrow is a first step and repositioning the definition of 'international politics' is a necessary theoretical adjustment so that this alternative approach can better describe and explain international political realities. By defining the subject of international political theories as 'all political acts and actors and that effect politics at the supra-state level' the alternative approach allows the events that many scholars agree influence international affairs to be incorporated into a theoretical framework as essential elements for describing, analysing and explaining international politics. Having identified the subject of the theory, the next step is to define the significant elements of the subject of the theory. While various actors have been mentioned in the examples above – states, corporations, terrorists, and democratic governments – the section that follows outlines the most important elements interacting within the system in greater detail and defines the nature and goals of the actors that inhabit the international political sphere.

Defining the Elements of the System

The previous chapter argued that the elements of the international political system, being the political actors themselves, are next to be defined once the subject of the theory is outlined. As in the previous section, this section will first outline the realist perspective before offering the perspective of the alternative approach. While the differences between the definitions of 'international politics' offered by realists and this alternative approach have been mirrored or outlined to some extent in the international relations literature previously, the types of actors defined in this alternative approach are very different indeed from what realists, and most other international political theorists, employ in their analyses. The reasons for this departure from traditional realist theory will be shown to be necessary in both the light of the already offered definition of 'international politics' and the forthcoming explication of the structure of the system in which the elements of international politics interact. Thus, this section will proceed by first laying out the two competing perspectives.

The Realist Perspective

Realists do not deny that there are many and complex actors involved in international politics. What is disputed by realists and where their theories are limited is the extent to which any of these actors are considered significant enough as to warrant theoretical concern. Clearly there is a focus on states by realists, sometimes exclusively but not always, but the goals ascribed to the states can be very different. Compare structuralist Waltz who writes:

> I assume that states act to ensure their survival...Survival is a prerequisite to achieving any goals that states may have, other than the goal of promoting their own disappearance as political entities. The survival motive is taken as the ground of action in a world where the security of states is not assured...[753]

...with the classical realism of Morgenthau who argues:

> ...the landscape of international politics is the concept of interest defined in terms of power...We assume that statesmen think and act in terms of interest defined as power, and the evidence of history bears that assumption out.[754]

Clearly where Waltz sees survival as the aim of states Morgenthau sees the pursuit of power and the pursuit of interests defined by power as the state's main goal. While both take the state as the key element of the international political system, both also ascribe different goals and motivations to the behaviour of states. The logic of Waltz, though, seems inescapable – the state or, indeed, any other actor, must survive in order to consider a further move in the international arena – Morgenthau's perspective

---

[753] Waltz. 1979, pp.91-92.
[754] Morgenthau. 1993, p.5.

214

is not without support, either. Neoclassicalist commentators like Gideon Rose note that "external behaviour [depends] on the means at the disposal of national decision makers", supporting Morgenthau's claims to national power determining the trajectory of state behaviour.[755] Others, like the Athenians described by Thucydides, describe a world much like the clashes of power that Morgenthau outlines, the Melians having no choice but to succumb to their more powerful challengers. But these, too, may be seen as motivations also described by Waltz. After all, power is but a means by which a state can ensure the survival envisaged by the neorealists. Whatever the realist perspective, states and the goals of states remain the central concerns of realist theorists when it comes to describing the elements of international political system.

It is pertinent, though, to consider momentarily the place of other international political actors in the realist international system. Whilst they may not be considered central, other actors do exist in the imagination of realists and are – in some approaches – ascribed motivations of their own. Waltz, for example, admits that "states are not and never have never been the only international actors" and adds that "the importance of non-state actors and the extent of transnational activities are obvious".[756] Further, while some realists argue that non-state actors such as international institutions have "no effect" on international relations between states, most do not ascribe to this extreme position and prefer to suggest, as Robert Gilpin does, that impacts are possible, though less common than liberalists imagine.[757] Yet realists are explicit in rejecting focus on actors that depend in most circumstances on states for existence and survival. The international institutions that liberals suggest play a significant role in international politics are formed through the alliance of states. Even those institutions that have their own bureaucracies and some independent power must be understood to have gained both via the surrender of the same by state members and it is clear that, at any time, the withdrawal of support by member states would see the institution disappear. In the case of corporations which, in the modern globalised political system, exert significant power, particularly in the developing world, but are generally ignored by the realists who would submit that corporations can only exist if there is a state for them to be incorporated within. While states can and did exist without

---

[755] Rose. 1998, p.162.
[756] Waltz. 1979, pp.93-94.
[757] Donnelly. 2000, p.132; pp.136-137.

corporations and states did and do exist outside of international institutions, both corporations and institutions – at least as we understand them today – cannot exist without the pre-existence of states. Thus, realists tend to place far more weight on the analysis of states and, where such non-state actors are acknowledged in the realist literature, the focus is on the role of states, state interests and state actions in establishing, maintaining or destroying those actors.

Yet the previous chapter of this book offered three cases where this preferencing of states has contributed to challenges for realists in describing, explaining and even predicting short-term events in international politics. In the example of the outbreak of World War One the standard realist explanation places great emphasis on the machinations and interests of state actors in Europe in the first years of the twentieth century. As argued in 'The Balkan Bullet with Butterfly Wings', a conventional account of the outbreak of the war runs similarly to the following:

> Austria-Hungary [is] drawn into conflict with Serbia; Russia mobilizing to assist Serbia; Germany moving to support Austria; France, bound by treaty to Russia, moving to counter Germany; and Britain moving to support neutral Belgium and, in some interpretations, France.[758]

Yet such accounts which certainly explain the *order* of the rush to war and offer reasons why major state actors became involved, the account is largely the 'big picture' surrounding the immediate events that triggered the outbreak of the conflict. As the previous chapter put it, sub-state and even individual level causes and actors must be considered in any explanation of the outbreak of the war. As has been argued elsewhere:

> [a] few small changes in the historical, cultural, or social realities of the time would have seen either a completely different series of events lead up to the war or, perhaps and more interestingly, the war not occur at all.[759]

The realist commitment to the explanation of international events through a focus on states and state interests blinds the analysis to the sub-state events and realities that are the immediate cause of a conflict like World War One. Realist explanations are

---

[758] Kissane. 2006, p.97.
[759] Kissane. 2006, p.100.

standard for explaining the outbreak of world war on the Balkans but these explanations can be greatly improved by making reference to the thus far excluded elements this book's alternate analysis suggests also play a significant role.

Look also to the manner in which realists explained the end of the Cold War and the collapse of the Soviet Union. As the previous chapter outlined, the realists largely failed to predict the end of the decade's long ideological conflict between the East and West even in the weeks and months immediately before the events occurred. Leading realists continued to publish articles theorising "Soviet doctrine" and specifying responses for the West in the face of the Soviet threat at the same time that both the doctrine and the threat were crumbling. This book argued that the realists were essentially theoretically blind to the impact of sub-state factors that would push for the collapse of the Soviet Union and the 'soft' pressure from groups, both within and without the Soviet Union, which assisted in the fall of the Soviet regime. By failing to account for the obvious impact that such groups, actors and – significantly in this case – such *ideas* could have in the collapse of a superpower and the establishment of a new democratic order in the east of Europe, the realists were left embarrassed and struggling to offer viable explanations for how they so conclusively failed to explain or consider the potential for one of the major evolutions in twentieth-century politics.

The post-Cold War integration of Europe presents another problem for realists who maintain a singular focus on states as international actors. The modern European Union is a striking example of a non-state actor that exerts state-like power in the international arena. Indeed, considering the power and sovereignty granted to this international institution by the member states, and keeping in mind the variances between states in terms of power and resources, the European Union can be argued to be more 'state-like' than many states. Peter van Ham argues that "modern project of European integration is incorporating more and more "state-like" functions such as economic, monetary and foreign and security policy" and, considering the representation of pan-European interests in bodies such as the World Trade Organisation and the Mid-East Peace Quartet, it is clear that the European Union is a significant non-state-but-state-like actor in modern international relations.[760] Indeed, how does one analyse the tran-

---

[760] Peter van Ham. 2001. 'Europe's Postmodern Identity: A Critical Appraisal.' *International Politics* 38(2): 229-252, p.229.

sitions in twenty-first century politics in the East of Europe, the post-Yugoslavian Balkans or within the security dialogue surrounding Russia's western front *without* reference to this non-state actor? The answer, of course, is that the power ceded to the European Union and the ability of Brussels to influence domestic and international policy in European and non-European states alike must be considered in assessing these and many others elements of today's international political system. Considering only states or constructing an explanation that attempts to account for the actions of the European Union as a manifestation of the state interests of 27 individual states turns the theorising of international politics from parsimonious to extravagant.

A final and even more recent example of the necessity of the assessment of non-state actors by analysts and theorists of international politics can be found in the attacks of September 11th 2001 on the United States by elements of the al-Qaeda terrorist group. The response by the United States – to strike, make war on and occupy the state of Afghanistan – is difficult, if not impossible, to explain without reference to the bin Laden-led terrorist group. While it is now clear that there were certain ideological tenets shared by both Afghanistan's Taliban and al-Qaeda, the latter's actions were unsanctioned by the former and served no part in advancing the state's interests. To analyse the terrorist attacks as the act of a state – perhaps Afghanistan or even Saudi Arabia – on another state is to ignore the reality. It is only by incorporating the existence, ideology and significance of a non-state actor into one's analysis that a reasonable representation, explanation and response can be imagined, something that a sole-focus on states as significant actors in international relations explicitly precludes. Clearly, then, there is a place for non-state actors in the theorising of international politics. How this place is defined and the means by which such elements are included are outlined in the following paragraphs where a novel solution to the problem of incorporating such disparate groups into the same international system is offered.

The Perspective of the Alternative Approach

As foreshadowed above, the alternative approach offered here incorporates a broader range of actors into its theoretical foundations. Rejecting the 'state only' and even the 'states predominately' approaches of realists, the alternative approach offered herein incorporates all actors that impact on the international political system. The examples above depict some of these including international institutions, regional bureaucracies, regional political and economic institutions, corporations and terrorist groups. Further, however, this approach draws individual humans into its analysis for the reason that they have the potential to influence international affairs, the outbreak of World War One being an example of this influence in action. As a result, there are many more actors demanding to be assessed in this approach than the roughly 200 similarly-focussed states that a realist would consider in analysing international affairs. Indeed, in today's world there would be in excess of six billion actors who are potentially relevant to be assessed at any one time. While this alternative approach does not attempt to construct an algorithm incorporating these billions of individual components it is possible to speak in broad terms as to the nature, motivations and interests of all of these international actors.

Realists are clear in what constitutes a state or state-like entity for the purposes of their approach. This specificity is non-arbitrary and essential in allowing the scholar to theorise international politics. In broadening the type and number of international actors to better reflect the international reality, a similar level of specificity is demanded for theoretical integrity. The alternative approach offered herein will speak of international actors, generally, as being those actors whose actions have an effect on politics at the supra-state level. As it will be argued, every one of these billions of international actors maintain the potential to significantly alter the course of international politics thorough their actions or through a failure to act. Yet, at the same time, it is impossible to give a detailed account of each of the actors, their motivations, their interests and their goals. Indeed, an effort to describe even the most basic elements of even half of these actors would be a task measured in decades.

In moving beyond realism and recognising the power and influence on international politics of non-state actors this alternative approach is acknowledging the dissemination of power and influence from state actors to others in the international system, a transition that has most recently been noted by Richard Haas. Haass, President of the Council of Foreign Relations, outlined a similar devolution of power in his 2008 *Foreign Affairs* essay, 'The Age of Nonpolarity', when he argued that power in modern international politics is now found in many actors in many different areas of the international system.[761] This is not to suggest that it is only in the present that this reality has existed – it has always been present in international politics – but only that it is somewhat more obvious in a globalised world to recognise it as such. While arguing that there are certainly six major powers in the twenty-first century international polity - China, the EU, India, Japan, Russia and the US – there are many other actors that exert significant influence over international reality:

> In addition to the six major world powers, there are numerous regional powers: Brazil and, arguably, Argentina, Chile, Mexico, and Venezuela in Latin America; Nigeria and South Africa in Africa; Egypt, Iran, Israel, and Saudi Arabia in the Middle East; Pakistan in South Asia; Australia, Indonesia, and South Korea in East Asia and Oceania.[762]

Haas continues, listing a melange of actors large and small that maintain and exercise international power and influence including the IMF, the UN and OPEC, as well as media outlets (BBC, CNN and al-Jazeera) and terrorist militias such as Hamas and Hezbollah. [763] While not going as far as to introduce the notion of individual humans as political actors, Haas rightly concludes that international politics "is increasingly one of distributed, rather than concentrated, power" and that the key to understanding this more complicated international politic begins with recognition of its fundamentally different, nonpolar nature.[764] What is also necessary, though, is to understand the basic motivations of all of these actors in international politics, a task which is assisted by defining the relationships between these actors.

Defining The Relationship Between Elements

As suggested in the previous chapter, once a theorist has outlined the subject of their concern and the elements relating to that subject, it is then necessary to outline the relationship between the elements or, in other words, define the structure of their relationship. In terms of international relations theory, once a theorist has described what is, in fact, "international relations" and what actors are "international actors", the next step in constructing a theory is to outline the relationship between those international actors by defining the nature and structure of the international system. Previous chap-

---

[761] Richard Haass. 2008. 'The Age of Nonpolarity.' *Foreign Affairs* 87(3): 44-56.
[762] Haass. 2008.
[763] Haass. 2008.
[764] Haass. 2008.

ters have made clear that the structure of international politics favoured by the realists is anarchic. Realist examples – from Thucydides through Machiavelli and Hobbes, through Carr, Morgenthau, Mearsheimer and Waltz – have relied on anarchy as the base structure upon which to build their realist theories. While some have employed anarchy as merely a background and others, particularly the offensive and structural realists, have allowed for anarchy to play a rather more significant role in their explanations, anarchy remains the basis upon which realist international relations theory is built. Anarchy is not simply *an* assumption common to most realists, it is *the* common assumption for *all* realists. More broadly, the assumption of anarchy in international relations theory is spread widely: liberalists, constructivists and radical theorists mostly endorse the assumption of anarchy, if with different emphasis and intent at times. This section will present in two parts first a short summary of the role of anarchic structures in realist theory and then the structure of international politics assumed by the alternative approach outlined herein. It will be clear that while – at first glance – the structure of international relations suggested here could be mistaken for anarchy at first glance, the specific, important and subtle differences between realist anarchy and the suggested international political complexity have far ranging implications for the theorising of international relations and the explanation of events in the international system.

The Realist Approach

The primacy of anarchy as an assumption about the nature of the system in realist theory should now be beyond doubt. The previous chapters of this book have demonstrated the consistency with which this is held to be a fundamental truth about international politics by realists whether ancient or modern. The purpose of this short review is simply to demonstrate for a final time the centrality and adherence to the notion of an anarchic international system and to allow for a close comparison between this existing realist approach and the alternative approach outlined below.

As Legro and Moravcsik have argued, anarchy is one of the three assumptions that realists typically make.[765] Though the pair describe the assumption of actors within

---

[765] Legro and Moravcsik. 1999, p.12.

an anarchic system as "the first and least controversial assumption of realism", it is part of the purpose of this book to outline exactly why it is – or should be – controversial and questioned by international relations scholars.[766] In The first chapter of the book it was argued that classical realist positions described by Thucydides, Hobbes and Machiavelli and expounded in the form of theories by Carr and Morgenthau all endorsed anarchy as a base assumption in international relations. The work that was built on their classical foundations, notably the structural realist response and the counter-response of the neo-classicalists, served to cement this assumption further into the standard realist approach to international relations. Whether serving as a background enabling element – in the advice of Machiavelli, for example – or as a key to explaining and predicting the likelihood of certain events in the international system, as in the work of the structural realists, anarchy has played a part in the development and evolution of realism in both its classical and structural forms.

So, too, has this book explained the key role anarchy plays in the other branches of the realist paradigm. Consider the Prisoner's Dilemma, for example, where the constructed anarchy of the jailhouse serves as a central feature for the 'players' to manage, use or abuse in making their choices. It is seen also in the offensive realism of John Mearsheimer; indeed, Mearsheimer states clearly that it is the foundational assumption of his approach to the analysis of international affairs. In a world guided by offensive realist precepts, the first thing that must be understood by policy makers and political practitioners is that their political world is one without rulers or rules:

> [L]eaders have little choice but to assume worst case about other great powers' intentions. The reason for believing the worst is that there is no higher authority that states can turn to if they guess wrong about another state's intentions. States operate in an anarchic system, which means that they have nobody to turn to if they assume that another state has benign intentions, but that judgment proves wrong. As I said in my book, if you dial 911 in the international system, there is nobody at the other end.[767]

Indeed, to extend the analogy, there is not only nobody at the other end of a hypothetical emergency call under anarchy but an person can never be sure that the friend they call for help when they can't get through to 911 is actually a friend. The uncertain, unpredictable and lawless anarchy in which Mearsheimer suggests world politics

---

[766] Legro and Moravcsik. 1999, p.12.
[767] Mearsheimer. 2006a, p.120.

takes place is key to understanding his offensive realist approach, as understanding the significance of anarchy is the key to beginning to understand realist international relations.

The Alternative Approach

There are two things that must be made clear in defining the alternative approach's perspective on the international system. First, the structure of the system must be outlined and, second, the properties and effects of a system structured in that way must be explained. As with the existing realist approach, there is a distinction between the structure – anarchic – and the properties and effects of that structure, being the competition, lack of trust, power hoarding and balancing by actors in the system. This alternative approach offers a similarly simple (at least in rhetorical terms) description of the structure of the international system and, as in realism, outlines a relatively more complex explanation of the properties and effects for the system and the actors alike of this system structure. The alternative approach outlined in the paragraphs to follow continues the pattern already laid out in this chapter wherein it seeks to recognise the more complex reality of the international political system. Just as it has been argued that the realists need to understand a broader notion of what constitutes the international political system and begin to consider the role played in international relations by a broader range of political actors, the alternative approach seeks to recognise not only the lack of overarching authority in the international system but also the more complex reality of international politics as a system.

Defining the Structure

Realists reduce the complexity of international politics to a single word: anarchy. The alternative approach's perspective on the international political system can also be reduced to a single word: complexity. The reality of international relations is complex and while it is the goal of the theorist to simplify reality, seeking parsimony at the expense of theoretical utility as the realists have done is sure to produce a less useful theory in the end. To say that the international system is complex, though, is to be just as broad and overly parsimonious; thus, while the alternative approach is founded on a system that is 'complex', the definition of what exactly a complex political system is remains of critical importance. Thus, for the purposes of this book and for the discussion of complex international relations and complex international relations theory that follows, a complex system is held to be:

> ...a system for which it is difficult, if not impossible, to restrict its description to a limited number of parameters or characterising variables without losing its essential, global functional properties.

Bernard Pavard and Julie Dugdale, writing as part of the European Union-backed COSI project which researched complex systems in the social sciences, add that it is necessary and:

> ...appropriate to differentiate between a complicated system (such as a plane or computer) and a complex system (such as ecological or economic systems). The former are composed of many functionally distinct parts but are in fact predictable, whereas the latter interact non-linearly with their environment and their components have properties of self-organisation which make them non-predictable beyond a certain temporal window.[768]

Obviously such a conception of the international system is an explicit rejection of the realist approach – the realist focus on states is a clear limitation in the number and variety of variables under examination yet the realists maintain that the system can still be adequately explained and predicted – but it is also a specific and natural fit with the previously outlined broadening of the notion of what is 'international politics' and who are 'international actors'.

Regarding this definition, it is necessary to highlight and offer explanation about three key words. First is the word 'system'. The word 'system' in international relations theory, so it has previously been argued, has meant, at different times and in different contexts, some three different things. As Jay Goodman argued, the world can either be used descriptively (for example, any bounded group of interacting parts), explanatively (for example, the system has an effect on the elements within the system) or methodologically (for example, a person employs 'system x' to arrive at a

---

[768] Bernard Pavard and Julie Dugdale. 2003. *An Introduction to Complexity in Social Science.* [26 May 2008} http://tinyurl.com/6x77hj.

conclusion or to facilitate analysis). In realism the first is generally employed by the classical realists and the second by the neorealists and offensive realists. In the alternative approach – where it will later be argued that the system facilitates and has a marked and measureable impact on the behaviour and prospects of its constituent elements – the word system is employed explanatively, that is, in the same way that Waltz and Mearsheimer employ the term. The system *does* have an impact on the elements of the system, not just in defining their relationships with each other but also the extent to which those elements can impact on the wider community of international political actors.

The second term in this definition to highlight is the definition's reference to 'parameters and variables'. In the context of a theory of international relations, these parameters and variables relate to the identified international actors. Where realists generally limit their analysis to the role and actions of states, a system in which the number of actors cannot be limited without misunderstanding the system under analysis demands the sort of broadening that the alternative approach provides. The actors and their capabilities form the parameters and variables that the definition above refers to.

The third term that requires definition is the reference made to the system's "global functional properties". This reference implies that the system itself has an impact on international politics in that it has certain properties that actors must either consider or have impact upon them. This is not at all a new notion; indeed, the neorealists and the offensive realists – not to mention some constructivist theorists, too – all endorse theories that describe an international reality in which the properties of the system as a system have some effect on the actors and their choices. Such systemic properties are 'global' in that they affect all elements in the system and impact on the capabilities of all international actors at every level. The systemic properties are 'functional' in that they serve a function, that is, they impact definitively on the international reality. Significantly, though, the properties of a complex system as this definition and approach describes are markedly different from those found under the realist's anarchy. Indeed, research into complex systems in the social sciences suggests that there are four significant properties of a complex system and all four have marked global and ongoing impacts on the actors in the system and the system as a whole. In the paragraphs that follow these four properties will be described, explained and explored.

The Properties of a Complex Structure

A system with the structure thus described has four major properties that impact upon the system and the actors existing and emerging within it. As outlined by Pavard and Dugdale, the four major properties of a complex system are (a) non-determinism and non-tractability, (b) limited functional decomposability, (c) distributed nature of information and representation and (d) emergence and self-organisation.[769] Common to all complex systems, these properties not only help to define complexity but also to shape the system and its evolution, too. Thus, in the following paragraphs each of the four properties outlined by Pavard and Dugdale will be considered in turn and have their effects described and explained in the context of international politics and the system described by this alternative approach.

Property I: Non-determinism and non-tractability

Pavard and Dugdale describe the first property of a complex system in the following terms:

> A complex system is fundamentally non-deterministic. It is impossible to anticipate precisely the behaviour of such systems even if we completely know the function of its constituents.[770]

This reality within the complexity of the system seems almost counterintuitive in a world where the general conception of science is that knowing *almost* everything about *almost* everything about a system (where the term is used in a broad sense) should allow us to predict *almost* the state of that system at a point in the future. As explained by Gleick, such properties "run against all intuition" for scientists, at least at first.[771] Even if one were to know completely what all of the actors within the system do – and remembering that in this alternative approach the number of potentially relevant actors runs into the billions – it would be impossible to predict the future of the system precisely, that is, with long-term confidence. This is not to say that short-term predictions cannot be near correct or that long-term predictions will always be wide of the mark; instead it is to say that many predictions about the future state of a

---

[769] Pavard and Dugdale. 2003.
[770] Pavard and Dugdale. 2003.
[771] Gleick. 1987, p.21.

complex international system are likely to be wrong and that the further out one predicts the more likely that the prediction will be incorrect. In the international political system, then, while we can perhaps predict with high probability the power of an actor such as the United States or China tomorrow, next week or next month, but attempts to predict the power maintained by such an actor in a decade's time or longer are much less likely to be accurate. Indeed, as the example from the previous chapter of realists speculating on the capabilities of the Soviet Union mere weeks before that superpower collapsed demonstrates, sometimes even the very short term can prove embarrassing for the most experienced international analysts.

Property II: Limited functional decomposability

Pavard and Dugdale describe the second property of a complex system thus:

> A complex system has a dynamic structure. It is therefore difficult, if not impossible, to study its properties by decomposing it into functionally stable parts. Its permanent interaction with its environment and its properties of self-organisation allow it to functionally restructure itself.[772]

The impossibility of decomposing the system into its constituent parts is illustrated by Pavard and Dugdale through the example of a car. A car, they write, is an example of a simple system that is decomposable. If you were to take the car apart, come to understand how the various components of the car (brakes, transmission, axles etc) work it is possible to develop an understanding of how the entire car works by simply combining each component.[773] Conversely, a complex system cannot be decomposed in this way. To paraphrase Douglas Adams, complexity lies outside of our normal vision: as opposed to stripping down a vehicle, "if you try and take a cat apart to see how it works, the first thing you have on your hands is a non-working cat". As Pavard and Dugdale explain:

> A principal obstacle to the functional decomposability of complex systems is the dynamic and fluctuating character of its constituent functions. The interaction with the en-

---

[772] Pavard and Dugdale. 2003.
[773] Pavard and Dugdale. 2003.

vironment, as well as the learning and self organisation mechanisms makes it unrealistic to regard such systems as structurally stable.[774]

In the context of the international political system, then, a theory that recognises the complexity of international relations must also avoid the temptation of attempting to focus on the elements of the system – the states, the institutions, the corporations, the NGOs and the individuals – and any attempt to draw conclusions about the system from an understanding of their motivations and goals alone. If the international system is a complex system then the realist focus on states and their attempt to describe, explain and predict international politics through understanding, analysing and modelling the actions of states is misguided. Indeed, it is doomed to describe an international politic that does not match the reality and the errors in explanation already highlighted in this book are testament to this.

Property III: Distributed nature of information and representation

Complex systems are necessarily distributed systems, that is, its resources are physically or virtually distributed on various sites.[775] Information about the system is not found in a single place and analysis of a single point or element in the system gives little information about other points in the system or the trajectory of the system as a whole. When information about the system is distributed, "neither the actors nor the observer can, at a given moment, give a deterministic plan" of the future of the system.[776] In essence, knowing a single part of the system or gaining information about many parts of the system does not mean that the system can be predicted or fully explained. Every element in the international political system has the ability to control the way that they distribute their own information locally, yet at a system level it is impossible to both control the transfer of information and to have access to all of that information. Actors seek to advance their own interests as they conceive of them, and actors interact with imperfect knowledge of each other's preferences and aspirations. Unlike a simple system consisting of only known quantities, predictable futures and limited choices for actors, the complex international political system so broadly dis-

---

[774] Pavard and Dugdale. 2003.
[775] Pavard and Dugdale. 2003.
[776] Pavard and Dugdale. 2003.

tributes information about the system and its actors that few quantities can be accurately tracked, few futures are predictable with any confidence.

Property IV: Emergence and self-organisation

Pavard and Dugdale describe the property of emergence and self-organisation in the following way:

> Emergence is the process of deriving some new and coherent structures, patterns and properties in a complex system. Emergent phenomena occur due to the pattern of interactions...between the elements of the system over time. One of the main points about emergent phenomena is that they are observable at a macro-level, even though they are generated by micro-level elements.[777]

While previous discussion of the properties of a complex system has made clear that the system is impossible to predict with certainty in anything other than the very short term, the property of emergence offers some hope for identifying trends in the system and drawing conclusions as to the probability of an event or action taking place. Argue Pavard and Dugdale, "emergent phenomena occur due to the pattern of interactions between the elements of the system over time".[778] As certain behaviours in certain circumstances emerge with regularity it is possible to suggest that such behaviours will continue to occur. This is not to say, however, that such suggestions take on the force of a 'law': they do not. Emergent behaviour may occur over and over again but it is not deigned to *always* occur and, indeed, the inherent nature of a complex system and its properties ensure that behaviour remains unpredictable. Also significant is that while patterns of emergence are noticed at the macro or system level, the drivers of this emergence are the actors at the micro level. In the context of the international political system, we can identify emergent behaviours (as realists have done with their studies of balancing and deterrence) at the macro level but we must also identify the micro level actors that drive this behaviour. That the international political system self-organises into a certain level of security and stability is no accident; the properties of this system, like any other complex system, are such that it is highly likely to occur.

---

[777] Pavard and Dugdale. 2003.
[778] Pavard and Dugdale. 2003.

Conclusion: A Summary of the Components of the Alternative Approach

This alternative approach to imagining the international political system is thoroughly different to the states-under-anarchy imagination of the realists. Where realists assume an anarchic reality this alternative approach embraces the complexity of the international system and recognises this not as something to be 'simplified away' but rather embraced and theorised from. Where realists focus on the largest political actors which, in the present time, are primarily composed of less than two hundred nation-states this alternative approach recognises the impacts that sub-state and transnational actors have and has thus expanded its scope of analysis to include the largest actors, the smallest actors and every actor in between. In a complex system where information and capabilities are distributed throughout billions of actors – and where each action may feedback into the system and spark everything from the outbreak of war to the arrival of peace – failing to assess the influence and power of any actors simply because they are not nation-states will leave the theorist offering analysis of a system that is far removed from the complex reality. As well, this alternative approach allows the analyst to imagine a system where future prediction is explicitly impossible but where – somewhat paradoxically – patterns of behaviour emerge over time and can be identified and correlated with certain circumstances. Thus, while not offering the analyst the 'billiard ball' certainty that exists in simple 'if X then Y' systems, the alternative approach correctly identifies the complexity and unpredictability of the international political system while leaving the possibility for emergent behaviours to be identified, correlated with system states and for the analyst to identify the *probable* among the infinite number of *possible* futures. The alternative approach outlined above is a better representation of reality of international politics but – like the realism it is intended to challenge – it must be tested before its utility is assured.

Testing the Alternative Approach

The alternative approach outlined above includes several assumptions about what actors are significant in international politics, the goals and motivations of those actors, the structure and nature of the international system, the properties of that system and the effect of these properties on the system as a whole, its constituent actors and for the analyst of international affairs who would employ this approach. While this book has argued that realism with its foundation of anarchy is an overly parsimonious approach to theorising international relations and is of little utility in analysing the complexities of international politics, the alternative approach offered herein is yet to be tested as an alternative. It is in this section of the book that the testing of the alternative approach will take place.

Drawing from the description of the international system above four key hypotheses will be developed. Each of the four will then be tested with reference to case studies from international political history. The cases selected to test the hypotheses include a combination of historical cases that realism has had difficulty in explaining as well as cases where realist explanations have proved sufficient in the past. The alternative approach will be shown to both better describe and explain events and actions that realism has previously described and capably explain events and actions that have proved problematic for realists in the past. As a result, a case for this alternative approach being superior to the realist approach will be made in the conclusion to this section and expanded again in the conclusion to this chapter.

Developing Hypotheses

From the explanation of the structure of the international system, the properties of that system and the number and type of international actors within it, hypotheses can be developed by which to test the approach against what is observable in the real world. This section will present four hypotheses developed from the approach outlined above, specifically related to the properties of the complex system that the alternative approach is founded upon.

Hypothesis I

The property of non-determinism and non-tractability makes prediction over the long-term impossible in a complex system. In a complex system with so many potentially influential actors, as in the international political system, attempts to predict the future trajectory of an actor, a group of actors or the political structure of the system is outside of the realm of possibility for the analyst and scholar. While some general assessments of the *probable* future may be inferred from studying emergent behaviours amongst actors and these can often be accurate, specific prediction – where a state of the system is defined for a future time and place – is rarely successful. Thus, the first hypothesis offered here relates to the unpredictability of the system:

> **H1: While probabilistic trends may be identified, long-term, specific predictions of the international system, both by international actors and international analysts, are likely to be inaccurate.**

Hypothesis II

The property relating to the limited functional decomposability of a complex system suggests that the study of individual elements or actors in international politics cannot inform the analyst as to the nature of the system. The focus on a single type or category of international actor, then, is bound to present an image of the international system that is flawed. We should find, then, that approaches that focus on only certain elements of the international system are likely to be flawed: the incompatibility of selective actor assessment combined with the inherent assumptions about the temporal permanence of those actors in the system mark such approaches as non-complex approaches. Drawing on this, the second hypothesis offered here relates to the focus of theoretical approaches to the international system:

> **H2: Analysis that seeks to understand international politics through reference to the actions, motivations or activities of a sub-set of actors cannot reliably describe the observable and complex international reality.**

Hypothesis III

From the complex system's property relating to the distributed nature of information and representation it is possible to develop a third hypothesis. As in all complex systems where information is scattered, relationships established between elements in the system are likely to be short-range, non-linear and contain feedback loops. International actors will be unable to trust their fellow actors having access to only limited

232

information about their intentions. From this property of the international political system we can extract the following hypothesis:

H3: Stable relationships between actors in the international system are possible, but relationships are frequently short-term, non-linear and weak.

Hypothesis IV

While the first hypothesis suggests that accurate *prediction* is impossible in a complex system we can also assume from the fourth property of such a system – emergence and self-organisation – that there exists a possibility to point to correlations between certain situations and certain behaviours by actors within the system. Emergent behaviour is a common feature of complex systems and, while it does not lead to a situation where all behaviour is explicitly predictable, it does allow for the analyst to suggest with some probability the likely future course of the system and the actors within it. As a result, the analyst should find certain behaviours repeated at all levels of the international system and by actors of all sizes. Structured as a hypothesis we can say:

H4: Certain behaviours emerge as commonplace patterns in the international political system over time, but they are subject to changes, which may be gradual or abrupt.

Testing the Hypotheses

Cases selected to test the hypothesis are drawn from two groups: first, the cases previously discussed in this book that have proven difficult or impossible for realists to explain adequately; and, secondly, cases that realists have already adequately explained. By examining both types of cases it will be shown that the alternative approach offers not only a credible explanation for the events, actions and behaviour that realists struggle with but also adequately explains – if in a different way and with a different focus – events, actions and behaviours that realism can already explain. The argument, then, is that the alternative approach and its non-anarchic foundation is a useful tool for the analyst to assess international reality and, while it is not yet

233

claimed to be completely refined or a replacement for realism, the tests offered below allow for – at the very least – the alternative approach to be considered an alternative research program in the Lakatosian tradition. In the paragraphs that follow each of the four hypotheses above will be examined in turn. In each case the hypothesis will be discussed first in relation to the alternative realist position before three cases from international political history are offered to test the assumption. Finally a concluding paragraph will assess whether the hypothesis holds or should be rejected.

Hypothesis I

Structural realist Kenneth Waltz has described the international system as "the realm of accident and upheaval, of rapid and unpredictable change".[779] Yet the same theorist has also admitted that his theory and, to his mind, all international relations theory is limited in its utility because of this. He writes:

> Theory obviously cannot explain the accidental or account for unexpected events; it deals in regularities and repetitions and is possible only if these can be identified.[780]

Waltz, like many realists, suggests that accidental or unexpected events and behaviours in international politics are distinct from the regularities of international relations and are thus outside of the realm of theorists within the discipline. Waltz is half right here: certainly a theory founded on anarchy such as neorealism is unlikely to be able to deal with international irregularities and accidental events. However, an approach that recognises the underlying complexity of the system *expects* that accidental events will not only play a part but a *significant* part in defining the trajectory of international politics. The difficulties that realists have found in predicting the future of international politics can be explained by the lack of attention paid to the small, sub-system and accidental irregularities. In this light, the first hypothesis can be considered with reference to situations and behaviour that realists have previously considered: predictions for a post-Cold War European landscape, predictions for the So-

---

[779] Waltz. 1979, p.65.

[780] Kenneth Waltz. 1988. 'The Origins of War in Neorealist Theory.' *Journal of Interdisciplinary History* 18(4): 615-628, p.615.

viet Union in the late twentieth century and early twenty-first century and Third Reich predictions on likely Allied responses to pre-World War Two expansionism. John Mearsheimer's offensive realist predictions on the future strategic and security landscape of Europe after the Cold War have been considered in the previous chapter and in greater detail in the article 'Offensive Realism and Central & Eastern Europe after the Cold War'.[781] The flaws in Mearsheimer's approach are significant and serve as evidence that predictions about the international system are likely to be wrong when those predictions are based on systemic anarchy and relations between states, and fail to consider the role of non-state actors and their potential effects on the system. Mearsheimer's argument in 'Back to the Future: Instability in Europe after the Cold War' is a study in how wrong such anarchy-based predictions can be: of the four distinct futures he offered not one can be said to have emerged in reality. Indeed, Mearsheimer concedes that his predictions are bound to be error filled, writing:

> ...political phenomena are highly complex; hence precise political predictions are impossible without very powerful theoretical tools, superior to those we now [in 1990] possess...later hindsight will undoubtedly reveal surprises and mistakes.[782]

This acknowledgement of the impossibility of predicting a complex international system did not stop Mearsheimer offering another 40 pages of predictions in that article, though the failure of his predictions does seem to confirm both the first hypothesis outlined above – as well as his own caveat on political predictions – by failing so obviously in describing the future of Europe. As the hypothesis suggests, long-term predictions of the international system by international analysts may be wrong.

Another series of long-term predictions that have been conclusively proved wrong surround the late twentieth-century predictions as to the future of the Soviet Union. The now-former superpower was held by many analysts to be both an ongoing rival to the United States and its NATO allies and a threat to world peace even weeks before the its collapse. Analysts like Charles Doran and Wes Parsons, writing in 1980, saw the Soviet Union as the rising power of the two global superpowers, the United States being in a decade-long decline.[783] The pair's representation of the evolution of

---

[781] Kissane. 2007b.

[782] Mearsheimer. 1990a, p.9.

[783] Doran and Parsons. 1980.

Soviet power was of a rising state actor that along with China was leading the world in terms of its power (as measured through national capabilities).

Kenneth Waltz, too, can stand as an example of an analyst that misread the trajectory of the Soviet Union. In 1988 – just a year before the fall of the Berlin Wall – Waltz argued that the Cold War was "firmly rooted in the structure of post-war international politics, and will last as long as that structure endures".[784] Only months later the Cold War was over, a superpower had collapsed and Waltz's confident 'business as usual' prediction was proven wrong. Again, a prediction about the future of the international system was proved wrong.

Predictions by international analysts in times of war have been proven equally invalid. In the years and months preceding the outbreak of World War Two poor predictions by both the Allied powers and the German government contributed to the war beginning when and how it eventually did. The Munich Agreement was an attempt on behalf of the non-German powers in Europe to broker a peace through the offer to the Germans of the Czechoslovakian Sudetenland. It was hoped, as British Prime Minister Neville Chamberlain announced after signing the agreement, that this would bring "peace with honour" to Europe and that it would secure "peace for our time". Obviously, with the outbreak of hostilities only a year later, the peace that Chamberlain hoped for and predicted failed to eventuate. The entrance of the British and French into a state of war with Germany, though, marked a further failure in analysis and prediction, this time on the behalf of the German Reich. Seizing on the assumed weakness of the Western European states in the face of the successful seizure of Austria and the Sudetenland, the German leadership did not believe that the British and French would declare war in the face of a German invasion of Poland. With the Molotov-Ribbentrop Non-Aggression Pact ensuring that the Soviet Union would offer no resistance on the German eastern front and in the belief that the other Munich Agreement states would not react as they had promised to the annexation of Poland, German forces rolled eastwards and found – almost immediately – that their leader's predictions were proven wrong. It would only be hours before German U-boats and British aircraft engaged the enemy in the sea and the air and states from as far away as Australia and Canada declared war on the Reich, too. Whether predictions by the

---

[784] Waltz. 1988, p.628.

British leadership as to the likelihood of ongoing peace in Europe after Munich or the predictions by the German leadership of the chance of a Europe-wide war as a result of their movement into Poland, the predictions and analysis on both sides about what would become the Second World War were flawed.

It is important, however, to differentiate in this discussion, as in the hypothesis it addresses, the difference between identifying trends in international politics and making specific predictions. Mearsheimer's four futures for Europe and Waltz's predictions for future Soviet positions were specific predictions about future realities of the system. Trends in the system, for example, declining US power or a re-emerging China, are different: they are neither specific or refer to a particular date. These trends are usually identified by the extrapolation of past and current data and are probabilistic; the predictions that are suggested herein to be inaccurate are those that are, perhaps based on such trends, made about a long-term, specific international reality. While it would be remiss to declare that all such predictions are most definitely wrong, the likelihood that a prediction will be inaccurate increases as the length of time between the present and the predicted future increases. Finally, it should be noted that the hypothesis is related only to long-term predictions. As has been proven for so many short-term encounters in the international system, well-informed actors can and do make reasonably accurate predictions about the trajectory of the international politic. However, it is the difficulties faced by actors and analysts in predicting the long-term future which suggests that the 'billiard ball' approximation of cause and effect and the 'if A then B then C' predictions of actors and analysts in international relations is something other than an anarchy with a limited number of significant actors; the complex reality of international politics means that such predicative algorithms will likely prove inaccurate in the long-term.

In a complex international system we expect that predictions are likely to be proven wrong. The inability to account for the actions, reactions, motivations, goals and agendas of billions of international actors and their effect on other actors renders prediction impossible. Whether predicting the future trajectory of a continent (as Mearsheimer attempted), a country (in the case of the Soviet Union) or the reaction of a small number of local rivals (as in the case of European calculations before World War Two), the small events and impacts of actors outside of the primary focus have

the effect of skewing any analysis. The failure by realists and other theorists to successfully predict post-Cold War European landscapes and to foresee the decline of
the Soviet Union is a direct result of the common assumption that the international
system is anarchic though, as has been noted earlier, this lack of predicative success
does not invalidate the realist approach altogether. Under anarchy the possibility of
prediction is maintained; as Mearsheimer implies, prediction in international relations
will be possible one day when superior theoretical tools are available.[785] Recognising
and assuming a complex international system, on the other hand, means that the
likely inaccuracy of long-term prediction in international relations is explained. A
'superior' theoretical or analytical tool will prove equally useless in accurately predicting international politics under complexity and the further 'out' the prediction is
made (that is to say the earlier a prediction is made) the more likely it will be ob-
servably incorrect.

Hypothesis II

In the past both natural science and social science were based on reductionism
whereby "the whole is understood by knowing the attributes and the interactions of
its parts".[786] In simple or closed systems reduction is a useful approach and the history of its employment in chemistry, physics, biology and economics is long and successful. James Gleick describes this Newtonian approach thus:

> Scientists [maintained that] given an *approximate* knowledge of a system's initial con-
> ditions and an understanding of natural law, one can calculate the *approximate* behav-
> iour of the system...Very small influences can be neglected...and arbitrarily small influ-
> ences don't blow up to have arbitrarily large effects.[787]

Reducing a system to its constituent parts and assessing the most significant of these
parts in order to ascribe qualities to the system and describe actions within it is a
strategy undertaken often by realists. The most common approach by realists is to
focus primarily on nation-states and, having ascribed them certain qualities and motivations (for example, Waltz ascribing survival as a goal of states), use those as a basis
for explaining events at the system-level. These ascribed qualities are also employed,

---

[785] Mearsheimer. 1990a, p.9.
[786] Waltz. 1979, p.18.
[787] Gleick. 1987, p.15.

238

for example, to describe the behaviour of other actors in the international system, international institutions being a stark example. From their understanding of nation-states the realists presume to understand the workings of the international political system and, while this may be valid under an assumed simple anarchy, it is far from valid under a more complex systemic reality.

Consider the case of the North Atlantic Treaty Organisation (NATO). The resilience of the NATO alliance in the absence of the previous threat from the former Soviet Union is one example of where the realist explanations fail and the second hypothesis held by the alternative approach does not. The NATO alliance is understood by realists to be a manifestation of the coincidentally congruent interests of its member states. More specifically, the NATO alliance is a security alliance and its nominal goal in the Cold War was, according to realists, to balance the threat of the Soviet-backed Warsaw Pact. With the collapse of the Soviet Union, the disintegration of the Warsaw Pact and the diminished strategic threat from the East of Europe, realist analysts believed that NATO would fold as an institution. The alliance's *raison d'être* had disappeared and – under anarchy – states will only continue with an alliance while their interests remain congruent. Yet the NATO alliance has survived nearly twenty years since the collapse of its rival and has even expanded to include some of the states that were previously enemies, a result that has left realist analysts seeking a new explanation as to why.[788] The fault in the reasoning of those surprised analysts is the way in which the evolution of institutions in the international system is assumed to be synonymous with the interests of states and that reactions to events (such as the collapse of the Soviet Union and the disappearance of a Warsaw Pact rival) should follow the same pattern as a solitary state. What was observed, in fact, was that the institution that is NATO reacted very differently than realist analysts expected; instead of folding it flourished and remains a significant actor in international politics – proof indeed that reducing international politics to the study of a single type of actor is bound to lead to poor analysis.[789]

---

[788] Kenneth Waltz has acknowledged that NATO "outliving its purpose" was a "strange case" for realists. See Waltz. 2000, p.18.

[789] John Mearsheimer was dismissive of notions that the NATO alliance and the Warsaw Pact would outlive the Cold War. He wrote that while "they might persist on paper" each would "cease to function as an alliance", a position that, in hindsight, is clearly mistaken. See Mearsheimer. 1990a, p.5.

The example of the establishment of the EU and the unprecedented peaceful integration of Europe discussed in the previous chapter also stands as an example where analysts remain surprised at the aberrant behaviour of states that should – judging on past history, interests and capabilities – be doing anything other than forming a closer union. Indeed, realists are unable to explain within the assumptions of their approach the integration by Europe into a continent-wide European Union and that the states involved are willingly and consistently surrendering sovereignty to another actor. In an anarchic, self-help international system where alliances are presumed to be short, narrow and essentially weak, the integration of Europe stands as a polar opposite: the alliance is nearly 60 years old, broad enough to encompass most of Europe and strong enough to boast the world's largest economy and be a rich home to half a billion people.[790] The states in the European Union are doing something other than what states are 'meant' to do under realist anarchy and the international institution that is the EU is acting contrary to how institutions are meant to act under anarchy. This would not be surprising if one assumes these states and that institution exist and are acting within a complex system. The realist parsimony that suggests that knowledge of the actions, motivations and interests of states can explain the wider system once again fails to demonstrate its utility here. Instead we see that the development of the European Union and its trajectory in international politics reflect more the complexities of the international system rather than an extension of the will of states in political anarchy.

Consider also the notion that the rationality of states can explain events in the broad international system. In the case of explaining conflict, as James Fearon has argued, "political scientists who have studied the origins of particular wars often have concluded that war can be a rational alternative for leaders who are acting in their states' interest".[791] Support for this position is found in a paper by Dan Lindley and Ryan Schildkraut who note convincing arguments for both World War One and the Iraqi

---

[790] John McCormick describes the evolution as a series of events that "will go down in history as one of the most remarkable achievements of the twentieth century". See McCormick. 2002, p.xi.
[791] James Fearon. 1995. 'Rationalist explanations for war.' *International Organization* 49(3): 379-414, p.379.

240

invasion of Kuwait being rational choices made by states pursuing interests.[792] Rationality is also assumed when discussing nuclear strategy with Kenneth Waltz's 'The Spread of Nuclear Weapons' and John Mearsheimer's 'Back to the Future' both being prototypical accounts where rationality in international relations is explicitly assumed.[793] The focus on states and their rationality may help explain some wars and some nuclear strategies but there exist examples of both that do not fit this narrow assumption. Consider, for example, the argument offered in the previous chapter regarding World War One: while realists, committed to rationality, have offered an explanation for this conflict there is a reasonable alternate explanation giving greater weight to the actions of sub-state actors working in a complex system. Similarly, while the rationality of actors with regards to nuclear weapons is often observed, there are occasions where actors choose to act in a manner that is largely irrational. States giving up their nuclear weapons programs, states choosing not to seek such weapons in the face of a nuclear-armed rival and states that share their nuclear technology with rival states. Where analysts assume that that states are rational and the system is a rational system, they are bound to find they are bound to find that the expected reality does not match what can and is observed.

The trend towards reductionism in the natural sciences has been arrested as the properties of chaotic and complex systems have become better known. Scientists realise that assuming that the properties of a part of a system are similar or the same as the properties of the entire system is not a valid analytical assumption for complex systems. As Gleick notes, "the laws of complexity hold universally, caring not at all for the details of a system's constituent [elements]".[794] While there are times where the qualities ascribed to certain elements work for all levels of the system, the exceptions outlined above suggest that this is not universal. Institutions and alliances do not always act like states or for states; states do not always act in what is thought to be their own best interests; and the system's trajectory cannot be explained reliably with reference to only the properties of a sub-set of actors. Knowledge of a certain part of the system does not offer clues as to the future of the system nor how that system works.

---

[792] Dan Lindley and Ryan Schildkraut. 2005. *Is War Rational? The Extent of Miscalculation and Misperception as Causes of War*. Paper presented at the Annual Meeting of the International Studies Association, Honolulu, United States, 5 March 2005, pp.1-52, p.5.
[793] Waltz. 1981; Mearsheimer. 1990a.
[794] Gleick. 1987, p.304.

The system itself has properties greater than the combined properties of its elements. Simply put, the whole is greater than the sum of its parts.

Hypothesis III

The third hypothesis is perhaps the one in which the realist approach and the alternative approach find the most common ground. In a complex system relationships between elements in the system are known to be non-linear, short term and weak in the sense that there is no permanency assumed. Similarly, realists have long assumed that the constraints of anarchy mean that relationships and alliances between states are limited in scope, timescale and are construed to be narrow, often relating to a single common interest. While the two approaches may maintain the same conclusion, however, the reasoning in each case is significantly different as the assumptions about the nature of the system in each case are in stark contrast. Under anarchy it is argued that an actor cannot be sure of any other actors true intention and that every other actor – even those who are 'friends' – may one day be enemies. As a result, alliances between actors are usually limited in scope and timescale by nervous actors on each side. In a complex system, however, it is not necessarily the intent or future intent of an actor that limits alliances and integration efforts but the nature of the system itself. With so many international level actors impacting upon each other, with feedback effects being felt throughout the system and with the information about capabilities being dispersed widely and even unobtainably across the system, alliances are frequently weak and short. As well, in a complex system relationships are expected to be non-linear and as unpredictable as any other part of the system. Just as an actor in a complex system cannot predict their own long-term future they (or an analyst) cannot predict the likely future of any relationship between actors. Consideration of the examples below puts this into perspective.

The Allied powers that defeated the Axis powers in Europe during the Second World War are a stark example of a short, single issue alliance in international politics. While there were dozens of nations allied against Germany and her Axis partners many of those allied states were uncommon bedfellows. The Soviet Union found itself allied with the United States, Britain and France, all states that had allied against the Soviet regime during the Russian Civil War at the conclusion of the First World War.[795] France and Britain were again allied after centuries of belligerence in the face of the greater threat of German expansion. The United States found itself in the remarkable position of actively supporting their ideological rival the Soviet Union through increased trade when – just years before – such a move would have been unthinkable.[796] Yet with the defeat of the German forces the alliance splintered. The United States and the Soviet Union settled into a 40 year Cold War, Europe was partitioned and former allies were occupied by the Soviet Union, a state of affairs that would continue for nearly half a century. The western sector of Germany became an ally when, weeks before, it had been part of the central Axis power in Europe while the eastern sector remained opposed to France, Britain and the United States while becoming allied with the Soviet Union. The relationship between the 'Big Three' – Britain, the US and the Soviet Union – was enough to defeat a force that had come to dominate a continent but lasted only a handful of years. The alliance between the East and the West is the epitome of the short, weak and indeterminate relationship between actors in a complex system. It would not be the last, however, as events in the Persian Gulf in the 1990s would prove.

The coalition of states that formed to eject Iraq from Kuwait in 1990/91 is again an example of a short-term coalition of likeminded actors who – when the goal is achieved – disband and return to their previous state of hostility and distrust. Thirty-four countries committed armed forces and an additional two – Japan and West Germany – provided financial support for the operation to liberate Kuwait and, as in the case of World War Two, the coalition partners narrowly constructed their goals and interests: where in Europe it had been the defeat and unconditional surrender of Germany in the Middle East it was the retreat and subsequent surrender of Iraq. Following the conclusion of hostilities in Iraq and Kuwait, the coalition disbanded and the actors returned to their sometimes-belligerent attitudes towards each other: Pakistan (which committed approximately 5,000 troops) and India (which offered re-fuelling facilities) continued to argue over the sovereignty of the Kashmir with the Kargil War breaking out in 1999; the United States (the major coalition partner) would soon fire

---

[795] See, for example, David Foglesong. 1995. *America's Secret War Against Bolshevism: US Intervention in the Russian Civil War, 1917-1920*. University of North Carolina Press: Chapel Hill.

[796] The program through which this support was channelled was known as the Lend Lease Program and was extended not only to the Soviet Union but also the Western European allies and China.

cruise missiles into Afghanistan (300 troops) and within a decade launch an invasion and occupation of that country; Britain (approximately 45,000 troops), Australia (1,800 troops) and the NATO states would join the United States in its 2001 war against Afghanistan; and Saudi Arabia (up to 100,000 troops) sought rapprochement with anti-coalition actors Jordan and the Palestinian Liberation Organisation, both of whom opposed the anti-Iraq intervention. The Gulf War coalition of 1990/91 is prototypical of relationships between actors in a complex system: short term, narrowly described and essentially weak in their nature. Indeed, how else would one describe a relationship which moves from armed forces fighting alongside each other to armed forces fighting each other in only a few years?

Yet, if we turn to examples of NATO and the EU once again, we find that there are relationships that seem to counter this short term, narrowly constructed and weak relationship norm under complexity. This alliance has outlasted its primary goal and has expanded in recent years to include some of the enemies it was meant to guard against. Furthermore, it was only in the period after the Cold War and a decade after the collapse of the Soviet superpower that the alliance operationalised its collective security mechanisms in the wake of the 11 September 2001 terrorist attacks on the United States. Thus, the relationship that was meant to protect against a superpower and that was expected to disband in the wake of that superpower's collapse continued to exist and evolved into a larger, more broadly focussed alliance now acting against a non-state actor in the shape of al-Qaeda. The continued relationship between NATO members stands in opposition to what is to be expected in a complex system. It might be argued that NATO is an aberration if there were not other examples in the international system of long-term relationships and alliances. The Australia-United States relationship, the Australia-United Kingdom relationships, the France-Monaco relationship and the relationship between the United States and Canada all stand as examples of long-term, broadly constructed relationships between actors in the international system and, perhaps, evidence that the hypothesis as to relationships under complexity fails its test.

For this hypothesis, then, we find that there are both incidents that confirm and to deny its veracity. Like the realists with their presumption of anarchy, the alternative approach suggests that relationships in international politics should be expected to be

244

short, weak and narrowly defined. Certainly in the example of the World War Two Allied powers this would seem to be the case, as it would also seem to be the case regarding the relationship in the Gulf War coalition in 1990/91. The NATO case, however, stands out clearly as an example of a remarkably stable international relationship which has not only existed in largely the same form for a long period but has done so even when its stated *raison d'être* has all but disappeared. This hypothesis, then, cannot be said to be confirmed, at least in its current form. In a complex system the longevity of the EU, the NATO alliance and the various bilateral relationships mentioned above are aberrations in a world where, as the third hypothesis suggests, relationships between actors are more frequently weak and of limited duration.

Hypothesis IV

Earlier hypotheses have suggested that the international system tends to be unpredictable in the long term. Examples of failures by analysts and actors to correctly predict the international system have been offered and, indeed, abound in the international system. For every actor that gambles and wins on the international financial market, for example, there are many that experience unexpected losses. Nation-states that win a long war against an equal become bogged down when facing a numerically, technologically and economically weaker foe. Realists like Kenneth Waltz feel confident enough to list 6 states and 5 corporations and demand, "Few states die; many firms do. Who is likely to be around 100 years from now?" – only to find that one of those states disappeared in little more than a decade while all the firms continue to exist nearly thirty years later.[797] Yet while accurate predictions about specific elements of the system may be impossible, the alternative approach does not suggest that trends will not emerge in international politics or that these trends cannot be identified. Rather, complex systems are partly defined by the emergent behaviours that develop within them. In this vein, the fourth hypothesis can be considered with reference to a behaviour that realists have long identified in international relations – power balancing – at the international level.

---

[797] Waltz. 1979, p.95.

Realists have long identified that international politics is regularly defined by actors seeking to balance against threats. Hans Morgenthau uses the term in at least four different ways in his book *Politics among Nations* but submits that, in general terms, 'balance of power' refers to the state where power is distributed among several actors with approximate equality.[798] The strategic East-West balance of the Cold War stands as a typical example of a balance of power, the eastern Soviet bloc balancing the power of the western US/NATO bloc. Note that the power or capabilities of each side of this 'balance' are not precisely equal but rather 'equal enough' to deter each side of the balance from threatening the other. Yet if the balance isn't perfect then the assumed applicability of the balance of power to the international system is. Morgenthau describes the balance of power in international relations as universal, offering multiple ways (divide and rule, compensations, armaments, alliances) in which the balance might be manifested.[799] Realists argue that this power balancing arises from the nature of both actors and the system they exist in for, as Waltz argues:

> Balance of power politics prevail wherever two, and only two, requirements are met: that the order be anarchic and that it be populated by units wishing to survive.[800]

Yet in a complex system the regularity of behaviour in a balance of power pattern is not unexpected. Waltz's claim to the necessity of anarchy is incorrect: emergent behaviour is an element of every complex system.

Emergent behaviours allow for probabilities to be developed for certain situations in international politics. Reliably accurate long-term prediction remains impossible under complexity, of course, but the emergent properties of a complex system allow for analysts to suggest that particular patterns will repeat in the system. The common occurrence of balance of power politics in international relations is an example of such emergent behaviour and has been recognised not only in systems where nation-states dominate but also in pre-Westphalian periods. Consider Machiavelli's description of Italian principalities where the power of the Venetians was balanced against by a coalition of less capable powers:

---

[798] Morgenthau. 1993, p.183.
[799] Morgenthau. 1993, pp.194-212.
[800] Waltz. 1979, p.121.

246

<blockquote>
King Louis was brought into Italy because of the ambition of the Venetians who wanted...to gain for themselves half of Lombardy...After having taken Lombardy, then, the King immediately regained the reputation that Charles had lost him: Genoa surrendered; the Florentines became his allies; the Marquis of Mantua, the Duke of Ferrara, the Bentivoglios, the Countess of Forli, the rulers of Faenza, Rimini, Pesaro, Camerino, and Piombino, as well as the people of Lucca, Pisa, and Siena, all rushed to become his ally.[801]
</blockquote>

If the system is assumed to be complex, then we consistently find that actors seeking survival (as Waltz assumed all actors were always doing) tend to act in the same manner as their predecessors. Unlike Waltz's conditions that any system that is anarchic and includes actors seeking survival will see actors seeking a balance of power, in a complex system all we can conclude is that some behaviour emerges as common and that, in the specific case of the complex international political system, that behaviour may be power balancing.

Note, however, that emergent behaviour is probable behaviour and not predetermined. Unlike the '*if* anarchy and actors seeking survival *then* balancing will occur' of structural realism the emergent behaviour in a complex system is not mandated and – drawing on the number of actors, their innumerable interactions and the uncertainties of the system – it is likely that there will be situations where balancing would usually occur but does not.

Analysts of international relations have found many examples where actors are expected to balance against other powers but chose instead to 'bandwagon' with the stronger actor leading, ultimately, to an unbalanced reality. As Randall Schweller explains "'the bandwagoning belief that 'nothing succeeds like success' has been at the heart of every bid for world mastery", citing Napoleon and Hitler as leaders who assumed such a notion.[802] He further discusses examples from Italy, Japan, Russia and Romania in World War Two which support the notion that there are times in international politics where actors deliberately avoid balancing and choose to bandwagon for, as Schweller argues, a "profit" in terms of security, treasure or land – and always with the expectation of gain. While Schweller does argue, in opposition to realists like Kenneth Waltz and Stephen Walt, that balancing and bandwagoning are not op-

---

[801] Machiavelli. 2005, p.13.
[802] Schweller. 1994, p.73.

posite behaviours, in a complex system we can recognise them both as emergent behaviours. Whereas under anarchy it is necessary for a scholar like Schweller to justify his argument on bandwagoning by reference to a new notion of 'balance of interests' under which both balancing and bandwagoning are legitimate strategic choices, such justifications are only necessary if the prior assumption is that the system is anarchic. If the system is assumed to be complex then bandwagoning and balancing can both be considered emergent behaviours and the fact that the choice of actor X in a certain situation chooses one or the other can be explained with reference either to the properties of the system itself or to human agency within the system. Schweller is correct that the recognition of balancing and bandwagoning as different-but-not-opposite behaviours by international actors demands a restatement of a key theoretical assumption; however, he chose to restate what is being balanced rather than restating his assumption about the nature of the system, which may have proved more useful.

In discussing and testing the first hypothesis it was argued that reliable prediction is impossible in a complex system – this remains the case. What is argued above is that certain behaviours in certain situations do recur and the possibility exists for suggesting that they will continue to occur in proximate situations in the future. Balancing behaviour by actors in international relations under anarchy is a given, according to realists, and the opposite of balancing is bandwagoning. Explaining why actors bandwagon instead of balance is a challenge for theorists working under the assumption of anarchy and, as Schweller's article demonstrates, requires a restatement of key planks of the theoretical platform. Alternatively, assuming a complex system eases this requirement: no behaviour is predetermined, no behaviour can be accurately predicted in the long term, largely due to individual and collective human agency, and both balancing and bandwagoning are likely behaviours for international actors under complexity. Analysts and scholars of international relations know that certain behaviours are common and that certain behaviours are repeated over time by international actors – but they also understand that there are aberrations and exceptions that do not fit their theories. Theories can be adjusted to incorporate and to try to explain these aberrant cases yet, as Legro and Moravcsik have argued in the case of realism, this can lead to the undermining of the parsimonious reductionism of realist theory by its own defenders.[803] If, instead, the theorist goes to the heart of their theory, understands how their base assumption of anarchy is part of the reason they now face difficulty in explaining what is observed in the system and, instead of renovating the traditional approach, rebuild their approach from a new foundational assumption then – and only then – will these 'aberrations' and 'exceptions' be seen for what they really are: the expected non-linearities, self-organisation and emergent behaviours of a complex political world.

Conclusion

This chapter has outlined an alternative approach by which to imagine and theorise international politics. Returning to first principles, this alternative approach began by defining international politics as encompassing all events that have impacts at the supra-state level. This definition of international politics implies a broad range and typography of international actors and, indeed, the alternative approach presented here broadens the number and type of international actors to include states, international institutions, corporations, non-governmental organisations, lobby groups, terrorist groups and individuals. All of these actors share two commonalities: first, they all seek to advance their own interests in the international system, though how each comprehends the interests differs; second, they all exist in the same international system. Significantly, this international system is not reducible to the anarchy that is assumed by realist theorists. Rather it is a complex system and actors are bound by four properties of systemic complexity: non-determinism and non-tractability; limited functional decomposability; the distributed nature of information and representation; and emergent behaviour and self-organisation. Considering these properties and the observable reality of international politics it is clear that this alternative approach is of some utility for describing and explaining events and behaviours in the international political system.

The alternative approach to imagining and theorising international relations outlined in this chapter offers an alternative research direction to the predominant but flawed realist paradigm. While there are obvious benefits to embracing this alternative approach there are potential objections that emerge, too. This alternative approach does

---

[803] Legro and Moravcsik. 1999, p.6.

not endeavour to offer the sorts of predictions about the future trajectories of world politics that realist scholars have and do; indeed, the alternative approach is explicit in stating the inherent inability of anyone to predict international relations reliability. Yet the alternative approach better explains the observable international reality: the small events that feedback into the system, the wars that begin by accident, the alliances that rise and fall and the trends in international politics that exist in spite of international uncertainty. The alternative approach is not designed to supplant realism but to add value to the discipline by offering a credible alternative for the analyst or scholar that seeks to describe and explain international politics. Complexity is at the foundation of all international relations and through this alternative approach that the observable complex foundation of international affairs can be recognised, theorised and operationalised. An approach based on the assumption of complexity adds value to the analysis of international relations by creating an expectation of probabilistic generalisations that provide better insights into international politics, while choosing not to recognise the foundational complexity of international relations, as realists with their assumption of anarchy continue to do, locks analysts into theoretical tribulations and predictive nightmares. By reassessing international political theory from its most fundamental assumptions scholarship, analysis and the discipline of international relations itself can only be improved.

CONCLUSION

That international politics is more complex than realists allow is not a new argument. Critiques of the realist approach to international relations have existed for centuries pointing to all manner of assumptions that realists make about the political system, the political actors and the motivations those actors have for the choices they make. Realism has been criticised for presenting a 'billiard ball' account of international affairs, for suggesting that human nature drives political action, for over-simplifying sometimes complex international events and for being outdated in a rapidly globalising and interconnected world. This book has offered a different critique of realism: that the base realist assumption on which all other assumptions are founded is wrong and that the anarchic international system does not exist. Rather than tearing at the secondary issues that sometimes unite but more often divide realists into their sub-paradigm groups, this book has argued that all realists make a similarly bad assumption about the nature of the international system. The problems that this book and others have identified as associated with the realist approach, then, are not related to secondary assumptions but to this misplaced faith in anarchy as the nature of the international system. As long as realists continue to place great faith in international anarchy their approach will continue to be plagued with problems of description, explanation and prediction.

As the French proverb warns, a theory cannot stop things existing. The highly developed classical and structural realist approaches are troubled by real situations that are difficult, if not impossible, to explain away. This book has presented the outbreak of World War One, the peaceful regional integration of Europe and the collapse of the Soviet Union as examples of events that realism has great difficulty in explaining if any attempt is made to do so at all. The realist theories outlined in this book – all of which are founded on an assumption of anarchy – cannot stop such events from existing but these events do provide good reason to reassess the realist perspective. Assuming that the international system is not anarchic, then, is one means by which the international relations investigator can propose an alternative theoretical approach.

Indeed, this book has argued that founding a theoretical approach on the assumption of a non-anarchic system, in this case a complex system, is a potentially superior means by which to describe, explain and predict international politics. While the book has argued extensively as to the potential promise contained in this approach it has not sought to provide a final or conclusive theoretical statement on this approach. Colloquially, though this book has broken the ground there remains work to be done before that ground bears the sweetest fruit.

In this conclusion to the book the likely direction and nature of this future work will be outlined and the ways in which this literature will fit within the wider discipline of international relations theory will be explained. Firstly, this conclusion will review the primary argument and examples raised in support of that argument within the book. Next, while the alternative approach and argument outlined here is innovative, this conclusion will point to other scholars in the field who are questioning either the role of anarchy in international relations theory or applying complex approaches and metaphors to shed light on politics at the international level. Further, this conclusion will suggest means by which an interdisciplinary approach to theorising international politics might succeed in developing a complex theoretical approach further and point to examples where such interdisciplinary approaches have already succeeded in the field. Finally, this conclusion will close by arguing that the approach that this book has outlined has the potential to prove very useful to theorists and analysts of international relations and, with further refinement, will lead to better descriptions and more realistic explanations of the complex environment within which international politics takes place.

Reviewing the Book and its Parts

Following the book's introduction, the first part of this work focussed on the various strands of theoretical realism that have come to influence significantly the discipline of international relations. The first section of this part considered the classical or biological realists.[804] Beginning with the Greek historian Thucydides, this section outlined the largely consistent classical realist approach to international affairs that spanned, in terms of time, the period between the Peloponnesian Wars of 400BC

---

[804] Anarchy and Classical Realism.

through to the Cold War of the 20th century AD. Thucydides stark retelling of the visit of the Athenian envoys to the island of Melos and the blunt power equation – the mighty take what they can, the weak accept what they must – recounted there set the stage for a series of classical realists who saw a world best explained with reference to the darker side of human nature and the doctrine of 'might makes right'. The strict win-at-all-costs strategies espoused by Niccolò Machiavelli, the need to escape a war of all against all urged by Thomas Hobbes and the structured, reflective political realism of Hans Morgenthau all fit easily within the broader category of classical realism. All, too, draw on a common conception of the international political system in that all embrace a notion of international anarchy, whether implied or explicit, upon which their own historical, philosophical and theoretical approach is established.

For Thucydides the anarchy of the system is evidenced in the utter helplessness that the islanders of Melos experience in the face of Athenian aggression. Logic, rational argument and offers of neutrality are of no use in the face of overwhelming force for, under anarchy, there is no arbiter for the citizens of Melos to appeal to, nor a central figure to whom one can call for respite. For Machiavelli this anarchy is a challenge to be overcome by an educated and ambitious Prince. Drawing on lessons from Italy and beyond the Medici scholar teaches how – even though the problems of anarchy cannot be overcome – the issues raised by anarchy can be mitigated by employing an amoral, power-seeking strategy. For Hobbes anarchy is all: life in the 'state of nature' he describes is essentially anarchy writ large. The largest is not safe from deadly attack from a weaker actor beside him, alliances are temporary and bound to fail, relatively safe commonwealths are sought as individuals are driven by the fear of something worse and life, he argues famously, is 'solitary, poor, nasty, brutish and short'. Finally, for Morgenthau, anarchy is a condition that the international theorist will never change but must acknowledge if their approach to international affairs is to prove of any utility. Anarchy, for Morgenthau, is the stage on which the play of international relations takes place: no matter how it is dressed or how the actors choose to move across it, the stage remains the fundamental reality of the play no matter how willingly the actors and audience choose to suspend their disbelief.

The second section of this realist review considered the Waltzian theoretical revolution in realism.[805] His structural realism, or neorealism, applied a self-styled scientific approach to international politics, prioritising the impact of the structure of the international system on state choices over the human nature explanations of the classical realists or the domestic influences favoured by some non-realists. Waltz offered a theoretical approach that was state-centric and where those states sought – above all else – to survive in the international system. Drawing on his twin classics, *Man, the State, and War* and *Theory of International Politics,* as well as a history of his scholarship across nearly 50 years, this second section presented the fundamental assumptions of neorealism and the significant departure from the classical approach that had stagnated in the face of criticism and a long Cold War. Though different in terms of the aims ascribed to actors and the significance of the international system, Waltz's structural approach continued to embrace anarchy as a fundamental property of international politics.

The anarchy of the neorealists is similar to that of the classicalists yet it takes a place in the theoretical approach that is far more significant. For Waltz and the structural realist anarchy is less a background to political action than a necessary driver of state actions in the international sphere. While, like Hobbes, the neorealists accept that anarchy is a dangerous state in which to live, neorealists operationalise this danger and theorise that actors under anarchy are driven by a desire to survive above all else. This fundamental aim of all actors has been questioned in recent times, particularly in the light of voluntary surrendering of national sovereignty as part of the European regional integration process, and in some cases neorealists have diluted their assumptions somewhat, yet the base assumption of anarchy has not been revisited; indeed, to remove the assumption of anarchy from the neorealist approach would be to render not another structural realist approach but rather a theoretical direction with little resemblance to neorealism at all. For Waltz anarchy must be recognised as influential and basic to the problem of explaining international politics: while he may reject the human nature-focussed explanations of the classicalists he remains in theoretical lock step, so to speak, when it comes to the nature of the international system.

---

[805] Anarchy and Neo-Realism.

254

The third section of this review of the realist literature considered three other realist approaches: John Mearsheimer's offensive realism, game theoretic realism in the shape of the Prisoner's Dilemma and neoclassical realism.[806] Mearsheimer's offensive realism, he admits, is a response and somewhat of an extension to Waltz's neorealism but with certain assumptions that differentiate the two approaches. To the basic neorealist framework Mearsheimer adds an assumption of an offensive military capability, an assumption of uncertainty about the intentions of others and an assumption that actors act rationally. In Mearsheimer's view these additional assumptions precluded the need for separate theory of foreign policy, a significant flaw he argued existed in the work of Waltz.[807] The Prisoner's Dilemma, on the other hand, stripped realism back to a series of fundamental rules in an iterated game. Like the offensive realists, the Prisoner's Dilemma assumes that competitors act rationally, on incomplete information and assumes rationality on behalf of the players. It differentiates itself, however, by refusing to identify a military component as essential to the politics of the game and by assuming equal payoffs and losses in all situations; the reality of international relations and the choices that actors must make suggest that each 'game' in the international arena is played for differing potential payoffs and losses. As well, the Prisoner's Dilemma presents a realist argument that involves just two players interacting in the international system where, in reality, the system involves many actors interacting continually across many issues. Finally, with regards to the neoclassical realists, this book outlined their links to the classicalism of Thucydides and Morgenthau, their focus on material capabilities in the mould of the structural and offensive realists and their focus not on actual or relative proportion of power or capabilities but on the *perception* of that power and capabilities by the state itself or others that interact with it. This third section of the literature review, then, presents three different realist approaches – both in relation to each other as well as the preceding classical and structural approaches – but, for all their variation, they all maintain the same assumption about the nature of the international system that all other realist approaches remain founded upon.

As with the classical and structural realist approaches, John Mearsheimer is explicit in recognising the international system as anarchic. Anarchy is ubiquitous and fun-

---

[806] Anarchy in Offensive Realism, Game Theory and Neo-Classical Realism.
[807] Mearsheimer. 2006a, p.112.

damental to the offensive realist approach, much in the same way it is to the structural approach of Waltz. For the Prisoner's Dilemma it is equally important: the players are left in a situation where there is no arbiter of right and wrong, no protection from the adverse actions of others and no means to guarantee that because one player acts in the interests of all that his opponent will act in the same, unselfish manner. The neoclassical approach also embraces anarchy though in a style more reminiscent of the earliest realists. Anarchy is the permanent nature of the system and serves as a background to calculations and perceptions of national material capability and relative state power. As is easily seen, then, no matter whether a realist chooses to embrace the classical or structural approach, the offensive or neoclassical approach or even the game theoretic approach, realists of all persuasions maintain anarchy as the heart of their theoretical methodology. The assumption of anarchy is "the first and least controversial" of any assumptions shared across the realist paradigm and, as this book demonstrated in the three chapters of its first part, there is not a significant realist theorist or realist approach that refuses to endorse anarchy's fundamental role in international politics.[808]

The second part of this book opened with a chapter under the heading, 'A Case for Complexity'.[809] It opened with a review of just what a theory of international relations is, what a theory seeks to do and draws on a cartographical analogy to illustrate the most significant of these. A theory of international relations, this book argued, is a simplification of the real world that partly describes but, more importantly, *explains* the observable world by drawing links and expounding the relationships between elements in the system under examination. It is here that the cartographical analogy is most useful: like a map, a theory of international relations should simplify reality so as to provide utility for someone who would interpret that reality. However, like a map, it is possible for a theory to oversimplify international politics to the point where the utility is lost. The quest for theoretic parsimony, then, is one that must be tempered by alertness to the effects of that parsimony: while parsimony is a goal of any theory of international politics it should not be sought at the price of theoretical utility.

---

[808] Legro and Moravcsik. 1999, p.12.
[809] The Limitations of Anarchy.

256

Though not the sole means by which realists have sought theoretical parsimony, the assumption of an anarchic international system is a major way in which complex international relations has been simplified. Having outlined in the previous part of the book the place of anarchy in realist approaches, this book then pointed to anarchy's role as a tool of parsimony. Beginning with Thucydides and his account of the Melian dialogue, for example, uses anarchy as a means by which to reduce international politics to a struggle between powers. Machiavelli, too simplifies the international system by appealing to anarchy and, in doing so, limits the choices available to the Princes he addresses. Hobbes uses anarchy to simplify a system where cooperation existed to one where cooperation – at least at the international level – is difficult to achieve if it is possible at all. EH Carr employs anarchy to construct a world of competitive security where cooperation is unlikely despite, as he notes, the fact that cooperation does exist and did at the time he wrote his *Twenty Years Crisis*. Morgenthau, too, uses anarchy as a base on which to build a model of an international system where states are the most significant actors, power is a tool of those states and the complex architecture of international governance organisations is largely sidelined.

Structural realists, offensive realists, game theoretic realists and neoclassical realists all too employ anarchy as a tool of parsimony. As the book argued, Waltz and the structural realists use anarchy as tool by which to reduce complex international politics to the interactions of powerful states alone. The structural focus on an anarchic realm makes for a simpler system though, as Waltz admits, not one that represents every single feature of the system. The offensive realists similarly reduce the complexity of international politics by assuming a competitive, militaristic anarchy that, while parsimonious, tends to downplay and even ignore the impact of economic ties and international institutions on politics at the inter-state level. For the game theoretic theorists employing the Prisoner's Dilemma as a realist tool the assumption of anarchy forms one of the few basic rules of the game. Along with the assumption of rationality, known potential payoffs, lack of complete information about the intentions of others and a limited time frame for decision making, the assumption of anarchy helps to simplify the international system to a one-on-one decision making game. Finally the neoclassicalists use anarchy as a tool of parsimony much in the way of the classical realists: it's a background for power struggles and the stage upon which perceptions of relative capabilities and competing power are assessed by nation-states.

Thus, all realists – from ancient Greek historians to modern game theorists – employ anarchy as a tool of theoretical parsimony, one that simplifies the international system for the utility of the analyst but does, in effect, leave the approach open to the criticism that it has *oversimplified* international politics. There is always a cost to theoretical parsimony but the challenge for the theorist is to ensure that utility is not sacrificed in its pursuit.

In order to establish the cost of anarchic parsimony to the utility of the realist approach to international relations three case studies of major events in international politics were presented. The three events – the outbreak of World War One, the end of the Cold War and the collapse of the Soviet Union, and regional integration in Europe – are major features of the political landscape of the twentieth and twenty-first centuries. The first, for example, led to what was, at the time, the largest conflict in the history of the world. The realist explanations for the outbreak of the Great War, however, are lacking in some significant ways. For example, the realists don't have good reasons why significant sub-state issues should be ignored in explaining the outbreak of war nor why, in other situations where factors similar to those blamed for the outbreak of war exist, war has not broken out. There is much that realists choose to exclude in explaining the outbreak of war in the Balkans and, while this lends great parsimony to their accounts of the period, it also leaves the realists open to significant criticism for their simplistic approach to a complex international event.

Consider, too, realist accounts for the end of the Cold War and the collapse of the Soviet Union that followed soon after. Most realists did not foresee the collapse of the Soviet Union or the end of the Cold War. Indeed, as this book explained, in the weeks and months before the collapse of the Berlin Wall and the disintegration of the USSR there was hardly a realist theorist who imagined that a superpower could fall even if the most western extent of its satellite reach would fall to democratic pressures. The focus of realists on states interacting in anarchy was a major reason why their explanations and forecasts were so inaccurate: by seeking explanations at the inter-state level the realists were forced to ignore significant sub-state and institutional factors. The realist focus on military power in an anarchic world, too, led to problems in terms of explaining the collapse of the Soviet Union. A superpower that had been in a 'cold' conflict with the West for decades imploded without a fight. As this book argued, anarchy and the other realist assumptions that followed it have proved a liability in explaining the events in Eastern Europe between 1989 and 1991. Further problems emerged for realists in analysing the regional political integration that has seen a small band of like-minded coal and steel producing treaty signatories expand into a pan-continental legal, political and social quasi-state power in the shape of the EU. Realists expect that that states in anarchy are loathe to surrender their sovereignty, particularly in relation to essential hard power aspects of the state including their military and their economy. While Europe's military integration is complex and slow-moving, the economic integration has seen many major international powers give up their national currencies, national central banks and much of the control over their national legislation. As this book argued, faced with a continent of some three dozen nation-states, scarce resources and a history of violent conflict, the realist naturally assumes that the 'natural order' will be maintained and competition will be the rule. These realist expectations, however, are shattered by the success of integration efforts in Europe and this – coupled with the case studies of the outbreak of World War One and the collapse of the Soviet Union – allowed this book to conclude that the parsimony offered by the assumption of anarchy has reduced the utility of the realist approach. What is needed, then, is an alternative foundation on which to build a theory of international relations.

Having outlined a variety of theoretical approaches groups under the realist paradigm, explained the significance of anarchy in each and all of these, pointed to anarchy's role as a tool of parsimony and suggested that this parsimony comes at too high a cost to analytical and theoretical utility, this book moved to describe an alternate assumption about the nature of the international system that would restore some of this lost utility.[810] An alternative approach was offered that began by assuming that international politics is not solely the domain of states but instead all political acts that effect politics at the supra-state level. In effect this also meant that the alternative approach assumed that the analysis of international politics should not be limited to the actions and interactions of states: all actors that exist, interact and effect politics at the supra-state level fall within the analytical scope of the alternative approach. With the number and type of these international actors far exceeding the approximately 200 nation-states that the realists consider, this book suggested that international ac-

---

[810] A Theory of Complexity.

tors can instead be thought of as being all actors with an international impact. The extent of the system and the actors within it thus defined, this book then went on to describe the structure of the international system in the methodology of the alternative approach.

Unlike the anarchy of realism, the alternative approach is defined by complexity. This complexity, in turn, has four significant properties that differentiate it from a realist system and define the relationships between the actors that exist within it: non-determinism and non-tractability, limited functional decomposability, the distributed nature of information and representation, and emergence and self-organisation. As was argued, where realists assume an anarchic reality this alternative approach embraces the complexity of the international system and recognises this not as something to be 'simplified away' but rather embraced and theorised from. From this foundation four hypotheses were constructed by which to extrapolate and test the utility of the alternative approach. The first hypothesis suggested that while probabilistic trends may be identified, long-term, specific predictions of the international system, both by international actors and international analysts, will be inaccurate. The second hypothesis suggested that analysis that seeks to understand international politics through reference to the actions, motivations or activities of a sub-set of actors will not describe the observable and complex international reality. The third and fourth hypotheses suggested that relationships between actors in the international system are usually short-term, non-linear and weak and that certain behaviours emerge as commonplace in the international political system over time, respectively. These four hypotheses – at least initially – were confirmed by basic testing against both the case studies that realists found difficult to explain and other examples from international politics. While not as developed as the realist approaches considered in the first part of the book, it was possible to conclude that it offers a credible alternative for the analyst or scholar that seeks to describe and explain the international politic as it *is* rather than as others imagine it *should* or *could* be.

The Book in the Wider Literature

While the critique of realism offered in the book is innovative it does fit into a wider literature within the discipline of international relations. Indeed, in recent years there has been an emerging trend wherein theorists and analysts draw on interdisciplinary sources and delve into chaos and complexity theories to assist in describing, explaining and predicting the international political system. This trend is not being led by critics of realism alone: analysts with interests in international institutions, sub-state actors and the interplay between domestic and international politics have all contributed to this emerging branch of research. In this section of the conclusion to the book selected researchers and research articles will be presented and the parallels in direction and conclusions will be highlighted. This section will place this book in the wider literature and demonstrate its value as a research project within it by first considering the wider social sciences before focussing on the specific discipline of international relations.

The trend in the social sciences towards applying complex analogies and drawing on the physical sciences – where such systems have been studied for decades now – is explained in Pavard and Dugdale's *Introduction to Complexity in Social Science*.[811] In this work the pair note the utility to social science of an approach that draws on the complexity research developed in the physical sciences, noting specifically that as assumption of complexity is especially suitable for social sciences where "oversimplification of models leads to non applicable results in real situations".[812] Such a conclusion, it should be noted, supports the key argument of this book wherein the various realist approaches are criticised for seeking excessive parsimony at the cost of any real-world utility. Their work within the European Commission-sponsored Complexity in Social Science (COSI) program was included as part of that program's long bibliography of authors and works falling into the broad category of 'studies of complexity in social science'.[813]

The bibliography of the COSI program is, while not exhaustive, a good guide to the interdisciplinary nature of complexity research in the social sciences. In COSI's bibliography one can find the work of physicists (for example, Murray Gell-Mann), sociologists (Kent McClelland), computer scientists (Jay W Forrester), philosophers (Paul Cilliers) and experts in international relations (Robert Axelrod). In a similar

---

[811] Pavard and Dugdale. 2003.
[812] Pavard and Dugdale. 2003.
[813] See the bibliography at http://www.irit.fr/COSI/papers/fulllist.php.

way the bibliography of this book draws on a broad range of non-international relations or political science sources in making its case. This book and the papers and articles related to it published by the author have quoted the sociologist/philosophers Bergman and Luckmann, the reporter of popular science James Gleick, meteorologists like Antonio Speranza, biologists such as Bruce Kendall and Lars Olsen, mathematicians such as David Ruelle and physicists like Mitchell Feigenbaum.[814] Such is the interdisciplinary nature of complexity research in the social sciences that there is not only a cross-over in terms of literature but variant fields quickly adopt the terminology and techniques of disparate sciences. Thus international relations researcher Robert Axelrod adopts computer simulations for theorising international relations and physicists Murray Gell-Man draws on examples and research in the biological sciences. This book, then, falls easily within the existing trend in the social sciences towards interdisciplinarity – particularly in relation to studies of complexity and its impacts – but it also fits squarely within the trend of applying complexity science to international relations research.

One edited work stands as clear examples of a trend towards the application of complexity theory to international relations. The 2006 book *Complexity in World Politics* (edited by Neil Harrison) drew together some of the scholars already considered in this book – J. David Singer, James Rosenau and Robert Axelrod – with others pushing the envelope of international relations theory and advocating the adoption of a complex approach.[815] Within this volume the utility of a complex systems approach is continually asserted. David Earnest and James Rosenau, for example, argue that complexity's "connotations of dynamism" are central to contemporary social science and point to the challenges and the potential benefits that complexity theory offers theorists of international relations.[816] Consider, too, Harrison and Singer's argument that complexity theory has the potential to revolutionise international relations theory

---

[814] See Dylan Kissane 2008a. *On the Problems in and the Possibilities for Mapping International Chaos*. Paper presented at the 3rd Annual Graduate Conference in Political Science in Memory of Yitzhak Rabin, Hebrew University, Jerusalem, Israel, 17th January 2008.

[815] Neil Harrison (ed.). 2006a. *Complexity in World Politics: Concepts and Methods of a New Paradigm*. New York: State University of New York Press.

[816] David Earnest and James Rosenau. 2006. 'Signifying nothing? What complex systems theory can and cannot tell us about global politics.' in *Complexity in World Politics: Concepts and Methods of a New Paradigm*, edited by N Harrison. New York: State University of New York Press, pp.143-163, pp.144-145.

by moving beyond an "internal" critique of international units, such as that offered by constructivists, or an "external" critique focussing on the international system, instead presenting a unified theoretical alternative dealing with both agents and structure.[817] Positive about the utility and potential of complex approaches to international politics, Harrison concludes the volume by arguing:

> The complexity paradigm offers a novel perspective on world politics at all levels that will generate new theories and models of issue-areas. It also encourages innovative methods for understanding political reality and advising policy makers[818]

Harrison concludes that the complexity approach "can increase our understanding of the complexity of world politics", a theme taken up by fellow researcher Emilian Kavalski.[819]

Kavalski's work in applying complexity theory to international politics has seen recent success. His 2007 article, 'The fifth debate and the emergence of complex international relations theory', makes a case for the complex approach and points to the broad range of issues in international relations where scholars have begun to apply a complex paradigm.[820] Kavalski points to applications of complexity theory in such disparate sub-fields as postmodernist international relations theory, international history, European integration, international development, state-building and security studies, and argues that complexity theory offers a means by which to better conceptualise the post-Cold War world.[821] Like this book, Kavalski is optimistic that a complex approach can provide "imaginative thinking on the complexity of human societies and their interactions", a theme he returns to in a second article published in late 2008.[822] Kavalski's 'The Complexity of Global Security Governance' furthers the

---

[817] Neil Harrison and J. David Singer. 2006. 'Complexity is more than systems theory.' in *Complexity in World Politics: Concepts and Methods of a New Paradigm*, edited by N Harrison. New York: State University of New York Press, pp.25-41, p.38.

[818] Neil Harrison. 2006b. 'Complex systems and the practice of world politics.' in *Complexity in World Politics: Concepts and Methods of a New Paradigm*, edited by N Harrison. New York: State University of New York Press, pp.183-196, p.193.

[819] Harrison. 2006b, p.193.

[820] Emilian Kavalski. 2007. 'The fifth debate and the emergence of complex international relations theory: notes on the application of complexity theory to the study of international life.' *Cambridge Review of International Affairs* 20(3): 435-454.

[821] Kavalski. 2007, p.442.

[822] Kavalski. 2007, p.451.

case for a complexity-based approach, noting that "the abstractions of complexity thinking offer relevant cognitive frameworks to address problems not difficult to prevent, but difficult to foresee".[823] Though this second article is limited to global security frameworks, when coupled with his earlier article Kavalski makes a strong case for the application of complexity theory to all major thematic and sub-disciplinary issues in international relations.

More broadly, this book sits alongside work such as Robert Axelrod's investigations of complexity in political systems and James Rosenau's interest in what he terms "fragmegration" and turbulence, the modern epoch of multiple contradictions in international politics. Rosenau's 1996 paper, *Many Damn Things Simultaneously*, is, like this book, a call for international relations scholars to look to the application of complex systems research in their work to overcome the obvious shortfalls in existing theoretical approaches.[824] He cites a number of others within the field of international relations – and, true to the style of social scientists described above, a number of physical and behavioural scientists, too – and, like this book, reverts to asking fundamental questions about the assumptions that international relations theorists make about the system they study. As he recounts:

> Look out the nearest window. Is there any straight line out there that wasn't man-made? I've been asking the same question of student and professional groups for several years now, and the most common answer is a grin. Occasionally a philosophical person will comment that even the lines that look like straight lines are not straight lines if we look at them through a microscope. But even if we ignore that level of analysis, we are still stuck with the inevitable observation that natural structures are, at their core, nonlinear. If [this] is true, why do social scientists insist on describing human events as if all the rules that make those events occur are based on straight lines?[825]

Considering the state of international relations theory and the review of the various realist approaches to international relations that have been outlined in this book Rosenau's question is indeed apt: why do realists look for a simple cause-and-effect

---

[823] Emilian Kavalski. 2008. 'The Complexity of Global Security Governance: An Analytical Overview.' *Global Society* 22(4): 423-443, p.441.

[824] James Rosenau. 1996. *Many Damn Things Simultaneously: Complexity Theory and World Affairs*. Paper presented at the Conference on Complexity, Global Politics, and National Security, Washington, D.C., United States of America, 13 November 1996.

[825] Rosenau. 1996. Rosenau is quoting Stephen Guastello.

explanation in a 'billiard ball' world of states when it is clear that the world is significantly more complex than such simple metaphors would allow? This book, then, fits within a larger trend of social scientists applying complex methods and metaphors in their work as well as a decade-old trend in international relations research specifically to do the same, a trend that has led some to conclude that the complex approach is international relations theory's 'fifth way'. Yet, as Rosenau and Axelrod do, this book also recognises that complexity theory is not a panacea for the woes of international relations theorists; this book opens the door to future program of research that can extend the key criticisms of realism and, perhaps, develop a complete complex theory of international politics.

Future Directions for Research

While a complete critique of the realist assumption of anarchy in and of itself there exists the possibility for future research to emerge from this book in at least two areas: first, further critiques of the assumption of an anarchic system in other theories of international relation and, second, the pursuit of the complex theory of international relations. Both of these directions finds a good foundation in this book and, in the paragraphs that follow, it is possible to outline briefly what sorts of research questions might be developed and the potential utility of embracing either of these research directions.

This book has deliberately limited itself to a concentration on realist theories of international relations. There were two major reasons for this limitation: the significance of the realist approach to the study of international relations and the time and resources available to the researcher to develop the book. With regards to the first of these, as has been made clear at a number of points in this book, realism is either the primary or the secondary theoretical approach employed by theorists, analysts and scholars of international relations. As such, it offers more scope for research and a wider literature on which to draw as compared to, for example, constructionist theories or even some institutionalist approaches. With regards to the second limiting reason, this book is the product of a doctoral program limited by the time allocated to research and the length of the final research product, this book. Limiting the book to consideration of realist approaches alone means that the realist theories can be considered in greater depth, a depth that would be impossible in the space and time allocated to the research had a broader range of theories been included in the critique. These limitations, though, are project related: there is no reason why the critique of the assumption of anarchy should apply to realist theories alone, especially when almost every theoretical approach in the discipline endorses the notion of an anarchic system.

Papers and articles published during the course of the research supporting this book have alluded to this possible research direction. In the article 'The Balkan Bullet with Butterfly Wings', for example, it was noted:

> Agreement on the anarchic nature of the system exists across most of the major theories of international relations. Realism, for example…has maintained the centrality of anarchy to its assessment of the international realm since its precepts were first outlined…Theoretical liberals also agree that anarchy forms a central tenet of international interaction, though they derive significantly different implications from the reality of an anarchic system…Even the so-called constructivists do not deny the *existence* of anarchy, only its implications and its construction.[826]

The article, like this book, limits itself to a critique of the realist approach to theorising international affairs but, in its concluding paragraph, allows for the possibility that those alternate theoretical approaches to be included as part of a wider review of the role of anarchy in international relations theory:

> It remains the argument of this article that this is unlikely to change while international relations studies persist with the notion that the international system is anarchic when, it would seem, there is at least a chance that it may be something else…Without a new paradigm, international relations will continue to misdiagnose the past, hampering its ability to explain the present and, one day, predict the storms which sweep the system as we know it today.[827]

Similarly the article 'A Chaotic Theory of International Relations?' impresses upon the reader the pan-paradigm nature of the assumption of anarchy before also concluding as to the likely utility of moving beyond the assumption of anarchy in international relations theory:

---

[826] Dylan Kissane. 2006. 'The Balkan Bullet with Butterfly Wings.' *CEU Political Science Journal* 1(4): 85-106, pp.87-88.
[827] Kissane. 2006, p.101.

> The possibility of moving beyond an anarchic or simple interdependent conception of the international system offers the international relations theorist the chance to move beyond the realist/liberalist dichotomy and reveal the reality of the system itself...It implies an analysis that is not limited to states or institutions alone but one that recognises the potential for much smaller units – individuals, terrorist groups, lobbyists – to impact the wider international system. This is something that anarchy based assessments of the international system (realism, neorealism, liberalism) cannot achieve...[828]

A third article, 'Offensive Realism and Central & Eastern Europe after the Cold War', makes a similar point: it is not enough to look to other anarchy-founded paradigms of international relations to counter problems with realist analysis.[829] As is argued therein, "what *can* assist [in overcoming problems with realist explanations] is a new assumption, a new founding point...what is needed is a new perspective".[830] Further research that advances the central critique of this book but with regards to other theoretical approaches in the discipline is, then, perhaps the most obvious direction for future research emerging from this book.

If the complementary critiques suggested above are the most obvious extensions of the research in this book it is also a first step towards a more significant contribution to the discipline of international politics. A theory of international relations that is founded on the assumption of a complex international system would be the ultimate extension of this book in terms of a contribution to the furthering of the discipline's understanding of the international politic. The development of a complex theory of international relations will allow for better analysis of real world politics, the integration of significant non-state actors into explanations of how, why and when events occur in the international system and the chance for international relations analysts to assess a globalised, increasingly integrated world system from a theoretical perspective that does not over-simplify to the point of losing much or all utility. As the French proverb at the opening of this conclusion states, theory cannot stop things existing but it can limit the extent to which that which exists is incorporated into theoretical calculations. While a complex theory of international relations will certainly – like all theories and as in the cartographical analogy in The fourth chapter – limit itself in some ways, a more inclusive theory founded on the assumption of a more

---

[828] Dylan Kissane. 2007c. 'A Chaotic Theory of International Relations? The Possibility for Theoretical Revolution in International Politics.' *Revistă de ştiinţe politice* 2: 85-103, p.101.

[829] Kissane. 2007b.

[830] Kissane. 2007b, p.400.

complex international environment should mean that more of those things that exist are able to be described and explained. As has been argued in work emerging from this book, there are significant challenges to the construction of a theory based upon the assumption of a non-anarchic system:

> In particular, the strengths of a theory which includes individual actors and accounts for their impact on the system is tempered by the knowledge that it may be a step-too-far for analysis of the system as a whole: including everything might just lead to explaining nothing. However, as this research program is in its early stages it would be premature to suggest that such obstacles are insurmountable.[831]

Extending the research direction developed in this book and overcoming these obstacles would allow for a significant contribution to international relations theory. It is surely the more difficult of the two branches for future research outlined in this conclusion but it would likely bear the most fruit.

Conclusion

This book opened by pointing to the long and distinguished history of realism in international relations. It went as far as to argue that – so influential has been realism in the study of international affairs – the history of international relations as a discipline might well be considered a history of the theoretical discourse of realism. Yet as this history was uncovered, the arguments of theorists from the earliest days through to the present were presented and their explanations of major international events were submitted two things became clear: all realists embrace the notion of an anarchic international system as fundamental to their theoretical approaches and all realists face significant problems in describing and explaining major events in that international system. This book argued that it was this first point of agreement that may be to blame for the shared outcomes of the second point and that these problems might be overcome if only the realists would assume something other than anarchy as the nature of the international system. This alternative assumption – a complex international system sharing many of the attributes of complex systems identified in other fields of natural and social science – and the systemic properties that arrive with it were shown to be an alternative to the anarcho-realist approach. While not as devel-

---

[831] Kissane. 2007c, p.102.

oped as the realist paradigm it would seek to displace, the door was opened to further critiques of anarchy-based theories of international politics and a direction for the development of a complex theory of international relations was delineated.

This book, then, while recognising the history and contribution of realist theory and realists theorists to the discipline of international relations lends weight to the argument that realists will be less significant in the future than they have been in the past. Today's world is more complex, more integrated and driven by elements with more interconnections and interdependence than the analysis of states under anarchy provides. Realist John Mearsheimer once described the production of sound theories as the essence of the study of international relations and warned analysts, scholars and researchers that "we need to be deeply engaged with the real world, and to be constantly thinking about how well our theories explain what is happening in the world around us".[832] On this point this book concurs with Mearsheimer, though, if the argument presented here proves valid, the implications of such engagement and critical thinking for realists like Mearsheimer might end up being a little less than welcome.

---

[832] Mearsheimer. 2006b, p.242.

REFERENCES

Axelrod, R., *Effective Choice in the Prisoner's Dilemma.* The Journal of Conflict Resolution, 1980a. **24**(1): p. 3-25.

Axelrod, R., *More Effective Choices in the Prisoner's Dilemma.* The Journal of Conflict Resolution, 1980b. **24**(3): p. 379-403.

Axelrod, R., *The Emergence of Cooperation Among Egoists.* The American Political Science Review, 1981. **75**(2): p. 306-318.

Axelrod, R., *The Evolution of Cooperation.* 1984, New York: Basic Books.

Axelrod, R. and R.O. Keohane, *Achieving Cooperation under Anarchy: Strategies and Institutions.* World Politics, 1985. **38**(1): p. 226-254.

Bacevich, A. *The New American Militarism: How Americans Are Seduced by War.* 2005 [cited 2007 22 October]; Available from: http://tinyurl.com/2lnsta.

Badie, B., *Realism under Praise, or a Requiem? The Paradigmatic Debate in International Relations.* International Political Science Review, 2001. **22**(3): p. 253-260.

Baev, P., *Review: The Tragedy of Great Power Politics.* Journal of Peace Research, 2002. **39**(5): p. 641.

Baldwin, D., *Neorealism and Neoliberalism.* 1993, New York: Columbia University Press.

Bank, World. *Life Expectancy.* 2008 [cited 2008 13 May]; Available from: http://tinyurl.com/672cyc.

Beeson, M., *Rethinking regionalism: Europe and East Asia in comparative historical perspective.* Journal of European Public Policy, 2005. **12**(6): p. 969-985.

Berger, P. and T. Luckmann, *The Social Construction of Reality: A Treatise in the Sociology of Knowledge*. 1971, Hammondsworth: Penguin.

Blum, Y., *Russia Takes Over the Soviet Union's Seat at the United Nations*. European Journal of International Law, 1992. **3**(2): p. 354-361.

Bodin, J., *Six Books of the Commonwealth*. 1955, Oxford: Basil Blackwell.

Booth, K., *Security in Anarchy: Utopian Realism in Theory and Practice*. International Affairs, 1991. **67**(3): p. 527-546.

Borrie, J., *Cooperation and Defection in the Conference on Disarmament*, in *Thinking Outside the Box in Multilateral Disarmament and Arms Control Negotiations*, J. Borrie and V. Randin, Editors. 2006, United Nations Institute for Disarmament Research: Geneva. p. 89-108.

Börzel, T., Private Actors on the Rise? The Role of Non-State Actors in Compliance with International Institutions. 2000, Otto Suhr Institute for Political Science, Free University of Berlin.

Bright, J., *Speeches*. 1869, London: Macmillan & Co.

Brooks, S. and W. Wohlforth, *Power, Globalization and the End of the Cold War*. International Security, 2000. **25**(3): p. 5-53.

Brown, M., et al., eds. *Theories of War and Peace: An International Security Reader*. 1998, MIT Press: Cambridge.

Brown, M., S. Lynn-Jones, and S. Miller, eds. *The Perils of Anarchy: Contemporary Realism and International Security*. 1995, MIT Press: Cambridge.

Bugge, P., *The nation supreme: The idea of Europe 1914-1945*, in *The History of the Idea of Europe*, K. Wilson and J.v.d. Dussen, Editors. 1996, Routledge: London. p. 83-149.

Burns, C.D., *Review: The Twenty Years Crisis, 1919-1939: An Introduction to the Study of International Relations*. Ethics, 1940. **50**(3): p. 344-346.

Bury, J. and R. Meiggs, *History of Greece to the Death of Alexander the Great*. 1975, New York: St. Martin's Press.

Buzan, B., *From International System to International Society: Structural Realism and Regime Theory Meet the English School*. International Organization, 1993. **47**(3): p. 327-352.

Buzan, B., C. Jones, and R. Little, *The Logic of Anarchy: Neorealism to Structural Realism*. 1993, New York: Columbia University Press.

Caporaso, J., *International Relations Theory and Multilateralism: The Search for Foundations*. International Organization, 1992. **46**(3): p. 599-632.

Carlyle, T. *On Heroes, Hero-Worship, and the Heroic in History*. 2008 [cited 2008 6 May]; Available from: http://tinyurl.com/57d9nn.

Carpenter, F., *The Inner Life of Abraham Lincoln: Six Months at the White House*. 1995, Lincoln: University of Nebraska Press.

Carr, E.H., *The Twenty Years Crisis 1919-1939: An Introduction to the Study of International Relations*. 2001, New York: Palgrave.

Cha, V., *Alignment Despite Antagonism: The United States-Korea-Japan Security Triangle*. 1999, Palo Alto: Stanford University Press.

Cha, V., *Abandonment, Entrapment, and Neoclassical Realism in Asia: The United States, Japan, and Korea*. International Studies Quarterly, 2000. **44**(2): p. 261-291.

Cha, V., *Nuclear North Korea? A Debate on Strategies of Engagement*. 2003, New York: Columbia University Press.

Checkel, J.T., *The Constructivist Turn in International Relations Theory.* World Politics, 1998. **50**(2): p. 324-348.

Chernoff, F., *The Study of Democratic Peace and Progress in International Relations.* International Studies Review, 2004. **6**(1): p. 49-78.

Chomsky, N. *The Israel Lobby?* 2006 [cited 2007 1 May]; Available from: http://tinyurl.com/jvoam.

Christensen, T., *Threats, Assurances, and the Last Chance for Peace: The Lesson's of Mao's Korean War Telegrams.* International Security, 1992. **17**(1): p. 122-154.

Christensen, T., *Useful Adversaries: Grand Strategy, Domestic Mobilization, and Sino-American Conflict, 1947-1958.* 1996, Princeton: Princeton University Press.

Christensen, T., *Perceptions and Alliances in Europe, 1865-1940.* International Organization, 1997. **51**(1): p. 65-97.

Christensen, T., *China, the US-Japan Alliance, and the Security Dilemma in East Asia.* International Security, 1999. **23**(4): p. 49-80.

Christensen, T., *The Contemporary Security Dilemma: Deterring a Taiwan Conflict.* The Washington Quarterly, 2002. **25**(4): p. 7-21.

Christensen, T. and M. Glosny, *Sources in Stability in US-China Security Relations,* in *Strategic Asia 2003-04: Fragility and Crisis,* R. Ellings, A. Friedberg, and M. Wills, Editors. 2003, National Bureau of Asian Research: Washington DC. p. 53-80.

Christensen, T. and J. Snyder, *Chain gangs and passed bucks: Predicting alliance patters in multipolarity.* International Organization, 1990. **44**(2): p. 137-168.

Clinton, B. *State of the Union Address*. 1994 [cited 2007 21 February]; Available from: http://tinyurl.com/25psdv.

Clyne, M. *Harvard's Paper on Israel Called 'Trash' by Solon*. 2006 [cited 2007 1 May]; Available from: http://tinyurl.com/26ord4.

Connon, B., *Beverley Nichols: A Life*. 2005, Portland: Timber Press.

Connor, W., *Thucydides*. 1984, Princeton: Princeton University Press.

Coogan, P., *Review: The Tragedy of Great Power Politics*. The Journal of Military History, 2002. **66**(3): p. 916-917.

Cooper, R., *The Breaking of Nations: Order and Chaos in the Twenty-First Century*. 2004, New York: Grove Press.

Copeland, D., *The Constructivist Challenge to Structural Realism: A Review Essay*. International Security, 2000. **25**(2): p. 187-212.

Corbett, P., *Review: The Twenty Years Crisis by EH Carr*. Pacific Affairs, 1941. **14**(2): p. 237-238.

Cox, M., *Introduction*, in *The Twenty Years Crisis, 1919-1939: An Introduction to the Study of International Relations*, E. Carr, Editor. 2001a, Palgrave: Basingstoke. p. ix-lviii.

Cox, M., *A Guide to the Secondary Literature on E.H. Carr*, in *The Twenty Years Crisis, 1919-1939: An Introduction to the Study of International Relations*, E.H. Carr, Editor. 2001b, Palgrave: Basingstoke. p. lxiv-lxxi.

Dean, E., *Review: The Twenty Years Crisis; Britain; British Foreign Policy since Versailles by EH Carr*. The Journal of Modern History, 1941. **13**(1): p. 119-121.

Deutscher, I., *Mr. E.H. Carr as Historian of Soviet Russia*. Soviet Studies, 1955.
6(4): p. 337-350.

DeVoss, D. *Searching for Gavrilo Princip*. 2006 [cited 17 April]; Available from:
http://tinyurl.com/2jnswv.

Diez, T., S. Stetter, and M. Albert, *The European Union and Border Conflicts: The
Transformative Power of Integration*. International Organization, 2006. **60**(3):
p. 563-593.

Donnelly, J., *Realism: Roots and Renewal*. Review of International Studies, 1998.
24(3): p. 399-405.

Donnelly, J., *Human Rights: A New Standard of Civilisation?* International Affairs,
1998. **74**(1): p. 1-23.

Donnelly, J., *Realism and International Relations*. 2000, Cambridge: Cambridge
University Press.

Doran, C. and W. Parsons, *War and the Cycle of Relative Power*. The American Political Science Review, 1980. **74**(4): p. 947-965.

Doyle, M., *Kant, Liberal Legacies, and Foreign Affairs*. Philosophy and Public Affairs, 1983a. **12**(3): p. 205-235.

Doyle, M., *Kant, Liberal Legacies, and Foreign Affairs, Part 2*. Philosophy and Public Affairs, 1983b. **12**(4): p. 323-353.

Duffy, M. *Who's Who: Archduke Franz Ferdinand*. 2006 [cited 2006 14 April];
Available from: http://tinyurl.com/3csxza.

Dunne, A., *International Theory: To the Brink and Beyond*. 1996, Westport: Greenwood Publishing.

Earnest, D. and J. Rosenau, *Signifying nothing? What complex systems theory can and cannot tell us about global politics*, in *Complexity in World Politics: Concepts and Methods of a New Paradigm*, N. Harrison, Editor. 2006, State University of New York Press: New York. p. 143-163.

Ebner, G., *Review: Man, the State, and War: A Theoretical Analysis by Kenneth N. Waltz*. Military Review, 2003. **83**(1): p. 68-69.

Editors, The, *American Realism and the real world*. Review of International Studies, 2003. **29**(03): p. 401-402.

Elman, C., *Horses for Courses: Why Not Neorealist Theories of Foreign Policy*. Security Studies, 1996. **6**(1): p. 7-53.

Engerman, D., *The Kennan century*, in *Boston Globe*. 2004. p. D4.

Etzioni, A. *What is Political?* 2003 [cited 2008 9 April]; Available from: http://tinyurl.com/5srzwz.

Fearon, J., *Rationalist explanations for war*. International Organization, 1995. **49**(3): p. 379-414.

Feaver, P.D., et al., *Brother Can You Spare a Paradigm? (Or Was Anybody Ever a Realist?)*. International Security, 2000. **25**(1): p. 165-193.

Foglesong, D., *America's Secret War Against Bolshevism: US Intervention in the Russian Civil War, 1917-1920*. 19985, Chapel Hill: University of North Carolina Press.

Fox, W., *Theoretical Aspects of International Relations*. 1959, Notre Dame: University of Notre Dame Press.

Fox, W., *How Wars End*. 1970, Philadelphia: American Academy of Political and Social Science.

Fox, W., *Review: Theory of International Politics, by Kenneth Waltz.* The American Political Science Review, 1980. **74**(2): p. 492-493.

Freund, C., *Secrets of the Clinton Spectacle.* Reason, 2000. **31**(11): p. 22-28.

Friedman, T., *The Impact of Globalization on World Peace,* in *Burkle Center for International Relations Working Papers.* 2001: Los Angeles.

Fukuyama, F., *The End of History ?* The National Interest, 1989(Summer): p. 3-18.

Fukuyama, F., *Liberal Democracy as a Global Phenomenon.* PS: Political Science and Politics, 1991. **24**(4): p. 659-664.

Gaddis, J., *International Relations Theory and the End of the Cold War.* International Security, 1992. **17**(3): p. 5-58.

Gillingham, J., *European Integration 1950-2003: Superstate or New Market Economy?* 2003, New York: Cambridge University Press.

Gilpin, R., *The Richness of the Tradition of Political Realism,* in *Neorealism and Its Critics,* R. Keohane, Editor. 1986, Columbia University Press: New York. p. 301-321.

Glaser, C., *Structural Realism in a more complex world.* Review of International Studies, 2003. **29**(3): p. 403-414.

Gleick, J., *Chaos: Making a New Science.* 1987, New York: Penguin.

Goddard, S. and D. Nexon, *Paradigm Lost? Reassessing Theory of International Politics.* European Journal of International Relations, 2005. **11**(1): p. 9-61.

Grieco, J., *Anarchy and the Limits of Cooperation: A Realist Critique of the latest Liberal Institutionalism.* International Organization, 1988. **42**(3): p. 485-507.

Haass, R., *The Age of Nonpolarity.* Foreign Affairs, 2008. **87**(3): p. 44-56.

Ham, P.v., *Europe's Postmodern Identity: A Critical Appraisal.* International Politics, 2001. **38**(2): p. 229-252.

Harrison, N., ed. *Complexity in World Politics: Concepts and Methods of a New Paradigm.* 2006a, State University of New York Press: New York.

Harrison, N., *Complex systems and the practice of world politics*, in *Complexity in World Politics: Concepts and Methods of a New Paradigm*, N. Harrison, Editor. 2006b, State University of New York Press: New York. p. 183-196.

Harrison, N. and J.D. Singer, *Complexity is more than systems theory*, in *Complexity in World Politics: Concepts and Methods of a New Paradigm*, N. Harrison, Editor. 2006, State University of New York Press: New York. p. 25-41.

Harvey, V., *Some Problematical Aspects of Peter Berger's Theory of Religion.* Journal of the American Academy of Religion, 1973. **41**(1): p. 75-93.

Haslam, J., *E.H. Carr and the History of Soviet Russia.* The Historical Journal, 1983. **26**(4): p. 1021-1027.

Hellie, R., *The Structure of Russian Imperial History.* History and Theory, 2005. **44**(4): p. 1-22.

Hephner, R., *Where Youth and Laughter Go: The Experience of Trench Warfare from Petersburg to the Western Front.* 1997, Virginia Polytechnic Institute and State University.

Herz, J., *Rise and Demise of the Territorial State.* World Politics, 1957. **9**(4): p. 473-493.

Higgott, R. and A. Cooper, *Middle power leadership and coalition building: Australia, the Cairns Group and the Uruguay Round of trade negotiations.* International Organization, 1990. **44**(4): p. 589-632.

Hixson, W., *Parting the Curtain: Propaganda, Culture, and the Cold War, 1945-1961.* 1997, New York: St. Martin's Press.

Hobbes, T. *Leviathan, or the Matter, Forme, & Power of a Commonwealth Ecclesiasticall and Civil.* 2002 [cited 2006 1 November 2006]; Available from: http://tinyurl.com/yz47c6.

Hobbes, T., *Leviathan.* 2004, Whitefish, MT: Kessinger Publishing.

Hoffman, S., *International Systems and International Law.* World Politics, 1961. **14**(1): p. 205-237.

Hoffman, S., *An American Social Science: International Relations*, in *International Relations – Still An American Social Science?*, R. Crawford and D. Jarvis, Editors. 2001, SUNY Press: New York. p. 27-52.

Hoffmann, S., R.O. Keohane, and J.J. Mearsheimer, *Back to the Future, Part II: International Relations Theory and Post-Cold War Europe.* International Security, 1990. **15**(2): p. 191-199.

Holm, E., *High Politics and European Integration: From EMU to CFSP.* 2000, The Hellenic Observatory, London School of Economics and Political Science.

Holsti, K., *The Coming Chaos? Armed Conflict on the World's Periphery*, in *International Order and the Future of World Politics*, T. Paul and J. Hall, Editors. 1999, Cambridge University Press: Cambridge. p. 283-310.

Honig, J.W., *Totalitarianism and Realism: Hans Morgenthau's German Years.* Security Studies, 1996. **5**(2): p. 283-313.

Hook, G., et al., *Japan's international relations: politics, economics and security.* 2nd edition ed. 2005, Oxford: Routledge.

Hopf, T., *The Promise of Constructivism in International Relations Theory.* International Security, 1998. **23**(1): p. 171-200.

House, The White. *Victor Cha: Director for Asian Affairs, National Security Council.* 2007 [cited 2007 4 June]; Available from: http://tinyurl.com/2rmp2k.

Hume, D. *An Enquiry Concerning the Principles of Morals.* 2003a [cited; Available from: http://tinyurl.com/zj6pj.

Hume, D. *Dialogues Concerning Natural Religion.* 2003b [cited; 10th edition:[Available from: http://tinyurl.com/kr224.

Humphries, R., *Running on Soviet time,* in *The Japan Times.* 2000. p. 1-7.

Hunter, R., *A Forward-Looking Partnership.* Foreign Affairs, 2004. **83**(5): p. 14-18.

Jervis, R., *Deterrence Theory Revisited.* World Politics, 1979. **31**(2): p. 289-324.

Jervis, R., *Realism, Neoliberalism, and Cooperation: Understanding the Debate.* International Security, 1999. **24**(1): p. 42-63.

Jervis, R., *Mutual Assured Destruction.* Foreign Policy, 2002(133): p. 40-42.

Joll, J. and G. Martel, *The Origins of the First World War.* 2006, New York: Pearson.

Kaplan, M., *System and Process in International Politics.* 1957, New York: Wiley.

Kaplan, M., *Review: Man, The State, and War by Kenneth N. Waltz.* The American Political Science Review, 1959. **53**(4): p. 1125-1127.

Kavalski, E., *The fifth debate and the emergence of complex international relations theory: notes on the application of complexity theory to the study of international life.* Cambridge Review of International Affairs, 2007. **20**(3): p. 435-454.

Kavalski, E., *The Complexity of Global Security Governance: An Analytical Overview.* Global Society, 2008. **22**(4): p. 423-443.

Kennedy, P., *The Rise and Fall of the Great Powers: Economic Change and Military Conflict from 1500 to 2000.* 1987, New York: Random House.

Keohane, R., *Neorealism and Its Critics.* 1986a, New York: Columbia University Press.

Keohane, R., *Theory of World Politics: Structural Realism and Beyond,* in *Neorealism and Its Critics.* 1986b, Columbia University Press: New York. p. 158-203.

Keohane, R., *Ironies of Sovereignty: The European Union and the United States.* Journal of Common Market Studies, 2002. **40**(4): p. 743-765.

Keohane, R. and L. Martin, *The Promise of Institutionalist Theory.* International Security, 1995. **20**(1): p. 39-51.

Khalil, E., *Adam Smith and the Three Theories of Altruism.* Recherches économiques de Louvain, 2001. **67**(4): p. 421-435.

Kissane, D., *The Balkan Bullet with Butterfly Wings.* CEU Journal of Political Science, 2006. **1**(4): p. 85-106.

Kissane, D., *Realist Theory and Central & Eastern Europe after the Cold War,* in *3rd CEU Graduate Conference in the Social Sciences.* 2007a: Budapest, Hungary.

Kissane, D., *Offensive Realism and Central & Eastern Europe after the Cold War.* CEU Journal of Political Science, 2007b. **2**(4): p. 381-402.

Kissane, D., *A Chaotic Theory of International Relations? The Possibility for Theoretical Revolution in International Politics*. Revistă de ştiinţe politice, 2007c. **2**: p. 85-103.

Kissane, D., *On the Problems in and the Possibilities for Mapping International Chaos*, in *3rd Annual Graduate Conference in Political Science in Memory of Yitzhak Rabin*. 2008a: Hebrew University, Jerusalem, Israel.

Kissane, D., *Forecasting the Storm: Power Cycle Theory and Conflict in the Major Power System*. Europolis, 2008b. **2**: p. 10-43.

Klinghoffer, A., *The Power of Projections: How Maps Reflect Global Politics and History*. 2006, Westport, CT: Greenwood.

Klotz, A., *Norms in International Relations: The Struggle Against Apartheid*. 1995, New York: Cornell University Press.

Krauthammer, C., *The Unipolar Moment*. Foreign Affairs, 1990. **70**(1): p. 23-33.

Kuhn, S. *Stanford Encyclopedia of Philosophy: Prisoner's Dilemma*. 2003 [cited 2007 10 May]; Available from: http://tinyurl.com/2qjpmu.

Kurata, H., *Dialogue and Deterrence: The 1970s as Prototype*, in *North Korea Policy After the Perry Report Workshop*. 2000: Sigur Centre for Asian Studies, George Washington University, Washington, DC.

Lacy, M., *Security and Climate Change: The Limits of Realism*. 2005, New York: Routledge.

Lake, A. *From Containment to Enlargement*. 1993 [cited 2007 5 May]; Available from: http://tinyurl.com/ysy27l.

Landy, M., *Zealous Realism: Comments on Mearsheimer and Walt*. The Forum, 2006. **4**(1/6): p. 1-10.

Langdon, J., *Emerging From Fischer's Shadow: Recent Examinations of the Crisis of July 1914*. The History Teacher, 1986. **20**(1): p. 67-68.

Lapidus, G., *Contested Sovereignty: The Tragedy of Chechnya*. International Security, 1998. **23**(1): p. 5-49.

Laqueur, W., *A History of Terrorism*. 2002, New Brunswick: Transaction Publishers.

Lawlor, S., *Churchill and the Politics of War, 1940-41*. 1995, Cambridge: Cambridge University Press.

Layne, C., *The Unipolar Illusion: Why New Great Powers Will Rise*. International Security, 1993. **17**(4): p. 5-51.

Lazarus, N., *Playing Pin the War on the Lobby*. The Forum, 2006. **4**(1/5): p. 1-10.

Lebow, R., *The Long Peace, the End of the Cold War, and the Failure of Realism*. International Organization, 1994. **48**(2): p. 249-277.

Legro, J. and A. Moravcsik, *Is Anybody Still a Realist?* International Security, 1999. **24**(2): p. 5-55.

Levy, G. and R. Razin, *It Takes Two: An Explanation for the Democratic Peace*. Journal of the European Economic Association, 2004. **2**(1): p. 1-29.

Levy, J., *Alliance Formation and War Behavior: An Analysis of the Great Powers, 1495-1975*. The Journal of Conflict Resolution, 1981. **25**(4): p. 581-613.

Levy, J., *Domestic Politics and War*, in *The Origin and Prevention of Major War*, R. Rotberg and T. Rabb, Editors. 1989, Cambridge University Press: Cambridge. p. 79-101.

Lieber, R., *Are Realists Realistic about Foreign Policy?*, in *Annual Meeting of the American Political Science Association*. 2003: Philadelphia. p. 1-16.

Lindley, D. and R. Schildkraut, *Is War Rational? The Extent of Miscalculation and Misperception as Causes of War*, in *Annual Meeting of the International Studies Association*. 2005: Honolulu, United States. p. 1-52.

Locke, J. *Two Treatises on Government*. 2005 [cited; Available from: http://tinyurl.com/2rytcw.

Luard, T. *ASEAN: Changing, but only slowly*. 2003 [cited 2006 16 October]; Available from: http://news.bbc.co.uk/1/hi/world/asia-pacific/3173458.stm.

Lui, C. *Victor Cha '83, NSC's Asian Affairs Expert*. 2006 [cited 2007 4 June]; Available from: http://tinyurl.com/2uykxd.

Lukes, T., *Lionizing Machiavelli*. American Political Science Review, 2001. **95**(3): p. 561-575.

Machiavelli, N., *The Prince*. 2005, Oxford: Oxford University Press.

Macintosh, D. and M. Hawes, *The IOC and the World of Interdependence*. Olympika: The International Journal of Olympic Studies, 1992. **1**: p. 29-45.

Mann, M., *Has globalization ended the rise and rise of the nation-state?*, in *International Order and the Future of World Politics*, T. Paul and J. Hall, Editors. 2001, Cambridge University Press: Cambridge. p. 237-261.

Map, A.A. *Brooklyn Mud Map*. 2006 [cited 2008 20 February]; Available from: http://tinyurl.com/3x42jv.

Martin, L., *An institutionalist view: international institutions and state strategies*, in *International Order and the Future of World Politics*, T. Paul and J. Hall, Editors. 2001, Cambridge University Press: Cambridge. p. 78-98.

Martinich, A., *Hobbes: A Biography*. 1999, Cambridge: Cambridge University Press.

Maslin, J., *If the Going Gets Tough, Get a Pet or Start a War*, in *The New York Times*. 1997. p. B10.

McCormick, J., *Understanding the European Union: A Concise Introduction*. 2nd ed. 2002, New York: Palgrave.

Mearsheimer, J., *Conventional Deterrence*. 1983, New York: Cornell University Press.

Mearsheimer, J., *Back to the Future: Instability in Europe after the Cold War*. International Security, 1990a. **15**(1): p. 5-56.

Mearsheimer, J., *Why We Will Soon Miss the Cold War*. The Atlantic Monthly, 1990b. **266**(2): p. 35-50.

Mearsheimer, J., *The False Promise of International Institutions*. International Security, 1994. **19**(3): p. 5-49.

Mearsheimer, J., *The Tragedy of Great Power Politics*. 2001, New York: Norton.

Mearsheimer, J. *Through The Realist Lens: Conversation with John Mearsheimer*. Conversations With History 2002 [cited 2007 1 May]; Available from: http://tinyurl.com/29fdy4.

Mearsheimer, J., *EH Carr vs. Idealism: The Battle Rages On*. International Relations, 2005. **19**(2): p. 139-152.

Mearsheimer, J., *Conversations in International Relations - Interview with John J. Mearsheimer (Part I)*. International Relations, 2006a. **20**(1): p. 105-124.

Mearsheimer, J., *Conversations in International Relations - Interview with John J. Mearsheimer (Part II)*. International Relations, 2006b. **20**(2): p. 231-243.

Mearsheimer, J. *Curriculum*. 2007 [cited 2007 30 April]; Available from: http://tinyurl.com/2hezst.

Mearsheimer, J. and S. Walt, *The Israel Lobby and US Foreign Policy*, in *Faculty Research Working Paper*. 2006, John F. Kennedy School of Government, Harvard University.

Mesquita, B.B.d., et al., *An Institutional Explanation for the Democratic Peace*. American Political Science Review, 1999. **93**(4): p. 791-807.

Miller, E., *Questions that Matter: An Invitation to Philosophy*. 4th ed. 1996, New York: McGraw-Hill.

Mistry, P., *Africa's Record of Regional Co-Operation and Integration*. African Affairs, 2000. **99**(4): p. 553-573.

Modelski, G. and W. Thompson, *Seapower in Global Politics, 1494-1993*. 1988, Seattle: University of Washington Press.

Molloy, S., *Realism: A Problematic Paradigm*. Security Dialogue, 2003. **34**(1): p. 71-85.

Monroe, K., *The Heart of Altruism*. 1998, Princeton: Princeton University Press.

Morgenstern, O. and J.v. Nuemann, *The Theory of Games and Economic Behavior*. 1947, Princeton: Princeton University Press.

Morgenthau, H., *International Affairs: The Resurrection of Neutrality in Europe*. The American Political Science Review, 1939. **33**(3): p. 473-486.

Morgenthau, H., *The Evil of Politics and the Ethics of Evil*. Ethics, 1945a. **56**(1): p. 1-18.

Morgenthau, H., *The Machiavellian Utopia*. Ethics, 1945b. **55**(2): p. 145-147.

Morgenthau, H., *The Twilight of International Morality*. Ethics, 1948a. **58**(2): p. 79-99.

Morgenthau, H., *The Political Science of EH Carr*. World Politics, 1948b. **1**(1): p. 127-134.

Morgenthau, H., *The Mainsprings of American Foreign Policy: The National Interest vs. Moral Abstractions*. The American Political Science Review, 1950. **44**(4): p. 833-854.

Morgenthau, H., *In Defense of the National Interest: A Critical Examination of American Foreign Policy*. 1951, New York: Alfred A. Knopf.

Morgenthau, H., *Another "Great Debate": The National Interest of the United States*. The American Political Science Review, 1952. **46**(4): p. 961-988.

Morgenthau, H., *Politics in the Twentieth Century: Volume One - The Decline of Democratic Politics*. 1962a, Chicago: University of Chicago Press.

Morgenthau, H., *Politics in the Twentieth Century: Volume Two - The Impasse of American Foreign Policy*. 1962b, Chicago: University of Chicago Press.

Morgenthau, H., *Politics in the Twentieth Century: Volume Three - The Restoration of American Politics*. 1962c, Chicago: University of Chicago Press.

Morgenthau, H., *To Intervene or Not Intervene*. Foreign Affairs, 1967. **45**(3): p. 96-112.

Morgenthau, H., *The Pathology of American Power*. International Security, 1977. **1**(3): p. 3-20.

Morgenthau, H., *Politics among Nations: The Struggle for Power and Peace*. 6th ed. 1993, New York: Alfred A. Knopf.

Morrow, J., *Arms versus allies: Trade-offs in the search for security.* International Organization, 1993. **47**(2): p. 207-233.

Mosely, P., *The Kremlin's Foreign Policy Since Stalin.* Foreign Affairs, 1953. **32**(1): p. 20-33.

Mousseau, M. and Y. Shi, *A Test for Reverse Causality in the Democratic Peace Relationship.* Journal of Peace Research, 1999. **36**(6): p. 639-663.

Neiburg, M., *Warfare and Society in Europe: 1898 to the Present.* 2004, New York: Routledge.

Neumann, J.v. and O. Morgenstern, *Theory of Games and Economic Behaviour.* 1944, Princeton: Princeton University Press.

Newell, P., *Climate for Change: Non-State Actors and the Global Politics of Greenhouse.* 2000, Cambridge: Cambridge University Press.

Nye, J., *The Changing Nature of World Power.* Political Science Quarterly, 1990. **105**(2): p. 177-192.

Nye, J., *The Paradox of American Power: Why the World's Only Superpower Can't Go It Alone.* 2002, Oxford: Oxford University Press.

Nye, J., *Soft Power: The Means to Success in World Politics.* 2004, New York: Public Affairs Press.

Orkin, M., *Balanced Strategies for Prisoner's Dilemma.* The Journal of Conflict Resolution, 1987. **31**(1): p. 186-191.

Owen, J., *How Liberalism Produces Democratic Peace.* International Security, 1994. **19**(2): p. 87-125.

Owens, M., *Letters: Debating the Israel Lobby.* Foreign Policy, 2006. **156**: p. 4.

Oye, K (ed.), *Cooperation under Anarchy*. 1986, Princeton: Princeton University Press.

Pavard, B. and J. Dugdale. *An Introduction to Complexity in Social Science*. 2003 [cited 2008 26 May]; Available from: http://tinyurl.com/6x77hj.

Peffer, N., *Basis for Peace in the Far East*. 1942, New York: Harper & Bros.

Peffer, N., *The Far East: A Modern History*. 1958, Ann Arbor: University of Michigan Press.

Pichler, H.-K., *The godfathers of 'truth': Max Weber and Carl Schmitt in Morgenthau's theory of power politics*. Review of International Studies, 1998. **24**(2): p. 185-200.

Politics, D.o.I. *Full History of the Department of International Politics: Edward Hallett Carr*. 2006 [cited 23 November 2006]; Available from: http://www.aber.ac.uk/interpol/history/history_5.html.

Pollack, M., *International Relations Theory and European Integration*. Journal of Common Market Studies, 2001. **39**(2): p. 221-244.

Popper, K., *Conjectures and Refutations: The Growth of Scientific Knowledge*. 1992, London: Routledge.

Posen, B., *The Sources of Military Doctrine: France, Britain and Germany Between the World Wars*. 1986, Ithaca: Cornell University Press.

Powell, R., *Absolute and Relative Gains in International Relations Theory*. The American Political Science Review, 1991. **85**(4): p. 1303-1320.

Powell, R., *Anarchy in International Relations Theory: The Neorealist-Neoliberal Debate*. International Organization, 1994. **48**(2): p. 313-344.

Rademaker, S. *Countering WMD and Terrorism through Security Cooperation*. 2006 [cited 2007 3 May]; Available from: http://tinyurl.com/yqtcae.

Randle, R., *Review: Theory of International Politics, by Kenneth Waltz*. Political Science Quarterly, 1980. **95**(1): p. 136-137.

Randolph, B.C., *Review: The Twenty Years' Crisis, 1919-1939*. The American Journal of International Law, 1940. **34**(4): p. 761-762.

Ray, J., *Does Democracy Cause Peace?* Annual Review of Political Science, 1998(1): p. 27-46.

Ray, J., *A Lakatosian View of the Democratic Peace Research Program: Does it Falsify Realism (or Neorealism)?*, in *Progress in International Relations Theory: Metrics and Methods of Scientific Change*, M. Elman and C. Elman, Editors. 2003, MIT Press: Boston. p. 205-243.

Reeves, J., *The Interrelation of the Domestic and Foreign Policies of a Nation*. Annals of the American Academy of Political and Social Science, 1941. **218**: p. 1-8.

Reilly, D., *The Power Politics Game: Offensive realism in theory and practice*. Simulation and Gaming, 2003. **34**(2): p. 298-305.

Renshon, S., *High Hopes: The Clinton Presidency and the Politics of Ambition*. 1998, London: Routledge.

Rodman, K., *Think Globally, Punish Locally: Nonstate Actors, Multinational Corporations, and Human Rights Sanctions*. Ethics and International Affairs, 1998. **12**(1): p. 19-41.

Rogoff, K., *Europe's Quiet Leap Forward*. Foreign Policy, 2004. **143**(Jul/Aug): p. 74-75.

Rose, G., *Neoclassical Realism and Theories of Foreign Policy.* World Politics, 1998. **51**(1): p. 144-172.

Rose, G., *It Could Happen to Us.* Foreign Affairs, 1999. **78**(2): p. 131-137.

Rose, G. and J. Hoge, eds. *How Did This Happen? Terrorism and the New War.* 2001, Harper Collins: New York.

Rosecrance, R., *Action and Reaction in World Politics: International Systems in Perspective.* 1963, Boston: Little Brown.

Rosenau, J., *Many Damn Things Simultaneously: Complexity Theory and World Affairs*, in *Conference on Complexity, Global Politics, and National Security.* 1996: Washington D.C.

Rousseau, J.J., *Discours sur les sciences et les arts: discours sur l'origine de l'inégalité.* 1992, Paris: Flammarion.

Rubenstein, C., *Why we must stop Iran*, in *The Age.* 2006. p. 13.

Ruggie, J., *Continuity and Transformation in the World Polity: Toward a Neorealist Synthesis*, in *Neorealism and Its Critics*, R. Keohane, Editor. 1986, Columbia University Press: New York. p. 131-157.

Ruggie, J., *Third try at world order? America and multilateralism after the Cold War.* Political Science Quarterly, 1994. **109**(4): p. 553-570.

Russell, B., *Political Ideals.* 1917, New York: The Century Co.

Russell, B., *History of Western Philosophy and its Connection with Political and Social Circumstances from the Earliest Times to the Present Day.* 1993, London: Routledge.

Russell, B., *Political Ideals.* e-Book ed. 2003, Salt Lake City: Project Gutenberg.

Russett, B., *Cause, Surprise, and No Escape.* The Journal of Politics, 1962. **24**(1): p. 3-22.

Russett, B., et al., *The Democratic Peace.* International Security, 1995. **19**(4): p. 164-184.

Russett, B., T. Risse-Kappen, and J. Mearsheimer, *Back to the Future, Part III: Realism and the Realities of European Security.* International Security, 1991. **15**(3): p. 216-222.

Sagan, S. and K. Waltz, *The Spread of Nuclear Weapons: A Debate.* 1995, New York: WW Norton and Company.

Schlatter, R., *Thomas Hobbes and Thucydides.* Journal of the History of Ideas, 1945. **6**(3): p. 350-362.

Schmidt, B., *The Political Discourse of Anarchy: A Disciplinary History of International Relations.* 1998, Albany: State University of New York.

Schmidt, B., *On the History and Historiography of International Relations*, in *Handbook of International Relations*, W. Carlsnaes, T. Risse, and B. Simmons, Editors. 2006, SAGE: London. p. 3-22.

Schmitt, B., *The Origins of the War of 1914.* The Journal of Modern History, 1952. **24**(1): p. 69-74.

Schroeder, P., *Historical Reality vs. Neo-Realist Theory.* International Security, 1994. **19**(1): p. 108-148.

Schwartz, T. and K. Skinner, *The Myth of the Democratic Peace.* Orbis, 2002. **46**(1): p. 159-172.

Schweller, R., *Bandwagoning for Profit: Bringing the Revisionist State Back In.* International Security, 1994. **19**(1): p. 72-107.

SCO. *Brief introduction to the Shanghai Cooperation Organisation.* 2008a [cited 2008 6 May]; Available from: http://tinyurl.com/68lexv.

SCO. *Bishkek Declaration.* 2008b [cited 2008 6 May]; Available from: http://tinyurl.com/63qs98.

Security, International, *The Great War and the Nuclear Age: Sarajevo after Seventy Years.* International Security, 1984. **9**(1): p. 3-5.

Sells, M., *The Bridge Betrayed: Religion and Genocide in Bosnia.* 1996, Berkeley: University of California Press.

Shils, E. and M. Janowitz, *Cohesion and Disintegration in the Wehrmacht in World War II.* The Public Opinion Quarterly, 1948. **12**(2): p. 280-315.

Shimko, K., *Realism, Neorealism, and American Liberalism.* The Review of Politics, 1992. **54**(2): p. 281-301.

Singer, J.D., *The Levels of Analysis Problem in International Relations.* World Politics, 1969. **14**(1): p. 77-92.

Singleton, F., *A Short History of the Yugoslav Peoples.* 1989, Cambridge: Cambridge University Press.

Skinner, Q., *The Ideological Context of Hobbes's Political Thought.* The Historical Journal, 1966a. **9**(3): p. 286-317.

Skinner, Q., *Thomas Hobbes and His Disciples in England and France.* Comparative Studies in Society and History, 1966b. **8**(2): p. 153-167.

Slaughter, A.-M., A. Tulumello, and S. Wood, *International Law and International Relations Theory: A New Generation of Interdisciplinary Scholarship.* The American Journal of International Law, 1998. **92**(3): p. 367-397.

Smith, S., *Is the truth out there? Eight questions about international order*, in *International Order and the Future of World Politics*, T. Paul and J. Hall, Editors. 2001, Cambridge University Press: Cambridge. p. 99-119.

Snyder, G., *"Prisoner's Dilemma" and "Chicken" Models in International Politics*. International Studies Quarterly, 1971. **15**(1): p. 66-103.

Snyder, J., *Myths of Empire: Domestic Politics and International Ambition*. 1991, Ithica: Cornell University Press.

Snyder, R., *Toward Greater Order in the Study of International Politics*. World Politics, 1955. **7**(3): p. 461-478.

Speer, J., *Hans Morgenthau and the World State*. World Politics, 1968. **20**(2): p. 207-227.

Spiegel, Der. *UN Veto Powers Give Tehran Ultimatum*. 2006 [cited 2007 21 February]; Available from: http://www.spiegel.de/international/0,1518,408771,00.html.

St Exupéry, A.de, *The Little Prince*. 2000, New York: Harvest Books.

State, Department ot. *Thomus J. Christensen: Biography*. 2006 [cited 2007 8 June]; Available from: http://tinyurl.com/2c55m4.

Stein, A., *Coordination and Collaboration: Regimes in an Anarchic World*. International Organization, 1982. **36**(2): p. 299-324.

Stephens, J. and H. Butters, *New Light on Machiavelli*. The English Historical Review, 1982. **97**(382): p. 54-69.

Strauss, L., *The Political Philosophy of Hobbes: Its Basis and Genesis*. 1996, Chicago: University of Chicago Press.

Sundaram, V., *Scientific Man vs. Power Politics*, in *News Today*. 2006.

Talani, L., *European Political Economy*. 2004, London: Ashgate Publishing.

Taliaferro, J., *Security Seeking Under Anarchy: Defensive Realism Revisited.* International Security, 2001. **25**(3): p. 128-161.

Taylor, M., *Community, Anarchy and Liberty*. 1982, Cambridge: Cambridge University Press.

Thucydides, *The History of the Peloponnesian Wars*. 1998, New York: Prometheus Books.

Trade, Department of Foreign Affairs and, *Advancing the National Interest: Australia's Foreign and Trade Policy White Paper*. 2003, National Capital Printing: Canberra.

Tucker, R., *Professor Morgenthau's Theory of Political Realism*. The American Political Science Review, 1952. **46**(1): p. 214-224.

Van Evera, S., *The Cult of the Offensive and the Origins of the First World War*. International Security, 1984 **9**(1): 58-107

Van Evera, S., *Primed for Peace: Europe after the Cold War*. International Security, 1991. **15**(3): p. 7-57.

Van Evera, S., *Causes of War: Power and the Roots of Conflict*. 2001, Ithaca: Cornell University Press.

Vasquez, J., *The Realist Paradigm and Degenerative versus Progressive Research Programs: An Appraisal of Neotraditional Research on Waltz's Balancing Proposition*. The American Political Science Review, 1997. **91**(4): p. 899-912.

Verba, S., *Simulation, Reality and Theory in International Relations*. World Politics, 1964. **16**(4): p. 490-519.

Walt, S., *The Origins of Alliances*. 1990, Ithaca: Cornell University Press.

Walt, S., *International Relations: One World, Many Theories*. Foreign Policy, 1998(110): p. 29-46.

Walt, S., *The Ties that Fray: Why Europe and America are Drifting Apart*. The National Interest, 1999. **54**: p. 3-11.

Waltz, K., *Man, the State, and War: A Theoretical Analysis*. 1959, New York: Columbia University Press.

Waltz, K., *Theory of International Relations*, in *The Handbook of Political Science: Vol 8*, F. Greenstein and N. Polsby, Editors. 1975, Addison-Wesley: Reading. p. 1-86.

Waltz, K., *Theory of International Politics*. 1979, Reading: Addison-Wesley.

Waltz, K., *The Spread of Nuclear Weapons: More May Be Better*. The Adelphi Papers, 1981(171): p. 1-32.

Waltz, K., *Reflections on Theory of International Politics: A Response to My Critics*, in *Neorealism and Its Critics*, R. Keohane, Editor. 1986, Columbia University Press: New York. p. 322-345.

Waltz, K., *The Origins of War in Neorealist Theory*. Journal of Interdisciplinary History, 1988. **18**(4): p. 615-628.

Waltz, K., *The Emerging Structure of International Politics*. International Security, 1993. **18**(2): p. 44-79.

Waltz, K., *Structural Realism after the Cold War.* International Security, 2000. **25**(1): p. 5-41.

Waltz, K.N., *Realist thought and neorealist theory.* Journal of International Affairs, 1990. **44**(1): p. 21-37.

Waltz, K.N., *Man, the State, and War: A Theoretical Analysis.* 2001, New York: Columbia University Press.

Waltz, K.N. *Theory and International Politics: Conversation with Kenneth Waltz.* Conversations with History 2003 [cited 2007 12 February]; Available from: http://globetrotter.berkeley.edu/people3/Waltz/.

Warner, R.S., *A Paradigm is Not a Theory: Reply to Lechner.* The American Journal of Sociology, 1997. **103**(1): p. 192-198.

Wawro, G., *The Austro-Prussian War: Austria's War with Prussia and Italy in 1866.* 1998, Cambridge: Cambridge University Press.

Wayman, F. *Incidence of Militarized Disputes Between Liberal States 1816-1992.* 2002. New Orleans: Paper presented at the Annual Meeting of the International Studies Association.

Welch, D., *Why International Relations theorists should stop reading Thucydides.* Review of International Studies, 2003. **29**(3): p. 301-319.

Wells, H., *The Shape of Things to Come.* 2006, Adelaide: eBooks@Adelaide.

Wendt, A., *The Agent-Structure Problem in International Relations.* International Organization, 1987. **41**(3): p. 335-370.

Wendt, A., *Anarchy is what states make of it: the social construction of power politics.* International Organization, 1992. **46**(2): p. 391-425.

Wendt, A., *Constructing International Politics*. International Security, 1995. **20**(1): p. 71-81.

Whiteneck, D., *Deterring Terrorists: Thoughts on a Framework*. The Washington Quarterly, 2005. **28**(3): p. 187-199.

Wiener, J., *Quentin Skinner's Hobbes*. Political Theory, 1974. **2**(3): p. 251-260.

Wight, C., *Philosophy of Social Science and International Relations*, in *Handbook of International Relations*, W. Carlsnaes, T. Risse, and B. Simmons, Editors. 2006, SAGE: London. p. 23-51.

Wilde, N., *Machiavelli*. International Journal of Ethics, 1928. **38**(2): p. 212-225.

Williams, M.C., *Hobbes and International Relations: A Reconsideration*. International Organization, 1996. **50**(2): p. 213-236.

Williamson, S., *Influence, Power, and the Policy Process: The Case of Franz Ferdinand, 1906-1914*. The Historical Journal, 1974. **17**(2): p. 417-434.

Wilson, W. *President Woodrow Wilson's Fourteen Points*. 2006 [1918] [cited 2006 13 July]; Available from: http://www.yale.edu/lawweb/avalon/wilson14.htm.

Wirsing, R., *India, Pakistan, and the Kashmir Dispute*. 1998, New York: St. Martin's Press.

Wright, Q., ed. *Neutrality and Collective Security*. 1936, University of Chicago Press: Chicago.

Wright, R., *Non-Zero: The Logic of Human Destiny*. 2000, London: Little, Brown and Company.

X, *The Sources of Soviet Conduct*. Foreign Affairs, 1947. **25**(4): p. 566-582.

Zagare, F., *Rationality and Deterrence.* World Politics, 1990. **42**(2): p. 238-260.

Zakaria, F., *From Wealth to Power: The Unusual Origins of America's World Role.* 1998, Princeton: Princeton University Press.

Zinner, P., *The Ideological Basis of Soviet Foreign Policy.* World Politics, 1952. **4**(4): p. 488-511.

Zuckerman, M., *The Mullah menace,* in *Jewish World Review.* 2006.

***ibidem*-Verlag / *ibidem* Press**
Melchiorstr. 15
70439 Stuttgart
Germany

ibidem@ibidem.eu
www.ibidem-verlag.com
www.ibidem.eu